Sheldon Amos

The Science of Law

Sheldon Amos

The Science of Law

ISBN/EAN: 9783744666671

Printed in Europe, USA, Canada, Australia, Japan

Cover: Foto ©Suzi / pixelio.de

More available books at **www.hansebooks.com**

THE INTERNATIONAL SCIENTIFIC SERIES.

THE
SCIENCE OF LAW.

BY

SHELDON AMOS, M.A.,

BARRISTER-AT-LAW; PROFESSOR OF JURISPRUDENCE IN UNIVERSITY COLLEGE, LONDON;
AND IN THE INNS OF COURTS; EXAMINER IN THE UNIVERSITY OF LONDON.

AUTHOR OF
"A SYSTEMATIC VIEW OF THE SCIENCE OF JURISPRUDENCE;" "AN ENGLISH CODE,
ITS DIFFICULTIES, AND THE MODES OF OVERCOMING THEM," ETC.

NEW YORK:
D. APPLETON AND COMPANY,
549 AND 551 BROADWAY.
1875.

PREFACE.

As many of the topics treated in the present work are the same as those treated in my former work, "A Systematic View of the Science of Jurisprudence," it may be serviceable to point out distinctly the difference between the purposes I have had in view in preparing the two several works. This explanation will be the simplest mode of distinguishing their nature and scope.

The former work was written especially for Law students, including under this expression all who for the time are making Law the principal part of their studies, though by no means confining the expression to those studying with a strictly professional object in view.

The present work is designed for the instruction of all serious students, whether of the Physical or of the so-called Moral Sciences, whatever be, for the time, the prominent topic of their study, and whatever be the general or special object they have in view.

The wider and less technical scope of this work, as well as the preparatory acquaintance with scientific methods of thought I have held myself entitled to anticipate in my readers, has enabled me to dilate with more minuteness than I could elsewhere on the essential relations of Law to Morality, on the one hand, and to the general constitution of Society and of the State, on the other.

The present chaotic and anarchical condition of Ethical Science in this country places the speculator on Law or on Politics at the greatest disadvantage. He must step out of his path in order to work out for himself disputable theories, instead of having an armoury of incontrovertible maxims ready to his hand. He can hardly turn to account even the commonest moral term without seeming to be a partisan in a war embittered with all the passions of political and even religious fanaticism.

Not, however, that I have shrunk from moral investigations, when the natural course of my subject has forced them upon me. I have throughout insisted upon, and elucidated in all the ways I could, the position that a moral constitution of society is, in conception if not in time, anterior to, and independent of, a legal one; but that, apart from the strength, coherence, and permanence imparted by Law and Government, the most hopeful moral growths are too frail and feeble to endure, still less to come to maturity.

I have lost no opportunity of enforcing the doctrine that human society is built up by the play of mutual relations, and not only (though it is also) necessitated by the clash of conflicting interests; that, philosophically, no less than historically, a group of persons, and not the individual person, is the atomic unit of society; and that in thought, and in order of worth and of preference, if not in time, the State exists before any of its component groups, and the larger groups before the smaller. It is the characteristic end of Law, as an instrument of Government, to maintain the identity, the coherence, and the vitality of all the groups of which the State is composed, and to ascertain and regulate the relations of the several groups to one another, and to the State as a corporate whole.

In this work, as in my former one, I have abstained as much as possible from personal controversy. There may be a time for controversy, as there is a time "to every purpose under the heaven." But in a condition of society like the present, when a main intellectual stimulus is supplied by watching the periodical tilting-matches between authors among themselves, and between authors and critics, there is surely a time and place for the clear and uninterrupted exposition of what is believed to be truth, in all its proportions, and with the accumulated treasures it has acquired in the most opposite climates.

I have learnt too much in all schools of moral, legal, and political thought, to find it a congenial task to invite attention to the errors or shortcomings of any of them. It is hardly possible to assault an isolated position of a great writer without—even in spite of oneself, and (it may be) by an excess of scrupulous candour—misrepresenting and unduly depreciating him. The errors of writers who are not great are certainly not worth alluding to, however much the extent of their ephemeral influence may be lamented.

There are many indications that Law will shortly be recognized as an essential element in a complete general education. Among such unmistakable indications are the gradual abolition of some of the most antiquated technicalities of English Law through the operation of the Supreme Court of Judicature Act; the increasing demand that is being made on all sides for measures which, by simplifying the language and structure of Law, shall popularize its study; the bolder conceptions that are being entertained of the true range of the higher education, and of the claims of Politics, in some other than a party sense, to be included in that range; the special efforts that are being made by the three English Universities, by the Inns of Court, and by the Incorporated Law Society to widen, deepen, and extend the professional training of all who are desirous of sharing in it, whether they intend to practise or not; the increasing desire, suggested both by commercial interests and by considerations of social convenience, to assimilate, and therefore to study, foreign systems of Law; and, last not least, the attention that is being awakened in the most earnest and philanthropic minds to the claims of International Law as a means of reducing the probability, and diminishing the horrors, of War.

There are two senses in which a treatise or a lecture may be said to be *popular*. Either the treatise or lecture may be intended to serve as a substitute for real and serious study, by communicating the results of study in so clear and agreeable a form as to send the reader or hearer away full of a glowing and newly-discovered sense of his own acquirements, while it satiates his curiosity and paralyzes his industry; or the treatise or lecture may be intended to do no more or less than to translate technical terms back again into the terms familiar in common speech; to examine afresh the meaning and scope of conceptions which the persistent jargon of specialists has clouded; to bring men of various pursuits and tastes into intellectual contact with one another; and, by opening out to novices an unsuspected region of interest, to whet their curiosity and to stimulate them to further research.

It need not be said that it is the aim of this treatise, as I would have it that of all my lectures, to be *popular* in this latter sense and not to be so in the former one.

SHELDON AMOS.

9, *King's Bench Walk,*
    Temple.

CONTENTS.

CHAPTER I.

RECENT HISTORY AND PRESENT CONDITION OF THE SCIENCE OF LAW.

	PAGE
Order of Treatment	1
Influence of BENTHAM	3
Historical Position and Influence of AUSTIN	4
Sir H. S. MAINE's Work on Village Communities	5
History and Influence of English Common Law	7
Study of Roman Law in England	9
Influence of Modern Codes	10
Influence of International Law, Public and Private	11

CHAPTER II.

PROVINCE AND LIMITS OF THE SCIENCE OF LAW.

Subject-matter of Law	13
Functions of the State in the Creation of Law	15
Nature of Constitutional Law	16
Materials of the Science of Law	18
Universality of Legal Principles	19
Conflicting Theories of the Origin of Society	20
Permanence of Legal Topics	23
Permanent Ethical and Logical Elements in Law	24
Law as regulating the Relations of States	25
Private International Law as supplying permanent topics	26

CHAPTER III.

LAW AND MORALITY.

	PAGE
Opposition of the Regions of Law and Morality	29
Competing Moral Theories	31
Contrasted Modes of Operation of Law and Morality	33
Equity as a Means of Moral Adjustment	35
Distinction of Penalty and Compensation	37
Discretionary Penalties	38
Prerogative of Pardon	41
Moral Claims and Legal Rights	43
Limits of the Operation of Law	44
Law and Personal Liberty	45

CHAPTER IV.

THE GROWTH OF LAW.

Sir H. S. MAINE on the History of the Growth of Law	47
Definition of the term *Law*	48
Definition of the term *State*	48
Functions of the Supreme Political Authority in the Creation of Law	48
Sir H. S. MAINE on the Origin and Nature of Customs	49
Conversion of Customs into Laws	51
Influence of Judicial Forms	52
Contrast of the Functions of the Legislator and the Judge	53
Influence of Legal Fictions	55
Nature of English Equity	56
Equity an Universally Recurrent Phenomenon	57

CHAPTER V.

THE GROWTH OF LAW—(continued).

Nature and Grounds of Interpretation	59
Modes of providing for Necessity of Interpretation	61
Meaning of French term "*Jurisprudence*"	63
Use of Definitions, Illustrations, and Interpretation Clauses	65
"Extensive," "Restrictive," "Logical," and "Grammatical" Interpretation	67
Judicial Adoption of Customs	67
Incorporation of Foreign Law	68
Influence of Text-book Writers and Commentators	69

	PAGE
Functions of Judges in framing Rules of Procedure	70
Influence of the expression "Law of Nature"	73
Subsidiary Resources for the help of Judges suggested by the Authors of the French Code	74
Criticism of the *Projet* of the *Code* by the *Montpellier Tribunal*	74
Modes of Statutory Legislation	75
Classificatory Arrangement of the various Modes by which the Growth of Law is determined	77

CHAPTER VI.

ELEMENTARY CONCEPTIONS AND TERMS.

Objects of Law in respect of *Persons* and *Things*	79
History of the legal term *Person*	81
Artificial or Fictitious *Persons*	83
History of the legal term *Thing*	85
Meaning of the expression "Incorporeal Things"	86
Extensive Uses of the legal term *Thing*	87
Origin of conceptions of *Right* and *Duty*	89
Analysis of the conception of "Liberty"	90
Relations of *Liberty* and *Right*	91
Relations of *Moral* to *Legal* "Right"	92
Growth of the conception of "Legal Right"	93
Exact Analysis of a "Legal Right"	95
Crimes in relation to Rights	96
Definitions of terms *Right* and *Duty*	97
Nature of Political Liberty	98
Possibility of the State having Rights	99
Popular Uses of the term *Act*	100
Definitions of terms *Act* and *Event*	101
Nature and Province of *Will*	102
Intention as qualifying Acts	103
Analysis of *Intention*	104
Modes of ascertaining *Intention*	105
Presumptions in favour of *Infancy*	106
Presumptions in favour of *Insanity*	107
Judicial and Medical Aspects of *Insanity*	108
Drunkenness as affecting Imputability	109
Presumptions in respect of *Ignorance*	110
Classification of Forms of *Ignorance*	111
How far Ignorance is treated as excusable	112
Fraud as affecting *Intention*	114
Negligence as affecting *Intention*	115

CHAPTER VII.

LAW IN RELATION TO (1) THE STATE, (2) THE FAMILY, (3) THE OTHER CONSTITUENT ELEMENTS OF THE STATE.

	PAGE
Various Meanings of the term *State*	118
Analysis of the conception implied in the term *State*	119
Historical Development of the term *State*	121
The *State* in reference to *Government*	122
The Functions of the *State*	123
Law in relation to the *Family*	124
Requisites in a Law of *Marriage*	125
Legal and Political Aspects of *Divorce*	125
Relative claims of Men and of Women	127
History of the Mutual Relations of Men and Women	128
Legal Relations of Men and Women	129
The *Family* as a topic of Roman Law	130
Growth of the Village Community	131
Local and Central Government	132
Law in relation to *Religious Bodies*	134
Various forms of the Relationship between *Church* and *State*	135
Structure of the "Established Church of England"	136
Nature and Policy of *Endowments*	137
Modes of providing against Abuses attending *Endowments*	139
Theory of *Trusts* and *Trustees*	141
Various Modes of appointing *Trustees*	143
General View of the Legal and Political Functions of the State	146

CHAPTER VIII.

LAWS OF OWNERSHIP OR PROPERTY.

Early anticipations of Ownership	151
Progress of the Conception of Ownership	153
Moral Aspects of Ownership	155
Communism	159
Elements of a Law of Ownership	160
Children and Lunatics as Owners	161
Early Property in Land	163
History of distinction between *Real* and *Personal* Property	164
Divisions of Things	165
Land as a subject of Ownership	166
Ownership of "Incorporeal Things"	168

CONTENTS.

	PARA
Copyright	16
Analysis of a Right of Ownership	170
Description of Servitudes or Easements	172
Classification of Servitudes JUSTINIAN'S *Institutes*	173
Relation of Possession to Ownership	175
Analysis of Facts and Conceptions implied in *Possession* ...	176
Distinction between the "Right of Possession" and the "Right to Possess"	178
How the notion of *Ownership* is evolved out of that of *Possession*	179
Various and Inexact Uses of the term *Owner*	180
Development of the Conception and Fact of *Transfer* or *Conveyance*	182
Sir H. S. MAINE's Theory of the Roman *Will*	183
Restrictions on Rights of Ownership	186
Political Limitations upon Rights of Ownership	186
Modes of protecting Rights of Ownership	189

CHAPTER IX.

LAW OF CONTRACT.

Meaning and Purpose of *Contract*	190
Historical Origin of *Contract*	191
Essential Nature of *Contract*	192
Sir H. S. MAINE on Primitive Contracts	193
Relation of *Legal* to *Moral* Contracts	194
Analysis of a Legal Contract	195
Principle of Excluding Immoral Contracts	196
The Capacity for Making a Contract	198
The Form and Evidence of a Contract	200
Meaning of the "Consideration" for a Contract	203
Rights and Duties of Contractors	205
The Interpretation of Contracts	206
Lien and Suretyship	208
Theory of a Law of Bankruptcy	209
The Remedy of "Specific Performance"	210
"Vindictive" or "Exemplary" Damages	211
The Policy of the English Combination Statutes	212
Modes of Assessing Damages for Breaches of Contract ...	214
Meaning of term *Quasi-Contracts*	215
Nature of Implied Contracts	216
Marriage as a Contract	217
Sale as a Contract	218

xvi   CONTENTS.

	PAGE
Relation of a Contract to a Conveyance	219
Relation of a Contract to an Obligation	221
Transfer and Descent of Obligations	222
Nature of Negotiable Instruments	223
Nature of Agency or Mandate	224
Nature of Contracts of Assurance	225

CHAPTER X.

CRIMINAL LAW AND PROCEDURE.

Primitive Relation of Crimes to Civil Injuries	229
Sir H. MAINE on the Early History of Criminal Law ...	230
Essential Nature of a Crime	232
Functions of the State in respect of the Prevention of *Crimes*	233
Theory of the Distinction between *Crimes* and *Civil Injuries* ...	235
The Moral Element in Criminality	236
The Elements in a *Moral* and in a *Legal* Judgment	238
Relation of Criminal Law to Popular Sentiment	241
Meaning of terms *Dolus* and *Malice*	243
Mr. AUSTIN's Analysis of the Elements of Criminality	245
Theory and Grounds of Exculpation	246
Accessories to Crimes	350
Characteristics of the Statute of Treasons of EDWARD III. ...	252
Historical Account of the English distinction between "Felonies" and "Misdemeanours"	253
Policy of punishing *Attempts* to commit Crimes	254
Nature of the English offence of "Misprision of Treason" ...	255
Mr. R. S. WRIGHT on the English Law of Conspiracy ...	255
Lord MANSFIELD on English Law as a directly Moralizing Instrument	256
Evils attending the Multiplication of Police Offences ...	257
How far Representative Institutions are a Security against Invasions of Public Liberty	258
Enumeration of Securities for Public Liberty	261
Dangers to Public Liberty incident to Subordinate Legislation ...	262
Policy of Extradition Treaties	263
Nature and Limits of the Security implied in the Right of Bail	264
Description and Operation of the English *Habeas Corpus* Act ...	265
Nature and Value of the Institution of Trial by Jury	267
Mr. Fox's Libel Act	269
The French Verdict of "Extenuating Circumstances" ...	270

	PAGE
English and Continental Criminal Procedure	272
Mr. FROUDE on the Characteristics of Englishmen in HENRY VIII.'s time	274
Value of the *Confessions* of an Accused Person as Evidence	275
Theory and Ends of Criminal Punishments	278
Inexpediency of the Use of Harsh and Cruel Punishments	282
Worthlessness of Retaliatory Punishments	283
Principles of Adjusting Punishments	284
Use and Value of Discretionary Punishments	286
Relevancy of Evidence of Character	287
Treatment of Lunatics and Youthful Prisoners convicted of Crime	288

CHAPTER XL

THE LAW OF CIVIL PROCEDURE.

Proper Place of the Law relating to Civil Injuries	290
Elements and Objects of the Law of Civil Procedure	292
The Institution of a Legal Profession	294
General course of a Civil Trial	295
Nature and History of "Pleading"	296
Parallel presented by Roman and English Pleading	297
Rules of Evidence	299
Value of Presumptions in settling on whom lies the Burden of Proof	300
Policy of excluding and of restricting Evidence	302
Possibility of determining what are "Relevant Facts"	303
Meaning of the opposition between *Direct* and *Circumstantial* Evidence	304
Meaning of *Hearsay* Evidence, and the policy of excluding it	305
Evidence obtained out of Court	305
Use of Depositions and Answers to "Interrogatories"	306
Use and Value of Cross-examination	307
Policy of exacting Judicial Oaths	308
Use and Treatment of the Evidence of *Experts*	309
Nature, Value, and Morality of *Advocacy*	311
Distribution of Courts into Courts of Original Jurisdiction and Courts of Appeal	313
Distribution of Courts into Courts of Inferior and Courts of Superior Jurisdiction	314

	PAGE
Distribution of Courts according to the nature of their business	315
Value of Tribunals of Commerce	316
Theory of Costs	317
Conflict of Laws, or Private International Law	318

CHAPTER XII.

INTERNATIONAL LAW.

Use of term *Law* in the International sense	322
Mr. AUSTIN on International Law	323
Law and Morality in the International sense	323
Criticism of recent English use of the term *Law*	324
Analogy presented by Early Law	325
International and Customary Law	326
Evolution of a Supreme Political Authority	327
Contrast of International and National Law	328
Analogy of the State and a Human Being	329
The State a Composite Body	330
Analogy of a State and a Corporation	331
History of International Law	332
Value of a pre-existing Legal Ideal	333
Value of a pre-existing Moral Ideal	334
Influence of Chivalry	335
Feudalism, the Church, and Monarchy	336
Relations of European Sovereigns	337
The Method of GROTIUS	338
Functions of the Statesman and of the Text-book Writer	339
Recent Growth of International Law	340
VATTEL's Distinction between the "Necessary" and the "Voluntary" Law of Nations	341
Recent Multiplication of Topics	342
Professor BLUNTSCHLI and Mr. DUDLEY FIELD's Codes	343
Modern Views of Expediency and Justice	344
Influence of International Law on Wars	345
Theoretical Equality of States	346
Prevalent Indisposition to Peace	347
Indisposition to Arbitration	348
Real Obstacles to Arbitration	349
Limits of use of Arbitration	350
Modes of preventing Wars	351
Value of Schemes for Codification	352
Special Difficulties in the way of Codification	353

	PAGE
Actual force of International Law	355
Prospects of International Law	356
Organization of Professors	357

CHAPTER XIII.

CODIFICATION.

Spontaneous Growth of Early Law	360
Mr. J. S. MILL on English Law in the time of BENTHAM	362
Enumeration of Reasons for Codification	364
Sir H. S. MAINE on Ancient Codes	365
Various Uses of the terms *Code* and *Codification*	366
Meaning of the term *Digest*, as opposed to *Code*	367
Objections to a Digest	368
Advocates of " Progressive " Codification	369
Analogy of British-Indian Codes and of the Code of FREDERICK II.	370
Objections to Partial Codification	371
A Code as a Product of Logical Art	372
Analogy from the Structure of Modern English Statutes	373
Purpose of Definitions	374
Demand for Rigid Classification	375
Adaptation of Language to Law	376
Amendments of the Code, and Use of Definitions and Illustrative Cases	377
Fresh Legislation embodied in a Code	378
Heedless Use of Foreign Analogies	379
Contrast presented by English and Continental Law	380
BENTHAM's testimony to excellence of English Law	381
Characteristics and History of English Law	382
Characteristics and History of French Law	383
Roman Law as an Ingredient of French Law	384
SAVIGNY's objections to Codification in GERMANY	385
Political Objections to Codification	386
How far Statute Law expresses the sentiments of the Community	388
Disadvantages of Unwritten and of Customary Law	389
Illustrations from English Common Law and from Customary Systems of France	390
Relations of Customary Law to a Code	391
Relations of New Statutes to a Code	392
Principles for determining whether the time for Codification has arrived	393

CHAPTER XIV.

LAW AND GOVERNMENT.

	PAGE
Democratical Form of Modern Governments ...	396
Distinction between Administration and Legislation ...	397
The Use of Subordinate Legislation ...	399
Perils incident to the Secrecy of Local Legislation ...	400
Value of Popular Co-operation ...	401
Functions of the Statesman in respect of Legislation ...	403
Moral Influence exercised by Laws ...	404
Fallaciousness of the notion of making experiments in Legislation ...	405
Law as a fact by which the State is organized and Individual Character perfected ...	406

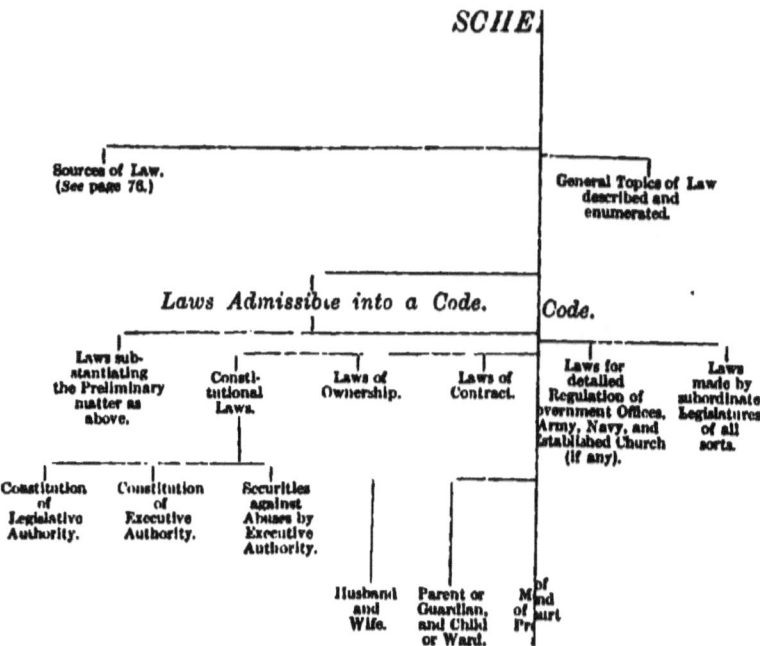

THE SCIENCE OF LAW.

CHAPTER I.

RECENT HISTORY AND PRESENT CONDITION OF THE SCIENCE OF LAW.

IN entering upon the treatment of any science it must always be a matter of doubt whether precedence, in the order of treatment, should be accorded to its history or to its nature and limits. It is obvious that both topics are essential to a complete elucidation of the science. The terms which a description of the science involves cannot be apprehended in all their integrity and distinctness, if no allusion is made to the progressive efforts by which they were, step by step, rescued by a line of thinkers from all the complications of popular language. Nor, of course, on the other hand, can this historical review be understood apart from all scrutiny into the nature of the materials and conceptions which the terms have more and more exactly represented.

The solution of the difficulty is to be found in starting boldly with one class of topics before the other, and in interpolating, by way of anticipation, such occasional explanations as may be necessary to give intelligibility to the whole. In this way each fresh chapter throws light upon all its predecessors, and the first chapter is never completely mastered till after the study of the last. In the present case it will be found most conducive to the purpose of precisely formulating the Science of Law to state briefly the condition in which that science stands in the present day, and to indicate the steps by which that condition has been reached.

There have been two main obstacles which, in this and in other countries, have, in different degrees, obstructed and perplexed the progress of scientific methods of thought in the matter of law. The one is the implication of law with morality; the other is the implication of abstract law with the individual character of each particular State as exhibited in its national customs. As to the first of these obstacles, the full nature of the difficulty can only be understood when, in a later chapter, the true and delicate relations of law and morality come under exact investigation. But, in the mean time, it is obvious that when the majority of persons use the terms "right," "ought," "duty," "crime," "malice," "fraud," they pay little attention to the construction which is put upon those important words in a Court of Justice. Still less are they thinking of the great logical exactitude in the use of every one of those terms which the practice of a Court of Justice demands. They use the words generally in a moral, rather than in a legal sense, or, at the best, in a legal sense more or less strongly tinctured with a moral sense.

It cannot be denied that the best and most philosophical thinkers of Germany, cognizant as they are of the true relations of law and morality, and of legal and moral terms, have to a certain extent contributed to this popular confusion by their reluctance to abstract, even provisionally, law from its moral surroundings. This abstraction has nowhere been so completely achieved as by Englishmen, after a fashion which will be shortly explained. The result of this philosophic tendency in Germany has been to merge the scientific treatment of law in the larger region of general ethical inquiry; and, consequently, instead of the Science of Law making an even and independent progress of its own, it has undulated with every wave of ethical speculation, and has consequently suffered the retardation incident to the growth of the most involved, because the most composite, branch of intellectual research.

The same dangers threatened the growth of a Science of Law in the hands of Bentham in this country, though they were obviated by the very causes which gave them birth. Bentham's characteristic method was to approach all moral and all legal rules in exactly the same attitude, and to test their value by one identical method—that of their conducing (as he expressed it) to the greatest happiness of the greatest number. The fact that a legal rule proceeded from a political sovereign, and that its infringement was punishable by that authority in a definitely prescribed way, while a moral rule proceeded (as Bentham held) from an indeterminate number of persons, and its infringement was only punishable at the hands of some of the number, with every feature of indefiniteness, indicates only differences in degree, and not in kind. Moral rules might gradually become as efficient as, or more efficient than, legal rules; and legal rules might, through non-execution or other causes, partake of all the imperfections of moral rules. There was no other morality but such as embodied moral rules of this class, and it differed from law only in the character of the imposing authority, and in the cogency of the "sanction" or "penalty." The direct effect of this mode of reasoning was to lose sight altogether of any permanent distinction and relation between law and morality, and thus to merge the Science of Law into the Science of General Ethics, as was being done from a directly opposite point of view by the great philosophers of Germany. But the indirect effect was very different. It was the annihilation of morality as a region permanently independent of law.

The next stage of thought evidently was the deliverance of law from the dead body of morality that still clung to it, and this was effected by Mr. Austin, who may be said to have been the true founder of the Science of Law, if indeed such an honour can ever belong to any one man, who can at the best be no more than the spokesman of his generation, and if he think at all, must needs take the next and only available step before him at the time.

It is true, however, that Mr. Austin combined in a peculiar degree the exact qualifications needed for the work before him. He thoroughly understood Bentham's work, and profoundly sympathized with it; but he also sympathized with much that to Bentham was intolerable. And yet he failed to sympathize with that element in foreign thought which would have led him astray from his appropriate task, and have deluged law with ethics and metaphysics. Mr. Austin apprehended to the full the use of the utilitarian test as applied to the political value of laws, and he recognized that the proper use of this test is an essential ingredient in the ethical judgment of the value of human actions. But he tried to discriminate with laborious and almost painful anxiety between the region of law and that of morality, claiming for the region of law a scientific character wholly peculiar and distinct. His sympathy with the writings of the Roman lawyers, in which he diverged notably from his master, led him at once to a comparative study of English and Roman law; and this again evolved the ideas which, being permanent and universal, give body and substance to the Science of Law. Had Mr. Austin not leaned more to a mechanical system of ethics than to a transcendental one, he must have incorporated more of German thought in his work than he did. But, fortunately for the progress of science then, he was just broad enough to free himself from Bentham, and just narrow enough to save himself from Kant and Hegel.

It was said that the other obstacle to the progress of the Science of Law has been found in the implication of law with the individual character of each particular State as exhibited in its national customs. There are two main modes in which law comes into being, one of which may be described as by ascending upwards, and the other as by descending downwards. The kind of law which ascends is formed out of customs spontaneously observed by classes of the population, either in certain places, or living under certain special conditions, or practising certain sorts of trades, professions, or occupations. The true relations of these customs to the law formed out of them will be exhibited further on, and the philosophy of the whole subject has been treated by Sir H. Maine in a most interesting way, in his lectures on "Village Communities." The other sort of law is that consciously imposed by the supreme political authority, or by the persons to whom a subordinate authority is delegated for this purpose.

All the law that comes into being through the mere practice of courts of justice belongs either to one or the other of these kinds, as qualified by the idiosyncracy of particular judges. The relation, however, of each of these kinds of law to the other depends generally more upon the discretion of judges than upon any fixed principle. Thus it may be laid down as an universal phenomenon that, while one large mass of every system of national law comes direct from the people, another large mass, constantly altering, controlling, supplementing, and superseding the former, comes directly from the Government. It need not here be said that both masses of law draw all their political force and validity from nothing else than the acquiescence and strength of the Government, however they may differ in their origin.

It is obvious, then, that that mass of the law which is most coloured by the medium of the popular usages amidst which it arose is most likely to be peculiar and estranged from the like mass of law in other countries; and in a country where that mass of the law is the most abundant and conspicuous, the alienation from all foreign systems of law is likely to seem most complete. Now, it is this state of things which exactly represents the condition of the legal system of England before the time of Bentham, of that of France before the Revolution, and of that of Germany, to a great extent, even at the present day. The case of England will illustrate that of the other countries, and will discover at once why it is that a Science of Law is only of extremely modern growth.

It is well known that up to the time of Bentham the law of England, and more especially the most antiquated portions of it, or the "Common Law," was obsequiously venerated on all sides, by judges, practising lawyers, legislators, and the general public, as the "perfection of human reason." If such a view seemed to shock common sense, when brought into glaring contrast with the actual anomalies, contradictions, barbarities, and irrational formalities which characterized every portion of the English Common Law, the difficulty was got over by ascribing all that was reasonable and precise to the Law, and all that was necessarily repugnant even to the acclimatized temperament of legal practitioners, to false interpretations of it. It is true, indeed, that the main structure of the English Common Law was so closely built into the very fabric of the English constitution, and even of English social and family life, especially in the department of the land law, the criminal law, and the county, municipal, and parochial institutions of the country, that it might well be conceived that nothing short of a national cataclysm could suffice to effect a thorough reform of the law without endangering the very basis upon which the whole State rested.

Just before the time of Bentham, English law had been, and still was, undergoing two great and important spontaneous modifications; one through the great development of commercial law, by which, as it were, a new and noble wing, built after the most approved models, was added on in a few years to the ancient edifice; and the other through the rapid expansion of the jurisdiction of the Court of Chancery. It remained for Bentham to use the battering-ram of the pure reason against what remained of the ancient system, and to compel every portion of it to justify itself by something better than its antiquity, its uncertainty, or its serviceableness to the lower interests of an inert legal profession. This proclivity of Bentham's necessarily involved a recognition of the principle that certain immutable logical and ethical principles underlie the laws of every country, and that the iniquitous condition of large—and those the most favourite—portions of English law proceeded from forgetfulness of these principles.

The first step towards the enucleation of a true Science of Law was thus indirectly facilitated by what had hitherto been one of the most serious hindrances to the conception of such a science. The hindrance was the implication of the national law with the formal institutions of the English people. It is obvious that in every country such an implication must exist, especially in the oldest portions of the law; but in a country which, like England, has, for so many hundreds of years, suffered no foreign conquest, and has generally guarded its insular ways and usages with almost sanctimonious reverence, the obstacles to a release of law from its surrounding incidents must be intensely powerful.

The feeble hold that the civil and canon law have had upon English Courts, and the jealous opposition to the introduction, in ever so diluted a form, into the Common Law Courts especially, of principles borrowed from them, present another striking point of contrast between the juridical situation of England and that of continental countries. It may well be, however, that the very enormity of the circumstances by which English law exhibited an aspect so markedly stagnant and barbaric, in comparison with its progressive political constitution so much in advance of every country of Europe, tended to precipitate the change. So soon as light was once let in upon the dark place, it poured in like a flood. The exact measure of Bentham's work in constructing the Science of Law is difficult to evaluate, as he combined in himself so many distinct faculties; generally attempting to reform the political substance at the same time that he laid bare the incongruities of the logical form of law. Nevertheless, in reforming, or endeavouring to reform, legal terminology and classification on principles of general logic, he was the necessary forerunner of Mr. Austin, to whom, as has been said, the conscious establishment of the legal science must properly be attributed. Indeed, it is scarcely possible to see how the science could have come into being at the time it did, without the previous existence of a body of truculent criticism directed against the abuses and scholastic puerilities which disfigured so large a portion of English law.

The revival of the study of Roman law in this country must not be omitted in recounting the main antecedents out of which the Science of Law has been evolved. This study, commended as it was in some memorable language of Mr. Austin's, has derived an important impetus from the scholarly and historical genius of Sir H. Maine.

There are two distinct directions in which the study of Roman law has already influenced legal thought, and is likely to influence it in the future. One of these is the improvement of purely logical conceptions through the comparison of the methods, terminology, and arrangement of the *corpus juris* with the traditional principles of English law. The mere habit of laying side by side two systems historically and ethically so remote from one another could not fail to discover elements of unity in them which, in fact, are the rudimentary principles of a Science of Law.

The other direction which the study of Roman law has taken has been of a more strictly historical kind. Through the pursuit of Roman law in an historical or antiquarian spirit, the relations of the national system of law to all the other phenomena of civilization in a country, and especially to the earliest phases of that civilization, have had much light thrown upon them. This light has been intensified through the recent study, in a spirit of comparative science, of the early customs of primitive communities all over the world. It may be that at present this process has been rather too hastily performed, and the generalizations arrived at may hereafter prove to have been premature and superficial. But the hopeful spirit in which any track of early modes of property, inheritance, testamentary disposition, succession, marriage, and criminal or civil procedure, is invariably followed out by modern investigators, points to the presence of a more and more conscious belief in the existence of a Science of Law. Undoubtedly the study of Roman law, as critically pursued of late years, must be credited with these favourable results and prospects.

On the other hand, it may be necessary in this place to interpose a caution, in order to guard against an over vehement tendency to exaggerate, by way of reaction, the importance of Roman law. If this study is to form an essential element in the legal education of every practising lawyer, it will be well that the method of teaching adopted should disclose of itself that the study is pursued, not for the purpose of gratifying antiquarian curiosity or even literary taste, but solely in subservience to the paramount object of promoting the scientific study of modern systems of law. If Roman law be thus studied in a strictly scientific spirit, with a view to the mastery of its form and methods, and not to the servile imitation of its precedents, the result can only be good. Foreign law and International law can be studied through no other medium than through Roman law, and no exposition of the Science of Law can be satisfactory which is not of cosmopolitan application.

The construction of modern codes, especially those already attempted for English-speaking or English-governed populations, must at once give the greatest impulse to the scientific study of law, and render that study a more and more indispensable condition. The history of Anglo-Indian legislation in this respect is very peculiar. The laws of British India have been recently re-modelled and re-published under the direction of a line of accomplished lawyers from this country,

Much of the law subjected to the process of reconstruction is identical with the law of England. A reflex influence has been experienced by the mother country upon itself, and the question is naturally asked whether the alleged impossibility or excessive difficulty of at once codifying English law is not rather due to the indolence of politicians, if not to the obstruction of interested persons, than to any real incompatibility between the English, when in their own country, and a well-arranged and intelligible system of law.

It is obvious that the increasing intercourse of modern States must in a variety of ways hasten the study of the Science of Law. The recent progress of International law, both public and private, is at once an augury and an expression of this tendency. If States are to have relations of ever-increasing intimacy with each other, there must be some uniform code, written or unwritten, by which the rights and duties of States are defined and circumscribed. Beneficial and essential as is such a code in times of war, it is equally so in times of peace. The construction of such a code must proceed upon some settled and generally recognized principles of logical classification, terminology, and ethical conceptions. The materials for these principles must, and can only, be drawn from a comparative study of the systems of national law actually prevalent in the different countries.

Hitherto the accidental prominence of Roman law in International law has hid from sight the essentially comparative character of any universal system of law. But as International law progresses to still finer developments, and trenches on regions of commerce and mutual co-operation wholly unknown both to the principles and to the language of the Roman law, some novel method must be discovered of expressing a common assent based upon common needs and aspirations. Such a method will evidently be a comparative one, and the elaboration of such a method presupposes the complete development of a Science of Law. In that region which is sometimes called Private International Law, and sometimes the Conflict of Laws, due as it is to the intercourse with each other of the citizens of different States, whether brought about through travel, commerce, continued residence, or even colonization, there has been increasingly felt the same pressing need to discover principles of utility and of justice to which the citizens of a variety of States and the tribunals of all States will pay deference. The discovery of such principles, to be successful, must rest upon a scientific investigation of the grounds, logical, social, and political, upon which all laws rest. Apart from such an investigation, the attempt in any given country to reconcile what is called "the conflict of laws" will always be exposed to the danger of favouring the interests or the prejudices of the citizens of the State where the law is applied. Thereby springs up, as has sprung up, an indefinite diversity in the private International law of each State, in the place of an identity of principle and practice, reflecting the identity of their moral claims.

CHAPTER II.

PROVINCE AND LIMITS OF THE SCIENCE OF LAW.

In order to ascertain what are the materials of the Science of Law, it will be well to cast a glance at the subject matter, in its rudest and most inartificial shape, to which the science relates. For this purpose the case may be taken of a nation in what may be called the early manhood of its life, after all the early struggles for its self-conscious existence or for its independence are over, and yet before it has developed within itself all the complicated machinery of a highly-organized commercial and social life. In such a State there must, by the very hypothesis, be a more or less steadily fixed government, whether that government approach more to a monarchical, or an aristocratical, or a democratical type. The stability of the State and its self-dependence imply agriculture, and agriculture implies property or ownership. The division of labour, again, which this economical condition presupposes, involves the habit of making contracts, even though they be of the most elementary form. The social condition cannot but rest upon a previously developed, though now strongly fortified, domestic condition, and this implies the fact of marriage, and the relations of husband and wife, parent and child, brother, sister, uncle, aunt, nephew, niece, and the like. The still remaining anarchical tendencies of certain individual members of the

State, lagging behind the rest, will generate occasional acts of violence threatening, directly or indirectly, the very life and existence of the State. These acts will excite the horror of all the more orderly members of the community, and will be denominated by some such term as *crimes*.

It is obvious that the characteristic classes of facts which have just been alluded to are so general and simple that their necessary occurrence at a certain epoch in the progress of every State may be predicted as a certainty. These facts, however, in themselves are of the utmost possible moment, and involve, by their permanence and universality, the elementary ingredients of a Science of Law.

It will be seen that these facts, looked upon as a whole, imply, first, a certain number of definite relations of persons to one another, whether as governors or governed, husbands or wives, parents or children, or as otherwise allied by blood or marriage. Secondly, these facts involve certain determinate relations between the persons in the community, in respect of the things (or physical substances) appertaining to the community as a whole. These things severally are owned by one or another, and not by the rest. The ownership of these things is the subject-matter of private arrangements and contracts between different members of the community. The violent or fraudulent abstraction of a thing owned from the owner may be one of the acts on the general prevention of which the very life of the community is held to depend, and as such is denominated a *crime*.

Again, the classes of facts already enumerated have two distinct sides to them, one touching the outward lives of members of the community, that is their *acts;* the other touching their inward lives, that is their thoughts and feelings. Over the former of these sides the whole of the community can, by its aggregate pressure, exert a considerable amount of force, of a specifically ascertained quantity and quality. Over the latter side, that touching the thoughts and feelings of individual members, the utmost direct pressure consciously exerted by the community is of the feeblest efficacy, and, at the best, indefinite and precarious in the highest degree. The sphere of action of the community with respect to the former, or the *acts* of men, is that of law. The sphere of action with respect to the latter, that is the thoughts and feelings, though not exclusive of acts, is morality. The relations of these two spheres to each other will be investigated in the next chapter.

In the mean time the following conclusions have been reached. It appears that the characteristic energy of every State consists in the reciprocal influence upon each other of the corporate whole and the constituent elements, in respect of certain definitely assignable classes of human action. These classes of action will either have reference to things or physical substances, as objects of ownership or use, or have no such reference. The actually subsisting relationship to each other of the corporate whole and the constituent personal elements depends upon the form of Government which casually happens to prevail.

The influence of the constituent personal elements of the State upon its governing authority, as representing, at any epoch, the corporate whole, is exhibited, first, in the selection (whether conscious or unconscious) of that governing authority according to its specific modifications; and, secondly, in the incessant control (conscious or unconscious) of that authority, by which the limits of its free action are at every moment defined. The influence of the governing authority, on the other hand, on the constituent personal elements of the State—that is, upon its so-called "subjects"—is exerted through two separate channels: one that of administration; the other, that of law. In other words, the purposes of Government are effected either through the medium of occasional and, as it were, spasmodic injunctions, or through general rules.

The limits within which any given governing authority can venture to issue occasional injunctions must be determined, as has already been seen, by its actual relations to all the constituent personal elements of the State. These limits will never be precisely determined in language, though they will be marked with tolerable exactness in fact, and instinctively appreciated by all persons concerned in either enlarging or protecting them.

The determination of these limits of administrative authority might be looked upon as forming one great branch of the general rules which constitute the other field of the appropriate activity of the Government. It composes a large portion of what is called "constitutional law." The anomaly, however, attaching to this extension of the term "law" is obvious, inasmuch as, if the name "law" be given to the body of general rules through which a Government exerts its appropriate activity, the same term "law" cannot be simultaneously applied to the limits affixed to its freedom of action. But this objection, when once understood, is of little practical importance. It is sufficient to establish that there are certain definite limits which circumscribe the free action of every governing authority, and that these limitations admit of being formulated into more or less precisely articulated propositions. Such propositions, capable as they are of being handled, interpreted, and enforced in Courts of Justice, have all the essential qualities that belong to the general rules framed by the governing authority itself for the guidance of the conduct of all persons submitted to its dominion.

The topics of these general rules or laws will be those matters which have already been described as essentially inviting the direction of the corporate strength of the community. Such matters are the relations of family life, so far as outward actions and public decorum are involved; the security of property; the protection of individual liberty; the enforcement of contracts; and the prevention of those violent and exceptional excesses denominated *crimes*.

At a very early period in the history of the community, the interest that each citizen has in the wise and effectual regulation of such matters as these becomes conspicuous to all, and more especially to those usually, or on the average, more advanced and intelligent members of the community who find themselves charged, through, it may be, a series of political vicissitudes, with the duties of Government. It is probable that these several and various objects will attach to themselves at different epochs a very unequal and disproportionate share of attention.

The security of property may alternate with security of the person as an object of governmental care; and the classification of crimes and civil injuries, or even of crimes and religious offences or sins, may be in the highest degree irregular and unsystematic. The vices, the selfishness, the ignorance of individual rulers will, from time to time, bring into relief some classes of laws to the disparagement or neglect of others. At one epoch a State will suffer from having too few laws, at another from having too many. Particular classes of persons may lose or gain at one period of legislation, and other classes may lose or gain at another. These eras and disasters are of none the lighter consequence, that they have been universal. It is in spite of them, and not by means of them, that States have finally endured and fought their way to a climax of intelligent legislation and conscious political life. In the case of such States, the heart of the people, as estimated from generation to generation, has been sound, and the heads of their rulers wise. The laws have gradually been adapted to promote individual liberty, and not to impair it; and the province of Government has been so mapped out as to make Government an institution conducive to the good of the people, and not a mere organ for the sacrifice of a nation to a class.

It will have been seen, in the above description of universal phenomena, that a purely abstract mode of treatment has been adopted. So far as universally confessed historical facts are pre-supposed, the truth of such facts is boldly assumed. But the main bases of the arguments are the elements of human nature itself as they are written not only in the venerable documents of ancient history, but on the face of every traveller's narrative, of every ancient body of laws, of every honoured institution subsisting in the midst of the national life of the most advanced countries of Europe. It is obvious, then, that the generality and permanence of the momentous facts above described affords the groundwork of a great science, the Science of Law.

This science is distinguishable from the Science of Ethics, to which it may be co-ordinated, as well as from the Science of Politics, to which it is subordinated. The materials of the science are: a description of (1) the essential institutions of human society, by the use of which the objects of that society are carried out through the medium of Government; (2) the nature, conditions, and limits of *law* as an expression of that side of governmental action which consists in the enumeration of general rules of action; (3) the accidents of law, such as language and interpretation, terminology, and devices for legislation.

When these materials are carefully scrutinized, it will be found that they are composed of elements as permanent and universal as the elements of human nature itself. All that is arbitrary and idiosyncratic for any particular State is banished from the inquiry. The surplus is as applicable to one State as to another; to the most immature system of law as to the most advanced; to an eastern as to a western community; to the modern as to the ancient world.

It is curious that this universality and permanence have been generally conceded to ethical truths, and have latterly been more and more freely conceded even to political phenomena, modified indefinitely, as these must needs be, by the excessive complexity of the conditions which constitute them. But the region of law has, up to a recent time, been held to be the natural home of caprice and irregularity. Some writers, indeed, such as Montesquieu and M. Charles Comte, have quoted the varying laws in the different countries of the world with almost an ironical gladness at their bizarre and parti-coloured appearance. It has been very generally held that Governments have been created by violence or accident, and have reflected the vices of their origin in the reckless selfishness of their legislation. It has been said again and again that force is the origin of all social institutions, and that the modes of directing that force have been determined in every State by the chance breath of political caprice or passion. It has been forgotten, or has escaped notice, that the caprice has been accidental and the order is essential.

It will be noticed that there are two distinct conceptions of human society which are both possible, if not both true, and that the existence of a Science of Law follows as a necessary consequence of the adoption of one conception, but does not follow from the adoption of the other. It may be said, on one theory, that the composition and action of human society, as exhibited in the State, is due to nothing else than the aggregation and mutual repulsion of a number of independent and self-conscious atoms which, by a gradual process of experience, have discovered that the largest measure of individual well-being is solely attainable through certain special modes of co-operation. These modes of co-operation take a variety of forms, but the most signal and important are those implied in the facts of government, ownership, the composition of the family, and contract.

According to the theory now under review every one of these facts is merely a device for carrying out ends believed to be beneficial. The facts might be made to vary indefinitely, and it is alleged to be conceivable that any one of them, and perhaps every one, might be absent altogether and a new set of devices take their place. It is held to be possible that the devices themselves will, at no remote period, be discovered to be rude and insufficient, and that many superior substitutes could be found for them, even if they do not already exist in certain societies, the constitution of which is as yet unexplored. The machinery by which each one of these classes of facts is called into being, and made to subserve its end, is physical force, taking the form of what is called law. The physically stronger part of the community compels the weaker to obey a certain form of governing authority, to recognize certain descriptions of ownership, to conform their lives to certain canons of domestic life, and to observe certain regulations of the market and the exchange. The rules, indeed, enforced by law are, for the most part, so transparently beneficial to all concerned that the pressure of law becomes very slightly felt, and the physical force which supports it is comparatively seldom called into play. Nevertheless, in the theory now being enunciated, force is not only present, but the main originator and upholder of every portion of the fabric of social order. It is obvious that, according to this view, there can only be a Science of Law in a very restricted sense. In the largest sense of the expression there can be none. Instead of law having any precise and determinate character impressed upon it and upon its operation, through the existence of a certain number of immovable social institutions, which react back as effectually upon law as law acts upon them, these institutions are nothing more than the creations of law itself, or rather the accidental shadows which law happens to cast.

The opposite theory of society starts with the conception that society is not developed through the conflicting passions of individual atoms striving to organize themselves after a fashion which shall best promote their own well-being, but is from first to last a subsisting organization made up of constituent groups reciprocally acting and reacting upon one another. The elemental forms and tokens of this organism are family life, ownership, and government. Each of these presupposes co-operation and contribution at all stages in the history of society, though under different forms; each of them implies the distribution of mankind into small groups rather than into large masses of individual atoms. It is difficult to say that any one of these original elements has precedence in point of time over any one of the others. It is more true to say that when once they are all found to be in existence, the State has then and there come into being. A very short time passes before another element—that of contract—implied in all progressive industrial co-operation, also comes to the surface.

There are thus formed in the primitive State a

certain number of elemental institutions which may be looked upon, not in any sense as the creation of law, but as existing independently of law; for the spontaneous arbitrary action of a primitive Government resembles what is now called "Administration" rather than law. It is true, however, that law, in the immature form of regulated usage, will be found to be one of the earliest of all the ingredients of the State. It will be, indeed, even from the first, the regulator and the guide of the other institutions with which it is contemporary, but is in no sense their parent or solitary guardian. Nevertheless, as time goes on, the support that law gives to the integrity of family life, to property, to industrial and commercial relations, and to Government, becomes important in the highest degree. Indeed, the prominence of the legal supervision exercised in a highly developed State over all these departments, affords an apology for the familiar notion that they are all the arbitrary creation of law and depend for their continued subsistence upon no greater or deeper sanction than that of physical force.

If it be true, then, as this last theory asserts, that in every State there are a limited number of great pivots, or turning points, round which human society revolves, and that law only plays a subordinate part in regulating and protecting the grand mechanism, it is obvious that a permanent and universal body of facts relative to law may be at once anticipated to result from the permanence and universality of the great groups of facts with which it happens to be mainly conversant. Experience and observation confirm this anticipation. Every known system of law, both of ancient and modern times, in all parts of the world, and in all stages of national development, distributes itself into the main divisions of laws determining (1) the nature, functions, and limitations of the governing authority; (2) the forms and conditions of ownership, whether of land or other things; (3) the relations of family life; and (4) the binding force of voluntary promises or contracts. These several topics afford a natural method of distribution applicable to every legal system whatever; and each several topic, according to its peculiar nature and to the incidents by which it is internally characterized, affords a distinct congeries of logical subdivisions which is invariably reproduced over and over again.

It is, then, in this identity of structure of human society in every State, that law discovers for itself the basis of its constantly recurrent methods of classification and its unchangeable conceptions. There are, however, certain other more obvious grounds for the permanence and invariability of legal ideas and methods which follow from the identity of man's physical, logical, and ethical structure in all times and in all parts of the world, within the limits to which observation has hitherto extended.

Law in its outward character consists of a body of commands addressed to individual members of the human race forming the component elements of a State. The issuing of commands involves the possibility of obedience or of disobedience, and therein supposes the presence of will, of liberty of action, and of the amount of intelligence needed to understand the purport of the commands. Attention is thereby compelled to the exceptional cases in which the terms of the command cannot be understood, whether through temporary incapacity, as infancy, error, or passing disease; or through permanent incapacity, as lifelong insanity; or in which the terms cannot be complied with through the pressure of external force, the interference of persons actuated by fraudulent motives, or the obstruction of physical facts creating the condition of impossibility.

Supposing, however, that the command can be understood and can be obeyed, there will be nevertheless cases presented in which the question has to be decided whether, as a matter of fact, the command, in a given case, was obeyed or not. Here are let in all the obstacles inherent in human nature itself to acquiring a correct knowledge of facts. All the current imperfections of human observation, all the insufficiency of language and expression, all the chicanery and double-mindedness, all the dulness of intellect, by which it becomes so hard to pass truth on unimpaired from hand to hand, are present to hamper the effort to apply and execute a single law. The several forms of these obstacles, however, are not peculiar to any one State nor to any one period, however their magnitude may vary. They are universally present, and can be classified under a comprehensive scheme.

But another and universal class of difficulties in executing a law has yet to be mentioned. It may be uncertain what is the form and intent of the law itself. If the law is written, the terms of the language in which it is written may admit of all sorts of ambiguity or vacillation in meaning, or, however certain the terms themselves, the opposed disputants may insist on different senses being put upon the whole text of the command.

If the law is unwritten, and has to be gathered either from traditional report or by reference to the rules which have been laid down on previous occasions in cases resembling the one now calling for decision, opportunity is presented for all sorts of logical conflict as to the import of the previous cases cited in illustration, or as to the value of the analogies insisted upon.

In other words, a series of logical processes is involved in the *interpretation* of every law, whether written or unwritten, and the correctness of these processes may furnish ground for indefinite doubt and argument. But these logical processes are permanent and universal, and the application of them to the interpretation of law imparts their own permanence and universality to the Science of Law.

It has thus been seen that the intellectual and the ethical nature of man in all nations tends to impart a scientific character to the study of the laws by which his social actions are regulated. The physical facts of his life and bodily constitution tend to the same end. His birth, his death, his age, his liability to diseases and accidents of all sorts, his capacity of locomotion, and his several relations to time, space, quantity, measurement, and the like, further discover fresh categories into which portions of the laws which regulate his conduct, and describe his situation, under varying circumstances, in relation to his fellows, necessarily fall.

Besides the elements of the Science of Law which are discoverable within the limits of a single State, and even of the most miniature one, there are others which are developed only in the course of time, as States multiply in number, and as their relations to one another become strictly defined.

The relations of States to one another are twofold in character. Either the Governments of the different States have relations to each other, or the individual citizens of the different States have relations to each other.

The first class of relations give occasion to what is called Public International Law, and the latter to what is sometimes called, with less precision, Private International Law.

It is plain that if the rules regulating the relations of States are true law in any sense, they are identical for all the States subject to them. The same ought to be the case with respect to the rules regulating the recognition of the laws of foreign States. But there are certain obstacles which have, in fact, prevented the uniformity of substance which might have been anticipated in this region of law.

The rules of the species of law last indicated come into being through the moral claim that is presented either by persons who, not being citizens of a given country, come to the courts of justice of that country, while sojourning there, to have rights recognized and protected which they have acquired in their own country; or by those who, being citizens of one country, but having acquired rights while sojourning in other countries, come to the courts of their own country to have those rights recognized and protected.

On every occasion for inventing rules applicable to these cases, the question is presented whether the courts of justice of a country shall recognize rights acquired either by their own citizens or by foreigners in other countries; or, in other words, whether the laws of other countries giving validity to those rights shall or shall not be held to be effectual in the courts of justice which are invited to interfere. The cases are generally further complicated by the nature of the processes and transactions out of which the asserted rights spring. Part of the transactions may have taken place in one country, and part in another, and the remedy may be sought for in a third. Or the person seeking the remedy, or against whom the remedy is sought, may be the citizen of one country, have his permanent residence or domicile in another country, and be temporarily sojourning in the country in which the remedy is sought.

It is obvious, from a mere enumeration and description of the cases which give rise to rules, that the purpose of the existence of these rules is always the facilitation of intercourse between the citizens of different States, and the prevention of practical injustice. These objects must be served in the highest degree, if the greatest possible uniformity of principle obtain in the courts of all nations in creating and applying the rules. In this way reasonable expectations are likely to be best satisfied, and fraudulent evasions of the law of any particular country are likely most effectually to be prevented. It happens, however, that, owing to the political jealousies that have hitherto kept apart the most considerable nations of Europe, and to the foolish prejudice with which individual nations have fostered principles of law familiar in their own courts, however alien to the practice of all other countries, there have hitherto been made only very imperfect attempts at uniformity either of principle or practice in this respect.

It is probable that an increasingly clear apprehension of the logical relations of the different branches of law, whether as touching upon ownership, contract, family life, or crime, will produce the effect of assimilating the substance as well as the form of the rules of law forming the so-called Private International Law of different countries. This end is perhaps one of the most practical and desirable that the Science of Law could set before itself, though it will need at every point the aid of the Science of Legislation. This subject will be recurred to again in the chapter on Laws of Procedure.

It appears, then, from the above investigation, that there is a true Science of Law based upon the irrefragable, permanent, and invariable facts of the constitution of human society, as exhibited in the state of the physical, logical, and ethical constitution of man. The objects of the cultivation of this science are, first, the ready understanding of every system of national law, through a firm hold being obtained upon its technical structure, its topics, its logical subdivisions, and the methods of its application; secondly, an orderly view of the whole system of law of any one country in order to its comprehensive amendment, reform, and intelligent reconstruction in obedience to the needs of a new political and social era; thirdly, the attainment of a clearly expressed, rational, and well developed system of Public International Law; and, fourthly, the reduction of the irregular, and sometimes chaotic, or arbitrary, rules of so-called Private International Law, as adopted in different States, to an uniform system, the same for all States.

CHAPTER III.

LAW AND MORALITY.

ON commencing the investigation of the basis of the Science of Law, it was noticed that there were two main avenues through which the whole social force of a national community is made effective towards the direction, and the constraint, of the impulses of the individual citizens of which it is composed. One of these avenues was said to be law, the other, to be morality. The constant confusion of these two conceptions, or the entire merger of one of them in the other, impresses the necessity of clearly marking out, at this stage, their respective provinces.

With respect to the bare fact that the two fields of law and of morality are different, not to say opposed, scarcely any one would be found to express a doubt. Casting an eye over the general activity of an advanced community, and the general range of the thought and occupations of a single individual man or woman, it is found that the thoughts, affections, and energies of home life, of social life, of industrial or commercial life, are the most absorbing and preponderating of the facts presented. It is law, indeed, which determines decisively the constitution of the family; which marks out the subject matter and the conditions of ownership; and which gives definiteness and precision, as well as what may be called physical validity, to business transactions

But within the limits described by law, there is a very wide scope for activity to which law cannot reach.

A man may be a bad husband, a bad father, a bad guardian, without coming into conflict with the rules of a single law. He may be an extortionate landlord, a wasteful tenant, a hard dealer, an unreliable tradesmen, and yet the legal machinery of the country may be quite powerless to stimulate or to chastise him. He may be, furthermore, a self-seeking politician, an unscrupulous demagogue, or an indolent aristocrat, and yet satisfy to the utmost the claims of the law upon him. Nevertheless it is just in the conduct of these several relationships that the bulk of human life consists, and national prosperity and honour depend.

"*Quid leges sine moribus?*" is the complaint of the old Roman poet, and the question may be asked with equal applicability in every age. It is vain to enact laws if the bulk of the community do not care to have them enforced. It is almost equally vain to enact them if they are scrupulously observed in the letter and broken in the spirit. It is of no good to prevent glaring frauds, if people are habitually and persistently treacherous. It is of no good to punish perjury, if people habitually lie. It is of no good to punish breaches of formal contracts, if the keeping of a common promise is the exception rather than the rule.

Admitting the existence of the vast field of morality as contrasted with that of law, a celebrated and probably inextinguishable controversy has existed as to the exact means through which moral considerations operate, and by which the conscience or moral faculty in man is finally appealed to. It is not strictly relevant to the present inquiry to plunge into the details of the controversy, but the nature of it must be indicated in order to mark the origin of the confusion between morality and law.

The just action of man in his moral relations with his fellows may be promoted either through fear of the consequences to himself of unjust action, or through cheerful obedience to the demands of a clearly recognized duty. The recognition of the duty when presented, and the disposition to obey its demands, may be due to the original constitution of man, or to the stimulus supplied by social contact, or to experience of the advantages of a ready and duteous obedience. One class of controversialists have resolved the whole motives to moral action into such as are supplied by the stimulus of hope or fear. Another class have imputed these motives to nothing else than the promptings of an universally diffused natural instinct. A third class again give what is due both to the original constitution of man and to the influence of social experience, but also attribute much to the contagious operation of a range of sentiments diffused throughout society in such a way as to result in a more and more certainly apprehended distinction between "right" and "wrong," and to produce by inheritance a characteristic change for the better in the actual constitution of man.

According to this last theory, morality, or the prevalence of moral sentiments and of duteous action, is a matter of extremely gradual growth in any community, and is, in fact, a joint product of all the other physical and social facts by which the community is characterized. This prevalent moral condition is, furthermore, extremely complex in its constitution. It reaches to every part of human life, thought, feeling, and action. Through the principles of association of ideas, operating upon the nervous sensitiveness of the physical constitution in an advanced social state, its effects are multiplied and intensified indefinitely on every side.

The conscience (which is a curt term to express the moral susceptibility of man) becomes, as it were, a refined organ of the most attenuated edge and the most delicate temper. Man needs no longer the promptings and support of his fellows to think, feel, and act as he ought. In the most desolate wilderness, in the hour of shipwreck, in the lonely mountain-top, he gives up his life for his fellows simply because he listens with keen attention to the voice of duty.

It must be conceded by all that if the above is a correct picture of the phenomena of morality as exhibited in a highly advanced country, the region of law is infinitely poor and narrow when contrasted with it. According to the theory that the existence of morality depends upon nothing else than a constantly inculcated experience of the personal disadvantage, in the long run, of immoral actions, it is difficult to draw any satisfactory line between the provinces of morality and law. They both touch outward actions alone. They both depend on the influences of fear, and, indirectly, on the presence of superior physical force. They both are capable of being digested into a body of rules or maxims. The only difference between the two is to be found in the persons by whom the physical pressure, in case of disobedience, is applied, and in the persons by whom the rules are from time to time constructed.

On the theory of morality here maintained, not only are law and morality different, but they are the complement, and, as it were, the very antitheses of one another. If morality looks to the thought and feeling rather than to the acts, though to the acts also, law looks pre-eminently to men's acts, and only to thoughts and feelings so far as is needed to explain the real character of men's acts.

If the force of law depends upon the physical

pressure, or "sanction," which is always ready to support it, the very excellence of morality is that it induces men to adopt a higher standard of action than that supplied by those persons nearest to them who are most capable of exerting direct physical pressure. The natural tendency of law is to generate fear; the natural tendency of morality is to make men brave.

It is true that obedience to law, by giving men leisure and freedom to be moral, co-operates with morality in making them brave; but the bravery comes from the morality and not from the law. This is seen at once when laws are multiplied unduly, or when they are unwisely made. Lastly, law is always capable of being digested into rules or logical propositions, and morality never.

So soon as it is attempted to bind up a moral principle into a logical proposition, the life of the principle is threatened, and the reign of casuistry is at hand. Every moral principle is tested and described solely by the circumstances which surround its application. It must rest with every man at the crisis of action to determine his own conduct. He may be largely helped in cases of doubt by the memory of previous examples, by the exhortations of moral teachers, and even by compendious maxims and rules; but no rule can be so universal as, of necessity, to demand his uncompromising submission. He stands alone in the presence of his trial, and no other man or body of men can relieve him of the awful responsibility. Others will judge him after the act, and he will judge himself; but, before the act, he has nothing but his firm grasp upon general moral principles and his own sensitiveness to the code of duty to rely upon.

Law, on the other hand, eminently deals in general rules; and hence, if these rules are properly published, no one need be in doubt at the crisis of action as to whether the act he is contemplating is legal or illegal. If he is in doubt, the difficulty comes not from the nature of law, but from the accidentally evil condition of the laws of his own country, a condition which is capable of indefinite improvement.

Thus, the characteristic of law is generality; of morality, individual application. It follows from this that the execution of law is always to some extent rude and unsatisfactory. The same penalty for a broken law is exacted from persons of an indefinite number of shades of moral guilt, from persons of high education and culture well acquainted with the provisions of the law they despise, and from the humblest and most illiterate persons in the country. The necessity of acting upon outward evidence, the value of which can be appreciated by the mind of average intelligence and sensitiveness to moral distinctions, increases this roughness and almost coarseness in the process of applying a law to a given case.

Various devices, indeed, are employed to correct the consequences of this want of refinement and elasticity. Such is "equity" in the older sense of the term, which seems to have been familiar to Aristotle. The purpose of this is to enable a judge, in any case in which the generality of a rule seems to press severely upon a particular person, to introduce, at his discretion, such modifications of the rule as may carry out the presumed general design of the law-maker with the smallest amount of deflection from the rigid language in which the law is couched, and yet with a more considerate regard for all the circumstances which surround the actual case than that language was capable of anticipating.

It is true that "equity," as administered in English Courts of Chancery, arose chiefly from the historical fact of a proved inaptitude of the English Courts of Common Law to provide all the remedies demanded without recourse to the special interference of the monarch through the medium of his chancellor; and it is also true that the development of "equity" has been due to the growth of a class of matters and relationships, to the complete adjustment of which the rules and machinery of the common law have proved to be more and more unequal; while, at the present day, the rules of "equity" are little less inelastic than rules of common law. Nevertheless, the method of supplementing the prevalent legal system by a subsidiary system of less rigidity, and of greater capacity for fine moral discrimination, is almost universal and indeed necessary in all advanced countries if law is in any measure to carry out the dictates of practical justice.

It may happen that the regular and the subsidiary system are administered by different judges and in different courts, as hitherto in England; or by the same judge sitting at different times in different characters, as at Rome; or by the same judge at the same time and just as the superior applicability of one or of the other system presents itself to notice, as in foreign countries and in some States of the American Union under modern codes. The disadvantages of such a subsidiary system as is implied in introducing the arbitrary discretion of the judge in the place of the fixed rules prescribed by the legislature, and in this way leaving the members of the community without a fixed guide for their actions or a reliable bulwark against the prejudices or vagaries of individual judges, are here recognized to the full.

There is needed, indeed, a systematized body of principles for the nicer adjustment of laws, as well as for the enunciation of laws themselves, and there must be a natural tendency in such a body of principles to become as rigid and inflexible as the rules which it is their purpose to qualify. Nevertheless, if the true nature of equity, as an essential supplement to law in all countries, be clearly understood; if it be recognized that, for the tracking of fraud and for the supervision of legal trusts, no bare rules of law can in themselves be adequate to the demand; if, on the other hand, the dangers of anarchy point to the importance of organizing principles of equity on a basis of regularity, uniformity, and stringency, in no way inferior to that on which law itself rests—then the existence of equity, so far from being considered as an unwholesome growth on a legal system, must be rather the symptom and proof of its complete development.

It scarcely need be said that the anomalies presented up to the present time in England, of administering law and equity in different courts, and of fostering, in many ways, the theory of a certain irreconcilable feud between them, is not only preposterous in its nature, but tends to the grossest injustice, delay, and inconvenience in its consequences to suitors.

The next signal mode of correcting the consequences following from the hard and rigid universality of legal rules is that of leaving to the judges, to whom the actual execution of laws appertains, the province of determining, within certain limits, the penalty to be exacted for the broken law. The penalty of a broken law generally has two aspects,—one, that of suffering to be inflicted on the transgressor, in order to reduce the probability of a repetition of the offence by himself or by another; the other, that of compensation to the person more immediately injured by the broken law for the loss or injury he may have thereby sustained.

As to some classes of laws, especially criminal laws,

the former aspect is the most conspicuous, or (as in England) the only one. As to other classes of laws, of what may be called a quasi-criminal nature, as laws for the protection of personal security and personal reputation, the two aspects of punishing the transgressor and compensating the sufferer are generally looked at together, and the amount and quality of the penalty may have to be determined by reference to both these considerations at once.

As to other classes of laws, again, as those conferring and protecting rights of ownership and of contract, which, in fact, are the largest portions of the law of every advanced community, and which give rise to the largest amount of litigation, compensation rather than punishment is generally treated as the object of the penalty.

The grounds of these common distinctions are not far to look for. In all cases the object is to prevent the infraction of law; but to increase the penalty beyond the exact amount needed for this purpose tends, in the long run, to promote impunity and lawlessness. With respect to matters touching upon the very existence of the community, as on politics and social organization, which are those with which criminal law is conversant, the danger to the community of the prevalence of crimes is out of all proportion to the special losses and suffering of individual persons. Hence comes the necessity of taking a standard for the measurement of the penalty wholly different from that supplied by the measure of compensation due in particular cases.

With respect to many matters of ownership and of contract, again, great as is the importance of the laws regulating them, yet the influence and means of owners and of contractors are sufficiently great to ensure, in the long run, the protection of their interests; and the measure of compensation due to them as great sections of society is, for the most part, sufficient as an effective penalty to prevent their rights being generally invaded. Rights of ownership, indeed, in all communities, are so important as to partake of both kinds of protection, the invasion of some classes of them falling under the cognizance of "criminal law," the invasion of other classes falling under that of "civil law," and, as such, being left for protection to the interference, by way of initiative, of the owners themselves, and the penalty being estimated by the measure of loss.

It is thus seen that the only region of judicial discretion in the assignment of the penalty for a broken law is where no question of compensation to the injured person is involved, or where this question is only of subordinate, or, at the most, of co-ordinate importance. It is in the region of criminal law and quasi-criminal law that discretion is mainly left to the judge to apportion the penalty in accordance with all the circumstances of the special case, and in this way he has an opportunity of correcting the hardship and practical injustice flowing from the rigid application of a general rule.

This discretion is, however, strictly limited by the legislature in all cases. In some countries, as in England, in the case of murder and high treason, no discretion in the selection or the modification of the punishment is left to the judge. If it be proved that the accused has done the act forbidden, with the mental intent requisite to conviction, there is no alternative but for the judge to pass the extreme sentence of the law.

The circumstances may differ by all the width that separates the accomplished and highly-educated poisoner from the agonized, abused, and ignorant mother destroying her child, knowing not what she does; and yet the judge has no alternative whatever to relieve him from passing the same sentence of death. With respect to other crimes, the judicial discretion is also limited, but the superior limit is generally affixed, and not the inferior one. Thus the penalty may vary from penal servitude for life to imprisonment for a day.

In some countries the responsibility is shifted from the judge to the jury, and, even in cases of technical murder, the jury are entitled to find a verdict of guilty, but to accompany it by some definite characterization in diminution of the penalty.

Whatever be the mechanism used, the purpose and consequences of leaving the measure of the actual penalty to be fixed at the time, and in view of the special circumstances of the case, are to leave free play for the consideration of the previous mental and moral condition and antecedents at the time of perpetrating the act.

It is true that other considerations may come in to direct the force and measure of the penalty besides that of regard to moral justice. The increasing or diminishing frequency of a particular class of crimes; the proclivity of certain classes of men (of whom the prisoner is one) to commit the crime in question, and the enhanced necessity of making the punishment exemplary; the extreme rareness of the whole circumstances, and the strong improbability or impossibility of their being presented again so as to favour the recurrence of such a crime; may also properly weigh with a judge in affixing the penalty.

But a scrupulous regard to moral justice as exhibited in an attentive consideration being given to the peculiar situation, temptations, opportunities, and previous character of the prisoner, is likely of itself to tend, quite as much as mere severity of punishment, to the diminution of crime.

As men come to feel that, in a court of justice, they will get what they really deserve, or, in other words, that the judgment of a legal tribunal reflects, with some approach to accuracy, the judgment of their own consciences and of the best, the truest, and the most tender-hearted of their fellow-men, their reverence for law becomes intensified, and their fear of breaking it becomes more effectually and constantly active. This subject is fully treated in the chapter on Criminal Law.

A third mode in which the rigidity of law, and its imperfect moral adaptability to individual instances, is corrected, is through an institution which has obtained in all the most civilized States of the World—that is, the Prerogative of Pardon, which is universally vested in the head of the executive. This prerogative, which probably at the first was little more than the expression of a certain overweening usurpation of the monarch over the realm of law, has become gradually restricted to the only uses which can justify the existence of so great, and apparently so extravagant, a claim.

If pressed to the full, the prerogative of pardon might imply practically a claim to override every law by the simple process of pardoning the transgressor of law, or of over-riding such laws as might be inconvenient in their operation to the person in whom the prerogative reposed. It is well known that the Tudor and Stuart kings of England affected, both practically and theoretically, to trample upon the liberty of the country and upon the co-ordinate powers of the two other branches of the legislature by proclamations, dispensations, and the unconstitutional exercise of the prerogative of pardon.

It was one of the articles of the Act of Settlement that a royal pardon should not be pleaded to an impeachment by the House of Commons. This clause, indeed, left the prerogative of pardoning a prisoner convicted on an impeachment where it was, and it does not seem that this prerogative can be usefully checked in any other way than by vigilant criticism of the responsible ministers of the Crown. The prerogative of pardon, indeed, when thus limited and guarded in its exercise, is the most important mode of correcting the frightful perversions of justice that might otherwise follow from an unfettered career of mere legal rules. If after the trial and conviction of a prisoner new evidence is produced, which could not be produced at the time —as through the accidental discovery of documents, the return from abroad or recovery from illness of an essential witness, the confession of another person—it would be an outrage upon public feeling to persist in punishing the person transparently proved, if not by the court of justice, at all events by the invincible eloquence of facts, to be guiltless. In such a case the only avenue to righting the sentence of the court must be sought through what is called the "prerogative of mercy" lodged with the Executive.

There are other cases in which the faculty of granting a remission or diminution of the penalty may also properly belong to the Executive. Thus, in cases of what are sometimes called "political crimes," in which the perpetrators of them are as often as not persons of virtuous habits and tendencies, and even, in some cases, of a heroic spirit of self-sacrifice, it must depend entirely upon the danger to the community to be apprehended from a repetition of such particular offences whether any and what penalty ought to be exacted. It may not be wise to leave to the judge the supreme decision of a question more of political circumspection than of simple moral insight. The usual, if not necessary, rule is to leave a considerable amount of choice of penalties to the judge, but to reserve to the

Executive the opportunity of entirely remitting, or, as political sagacity prompts, from time to time qualifying, the penalty exacted by the strict letter of the law. These remarks, while justifying the institution of the prerogative of pardon, none the less point to the essential importance of hedging round the exercise of this prerogative with all the safeguards which a vigilant legislature and an active public opinion can devise.

It has thus been seen that, while the region of law is necessarily and permanently different from that of morality, and while legal rules must, from their very nature, only imperfectly carry out the ends of moral justice, yet the necessity of adjusting, as far as possible, this inherent inadequacy has been fully appreciated in all highly-developed States, and the institution of equity, the discretionary faculty of punishment, and the prerogative of pardon are three notable devices for bringing the operation of laws into closer accord with the requirements of abstract justice. It remains to ascertain the true import of law as the nurse and support of morality, especially in the earlier stages of national development.

It has been observed that all the essential institutions of the State can be decomposed into government, the family, property, and contract. It was noted that the inquiry into the historical and ethical origin of these institutions has given rise to various schools of opinion, and though an approximation to agreement may be more and more expected, still it is probable that room for great divergencies of thought will be presented to the end of time. Nevertheless all the theories on the subject concur in the view of the extreme momentousness of each particular institution, and in appreciation of the indispensable place it holds in the progress of national life. Whatever place law occupies in the original foundation, or (as some say) the invention, of these several institutions, it must be confessed that the functions performed by law in marking out and giving stability to them are of the utmost importance.

It will shortly be seen, in speaking of the growth of law, that it is through the actual controversies that arise out of men's moral claims and moral situations, and which call for formal decision at the hands either of the governing authority or of accidentally selected umpires, that legal rules first come into being. It is because men are doubtful about what is and what ought to be that law comes in to determine what shall be.

From this time moral claims become converted into legal rights, and moral ties into legal duties. At first the course is vacillating, uncertain, and ofttimes retrograde; but the hardening and determining process is ceaselessly at work. Marriage loses all its more casual attributes, and has its forms, its limitations, and its social consequences impressed upon it in the most unmistakable lines. So likewise ownership and all its varying forms, its duration and conditions, its subject matter, its liabilities, and the modes of its acquisition, loss, and protection, become severely determined and lifted entirely out of the prior state of precarious sufferance. Contract, again, has all its forms, possibilities, and incidents sharply marked, to such an extent, indeed, that the legal features for a time seem to absorb or suppress the moral ones. The same process takes place, though more slowly and tentatively, with Government, legal limits being gradually imposed on the arbitrary disposition of the Government and the notion of a constitution superior to the actual governing authority gradually making its way.

In all this story of universal development it will be observed that law can only take under its shadow a very small portion of the inherent life and force of each institution, though to the whole institution it gives so much. Law, indeed, marks out the limits of the family, and provides general remedies for the grosser violations of the integrity of the family. But it can go, and does go, a very little way towards making good husbands and wives, fathers and mothers, sons and daughters, brothers and sisters. Law can create and define the relations of landlord and tenant, farmer and labourer; but it is well known how little it can do directly to guide landlords in the rent they morally ought to exact, or the compensation for improvements made by an outgoing tenant which they ought to allow, or to compel farmers to remunerate their labourers, build cottages for them, and exact work from them in the way least likely to render them paupers in their old age.

So with contract. The operations of the market must meet with some other stimulus and guide than legal rules, if men are to be scrupulously honest in keeping their engagements, in selling pure and unadulterated goods, in laying bare all the hidden vices of the things for which they are endeavouring to find customers. Law can do none of these things directly. Indeed, by trying to do them directly it may only weaken that force of morality which alone is equal to the task.

Law can do much, however, indirectly. It defines the field and the different portions of the field within which moral agencies are called to work. Law is the constant and visible representative of an universal interest outside the individual interest of each man and household. The best and most vigilant of men might be tempted to invade the moral claims of their neighbours if they were not forcibly reminded of the great and strong fence by which those claims are encompassed. In the same way the weak, credulous, and thoughtless might be easily seduced from time to time to part with their moral birthright of liberty, and to render themselves the contemptible slaves of the strongest in the neighbourhood, if the law did not stand by them, to remind them as much of their moral as of their legal rights, and to warn transgressors of their legal as well as of their moral duties. Thus it is well for all men, in the course of perfecting their moral nature, to have ever at hand a grand, visible, and practical witness to the claims of their brother men, to the subordination of the individual person to the State, and of the subserviency of all individual action and life to the accomplishment of the general aim of humanity.

Lastly, and perhaps more than all, it is in securing to individual men a free field of undisturbed work and life—in other words, in securing personal liberty—that law exhibits its main moral efficacy. Men cannot be virtuous unless they are free, and they cannot be free unless they are strongly guarded against the occasional licence or permanent selfishness of those who might impair their security. Nor is it only against the violent and the bad that this security for freedom is needed. It is needed likewise against the well-intentioned and conscientious, who have not learned to respect the solitude of the human spirit, nor to refrain from giving rein to their own capricious tempers and passions. Law respects and guards the liberty of all, and, before the law itself is broken, shelters the independence of the vile and worthless with as much jealousy and alacrity as that of the deserving and the rich.

It may be, indeed, that in all countries, and in this country at this day, there have been and are laws which seem to offend against all these principles, which sacrifice the liberty of the poor to the vices of the rich, or, in the name of free institutions, confiscate liberty in search of passing panaceas which have temporarily beguiled a dominant section. The whole story of law, as the story of every other department of human life, is the story of human error, but also the story of truth and of the resistance to error, not to say of triumph over it. It is by virtue of the good laws and not of the bad that States have progressed and nations continued to live; and it is because the vast bulk of the law in all countries, even the worst governed, has generally done more to secure human freedom than to impair it, that human civilization has progressed as far as it has.

CHAPTER IV.

THE GROWTH OF LAW.

THE history of the growth of law has had great light thrown upon it in recent times from a number of quarters. Sir H. Maine, in his work on "Ancient Law," has pointed out the bearing upon the history of early law, and upon the institutions which may be said to have preceded a condition of fully-developed law, of such monuments of ancient (especially of Roman) law, as still survive. The same eminent writer, in his work on "Village Communities," drawing his examples mainly from India, has attracted attention to an era, occurring in certain societies at all events, in which there is no true law in the severe sense affixed to the term by Bentham and Austin, but in which a reign of custom prevails so ubiquitously and so regularly as to present all the chief and most practically important phenomena of law.

The extreme variety of the actual forms of primitive society, whether in respect of the organization of the family, of the forms and conditions of ownership, or of the nucleus of government, have been recently made the object of extensive comparative research, to which Sir J. Lubbock in this country, and a succession of erudite writers abroad, have contributed.

The general result of these investigations touches a period in history anterior to the development of law in the strictly political use of the term, and therefore it would be out of place to do more than to allude to them here. The general phenomena of custom, however, as it constitutes the immediate antecedent of true law, and always exists side by side with it, ever supplementing and reforming it, strictly belong to the present inquiry.

A *law*, in the strictly political sense of the term,—for it is obvious that there are a variety of other senses, theological, ethical, and merely metaphorical,—is *a command proceeding from the supreme political authority of a State, and addressed to the persons who are the subjects of that authority*. By noticing with care the different elements which enter into this definition, it will be more easy to trace the steps by which the era of law in the fullest sense of the term is finally reached.

It is manifest, in the first place, that in every true State (a term which itself needs exact circumscription, but which may here be briefly said to denote "*an organized portion of the human family looked upon as a subject matter of Government*") there is at every moment of its existence a Supreme Political Authority—that is, a person or body of persons who at the time are generally obeyed by the bulk of the community. This authority possesses, by the hypothesis, the supreme power in the State, and can accompany all its commands by the application of physical force in the case of actual or threatened disobedience. It is said that all law is the expression of the will of this authority, or, as the definition has it, every law is a command proceeding from that authority. It is clear, however, that this assertion is only approximately true, because the larger mass of the law of every country has begun its growth long before the existence of the supreme political authority in being at any particular moment; and this mass of law was silently recognized, and indeed formed the support of some of the main institutions of the State, long before it attracted the attention of that authority. Therefore only by imputation can it be said to have proceeded from it.

It is true, however, that the supreme political authority might alter the whole law if it thought proper to do so, though if it attempted to do that, or any other act which was decisively unpopular, its own existence might be threatened. Nevertheless, the supreme political authority is generally largely occupied in devising changes of the existing law; and, as that authority is the only one from which the law can experience any conscious change, it is not incorrect to say that all the law of a nation proceeds from the existing political authority. Thus the complete development of such an authority is a condition precedent to the existence of true law.

It is, however, a matter of historical observation that, long before any supreme political authority has come into being, a series of practical rules determine the main relations of family life, the conditions of ownership, the punishment of the more violent forms of moral wrongdoing, and the adjustment of contracts. The mode in which such rules are formulated seems to be the following:—A spontaneous practice is first followed, and if good and useful, is generally copied over and over again, the more so as habit and association always render the imitation of an old and familiar practice easier than inventing a new and untried one.

It has been well observed by Sir H. Maine (" Village Communities," p. 58), in reference, at the least, to Aryan communities, that an important distinction has to be drawn between customs which do and customs which do not correspond to practices. "If a tradition be not kept steady by corresponding practice, it may be warped by all sorts of extraneous influences." It is, however, the peculiarity of the class of customs which are the true germs of future law, that they are being constantly brought to mind and tested by application to action. Customs prescribing the formalities and conditions of marriage are brought into distinct consciousness on the formation of every fresh family. The incessantly active vicissitudes of birth and death in every community call for an unintermittent series of decisions upon the competing claims of survivors in matters of ownership, and upon the responsibilities of those who may already be called " personal representatives " in matters of contract.

Government, again, is the most restless of all institutions, and the most intractable under the yoke of custom, and so far as its activity or its forms are regulated by traditional usage, the validity and integrity of those forms are being constantly exposed to the most searching and public test. While, then, it is true, as Sir H. Maine has well described it, that it is "naturally organized groups of men who are obstinate conservators of traditional law, but that the accuracy of the tradition diminishes as the group becomes larger and wider," it is also true that customs which share the nature, and are the germ, of law are, from the quality of their subject matter, far more than religious or social customs likely to be handed on in an unbroken integrity from one age to another.

The main machinery for the conversion of desultory and uncertain customs into fixed rules, needing only the complete development of Government to transmute them into true law, are the decisions which are constantly demanded for the purpose of ascertaining, for a practical purpose, the true purport and extent of an alleged custom. The decision may be called for at the hands of a casually selected arbitrator, or of a permanently constituted village council, or of some foreign and remote authority specially invited to interpose. The grounds of the decision may be either the personal memory of the judge or judges, as stored with past recollections and hearsays, or a view of general expediency, or considerations purely analogical in their nature. Whatever the grounds may be, the decision is something more than the custom which it is called to interpret and solidify. It furnishes the first of what may be styled a secondary range of customs running parallel with the original and actual ones. It becomes a precedent itself, and, from the particulars of its form and the solemnity of the circumstances out of which it has sprung, is likely to outweigh in authority the original material on which it is based. It needs only the complete institution of Government, and the recognition and public authorization of the judge, to perfect the truly legal character of these occasional decisions.

Though many writers have dwelt on the above phenomena as the typical modes in which true law comes into being in all self-developed communities, yet the generalization has not been sufficiently insisted upon that it is on the side of Procedure that all law is originally presented, and that it is the part of law dealing with Procedure which most pertinaciously resists the hand of conscious change and legislation. The process of a legal controversy, so far as that takes place before a public tribunal, affords the only occasion on which—in primitive communities, at all events—public attention is arrested by the presence of law. The large bulk of rules which are, in practice, observed are accepted without thought or criticism. They form part of the inseparable consciousness of the people, and prescribe the same sort of natural limitations to their activity as do the conditions of time and space and the inevitable accidents befalling human nature.

It is thus only when its peaceful order is violently

broken that a new-found consciousness of disorder brings with it the first craving after conscious order. A vindication of the existence of this order is sought for, and the public vindication by the judge, after careful and solemn inquiry, results in creating for all the beholders a new realm of conscious law. The outward circumstances of the trial, however inartificial and rudimentary, the forms of the proceedings, the rapt attention or earnest gesticulations of those concerned, the reference to the past, and the final and formal delivery of the sentence are all calculated to impress the imagination and give all the elements of form, colour, and substance by which the firmest associations are moulded and riveted. The formalities of the court of justice pass back into common life, and become the type upon which the outward solemnities attending the more important transactions of commercial and social life are fashioned.

It need not be said that all the circumstances that could combine to render institutions at once deeply rooted in the popular affection and unalterable in their structure meet here. The judge can rely, and must rely, more upon ancient precedent than aught else in elaborating his decision. He becomes more and more frequently and regularly assisted in his work by a number of persons permanently connecting themselves with his court, and making it the special and continuous occupation of their lives punctiliously to record the ceremonial and decrees of the court. The attendant populace become more and more familiar with the regular occurrence of antiquated forms, and proportionately attached to them. The slightest variation from them produces first astonishment, then pain, and lastly revolt. The purpose of law itself, as a subordinate instrument of human well-being, is lost sight of, or, if ever noticed, is rapidly forgotten. The preservation of the old and the repetition of the familiar

-become the sole considerations which operate on the minds of judges, of the attendant ministers of the courts, of suitors, and of spectators.

It is necessary thoroughly to allow for, and to understand, these persistent tendencies to conservatism in early, and indeed in all, procedure, in order to comprehend certain peculiar directions in which law manifests its growth. If the community progress, the law must needs expand and become a more and more exact expression of the moral sensibilities and economical habits of the people.

This expansion can only be effected in two ways —that of direct legislation, proceeding from the supreme political authority, and that of indirect legislation, proceeding from the judges who are called upon to execute the law. As to the former way, that of direct legislation, the meaning and method of it are sufficiently understood in the present day, when it is the main and, apparently, the most natural method of introducing changes of the law. But the large mass of the law of every civilized country has been developed in the process of executing law, though a variety of different methods have been consciously or unconsciously employed for this purpose.

It may be noticed, at the outset, that the supreme legislator and the judge are, from the nature of the case, very differently situated in respect of the contemplation of any new or old law. The legislator must needs put the general tendency and consequences of a law in a higher rank of importance than its occasional operation. If, on the whole, the law seems likely to promote a balance of good over evil, for him the law is a good one and should be retained or introduced.

The judge, on the other hand, having a vast number of laws to execute, some of them only on very few occasions, is more arrested by the special operation of a law in the particular instances which come before him, than by the general consequences of the law which he is less bound to think about. The special operation of a law he can inspect with a distinctness which no legislator, contemplating the circumstances of men's personal history and the accidents of human life only at a distance, can rival.

Nor is it alone the true bearing and effect of a law that can be better appreciated by him who executes than by him who makes, but a truer apprehension of the detailed wants of society and of the character of men and women, as affected by the general operation of laws, is likely to be acquired by the judge, who is ever in contact with society in its most concrete shape, than by the legislator, who only looks upon mankind in masses.

It is, of course, true that individual judges may happen to share in many of the characteristic qualities of the large-minded statesman, and the statesman may have a special faculty for correctly estimating the more minute conditions of human life. But these accidental divergencies will not affect the general result. Generally speaking, the tendency of the judge will be to understand law, and to explain it, in a sense the most adapted to the actual condition and work of mankind. This function is of supreme importance at a period when the legislature has not yet been raised into conscious activity; but it continues to be (as has already been shown) of no small importance, even when the legislature is constantly on the alert, and is incessantly engaged in composing fresh laws. In the earlier period, indeed, the judge is the sole law-making authority. In the latter period, his law-making function is of very considerable importance, however much it may be described under the name of mere "interpretation."

Assuming, then, that there is a natural proclivity in every rule of law to undergo a minute deviation in the course of its application—the deviation becoming afterwards a qualification in the form of the rule itself,—it remains to examine and enumerate some of the most celebrated methods by which this deviation is brought about.

It has already been seen that, inasmuch as judges are likely to exceed in intelligence the bulk of the community, in every court of justice there will be two rival forces at work, tending respectively to the conservation and to the modification of existing rules of law. The practice of *legal fictions*, by which the imaginative reverence for old symbols and formalities is deferred to while more or less perceptible change is introduced into the substance of the law, is now thoroughly understood, and has been fully commented upon. Sometimes, by the medium of a *fiction*, the legislature itself is imposed upon, and is lulled into acquiescence with a policy which, when distinctly presented to it, it would disown, or has actually disowned. Generally, however, the legislature is assumed to be indifferent, and it is rather the populace, or such parts of the more educated populace as bestow attention upon legal proceedings, that are the object of the snare. More frequently, the judges and all the ministers of the court who co-operate with them deceive themselves by tricks practised upon their own understandings. The value of the new rule seems so obvious, and yet the difficulties of introducing it by a bold step of conscious legislation so insuperable, that the self-deception readily wins its way, that what is useful must be real.

It is through a series of useful fictions that the English Courts of Queen's Bench, Common Pleas, and Exchequer have gradually encroached on the previously distinct jurisdiction of one another; that the strict entailment of property by which land might have been preserved from alienation for generations was judicially encroached upon; that a large branch of the prætorian jurisdiction at Rome developed itself; and that a variety of important doctrines—some useful, some pernicious—touching the prerogative of the English Crown, have acquired a symmetrical shape.

The nature of *equity* as a mode of judicial legislation has already been described in one of its aspects. It has been described as being originally a device employed by those who administer law by which to diminish the unjust consequences frequently resulting from the unflinching application of general rules. But the purpose of it as an universal method is larger than this.

It implies, first, the progressive recognition of a novel class of rights and duties, existing side by side with those existing under the ordinary rules of law—new rights and duties, the gradual product, under judicial nurture, of new social emergencies and a higher range of moral instincts.

Equity implies, secondly, a new and more elastic system of procedure, by which the artificial technicalities, the tedious ceremonies, and the precise verbiage familiar to an older age are summarily got rid of. This view of equity is presented in its most distinct form in England, where the different order of courts through the agency of which it came into existence suggested the use of a machinery borrowed rather from the refined but simple methods of the canon-lawyers than from the early barbaric experiments of primitive Englishmen.

Lastly, equity presupposes a superior habit of moral discrimination, by which fraud is capable of being followed through all its mazes, and even the private duties appertaining to some relations of life (as the duties arising out of guardianship, testamentary directions, and private partnerships) are made imperative upon those liable to them. In pursuit of like objects, equity endeavours to ascertain, with more precision and attention to the claims of moral justice than the ordinary law, the respective claims of a variety of persons in cases where those claims, as it were, cross and intersect one another.

In treating of equity as a conspicuous mode of judicial legislation, it might be questioned whether the presence of it is a mere peculiarity of certain very celebrated systems of law, or whether, rather, that presence may be properly regarded as a permanent and universal fact. It is true that equity, in all its main features, has been a striking characteristic both of the Roman and of the English law, though even here the differences it has exhibited are very observable. But the distinction between equity and the ordinary law is not preserved in any of the modern codes founded on the Roman law. It was gradually disappearing under the influence of Justinian's legislation in Roman law itself; and it is known that, apart from the direct influence of the Judicature Act of 1873, a number of causes—some spontaneous, some legislative—have long been co-operating in this country towards what is popularly known as the "fusion" of law and equity, which means the arrest of the further growth of equity, not only by finally consolidating the best principles belonging to each system, but by committing the administration of the conjoint system to one set of courts and judges. When this is accomplished, it may be said that equity, as a distinct mode of judicial legislation, will no longer be a proper subject for scientific inquiry.

But it is more than doubtful whether such an epoch can ever arrive. It would seem more likely and more conformable to the recorded results of experience that the alternative appearances of law and of equity as the mutual checks and corrections of one another are lasting and not transitory phenomena. However severely and peremptorily equity, and all the arbitrary judicial power implied in its exercise at particular epochs, may be controlled and discredited, there is reason to think its resurrection must be constantly waited for. So soon as a system of law becomes reduced to completeness of outward form, it has a natural tendency to crystallize into a rigidity unsuited to the free applications which the actual circumstances of human life demand. The invariable reaction against this stage is manifested in a progressive extension, modification, or complete suspension of the strict legal rule into which the once merely equitable principle has been gradually contracted. Thereupon follows not only a special logical method for the creation of a new series of modifying principles in obedience to the claims of a higher moral standard, but also a vast multiplication of channels for social and commercial activity, and a general conviction of the inadequacy of the existing law.

It is true that conscious legislation, proceeding from the supreme political authority, as well as other modes of judicial legislation, to be shortly enumerated, will compete, to an increasing extent, with the progress of equity. But it is impossible that the functions of equity can, by any of these rival forces, be entirely superseded. Equity works more assiduously and consistently than political legislation, and is more delicate, and perhaps more silent and obscure, than the judicial interpretation of written law which will immediately appear to be its more formidable competitor. Thus the history and the nature of equity may be properly held to be a permanent topic in the exhibition of the Science of Law.

CHAPTER V.

THE GROWTH OF LAW—(*Continued.*)

An instrument equally important with those mentioned in the last chapter, by which law grows through the very process of executing and applying it, is that of the *interpretation* of written law. The functions of interpretation are among the most arduous of the occupations of the judge; and the consideration of the topic is all the more momentous, as it involves an inquiry into the true nature and differences of written and unwritten law.

The grounds for interpretation are the following:—In the case of all law directly published by the lawgiving authority,—which may chance to be some extremely primitive one, existing at the earliest epoch in the national life of the community, and which has left behind it only some scattered monuments or almost illegible relics of its will,—there is needed the intervention of some official personage, for the purpose of affixing to words and sentences of uncertain intent the actual meaning which it was originally designed that they should bear.

The large mass of a nation's laws are made at one period, and are put into execution through a long series of following periods. In the case of any large and growing State, the laws are made in one part of it, as in the metropolis, and are put into execution at a vast variety of places, some of them indefinitely far removed from one another. Again, laws made by, or especially in view of, one class of men, speaking one language, actuated by one set of interests, and habituated to one way of life, are put into execution among men wholly alien, in all these respects, to the particular class of persons originally kept in view. It is obvious, at the same time, that the meaning of language is peculiarly susceptible of the influence of all the vicissitudes produced by time, geographical distance, climate, occupation, and general modes of life.

It thus comes about that only in the rare and almost impossible case of a legislator condescending to step down into the judgment-seat, and, as occasion required, to interpret his own laws, can the integrity of the meaning really intended by the legislator in the use of the words he employed be infallibly preserved.

These observations presuppose that (at least) the legislator is a man of a single mind, and really had a distinct and single meaning. In the case of modern popular legislation, proceeding, as it does, through the medium of prolonged debate and of innumerable compromises and amendments on the original proposition, it must be doubtful from the very first whether the law passed could be said to contain in itself any one and self-consistent meaning at all.

The problem, then, before the judge, may happen to be of a nature very difficult to solve. He has before him a given condition of facts, and he has a law quoted before him as applicable to that state of facts, and as determining the rights, duties, and liabilities of certain persons concerned. It may be that, through the vicissitudes and modifications of language above adverted to, either (1) the original language of the law has now contracted a variety of supplementary meanings, which render it doubtful which of the meanings the legislator intended at the time of composing the law; or (2), the original language of the law may have now lost some of its ancient shades of meaning, and it may be doubtful whether the only surviving meaning ought to limit the present application of the law.

In either of these cases the judge must have laid down for him by law a definite principle of interpretation for his guidance. He may be directed, for instance, to institute a historical and philological inquiry as to the exact changes which the expressions of the law have undergone in popular use since its enactment, and, in accordance with the result of this investigation, to revert to the true meaning of the terms intended by the legislator to be conveyed by them. Or he may be directed to consider the probable modification in his expressions which the legislator would have made had he been living at the present day, and had he shared in all the social conditions by which the judge himself is surrounded. Or the judge may be directed to consult the existing supreme political authority of the day in every case of difficulty, and, as it were, draw fresh inspiration, as needed, from the ever-living authors of all legislation. This last device, indeed, is adopted in the English Statute of Treasons of the twenty-fifth year of Edward III., and also in the North German *Landrecht*, according to which latter (*Introductory Section* 47), "If " the judge considers the meaning of a law to be doubtful, " he must, without naming the parties, lay his doubts " before the Legislative Commission." Frederick II. likewise, in his code, the predecessor of the *Landrecht*, forbade all *interpretation*, and, in the case of laws proving insufficient or ambiguous, provided for direct recourse being had to the legislature.

The last possible mode of meeting the difficulty

resulting from a change or uncertainty in language is to leave the judge to decide for himself in view of all the exigencies of the case. This discretionary power, when so left to the judge, may be used in a variety of ways.

He may either decide simply in view of the immediate suggestions of practical justice and convenience as presented by the actual situation of the parties before him. Inasmuch as these suggestions may lead him, in the next case which comes before him, to an entirely different conclusion, and to laying down a very different rule of law, it is obvious that to admit any test of this vague sort can only tend to a reign of arbitrary caprice, and, in fact, to general anarchy; for complete uncertainty in law differs little from the absence of all law.

Or, again, the judge may use his discretionary power in making the meaning of the law under discussion conform as far as possible to the analogy suggested by all those other parts of the law the meaning of which is indisputable. For this purpose he will have, on each occasion of deciding on a doubtful statute, to consult all such parts of the general law, written and unwritten, as seem likely, from the analogous character of the relations and transactions which they control, to have any bearing on the case in hand. For the same purpose current logical methods, moral assumptions, and legal maxims or modes of conception will all be resorted to in order to guide the judge in the elaboration of the rule for which the written language only affords imperfect hints.

It is not too much to assert that it is through this process, as directed and perfected by a highly organized legal profession, that the largest quantity of the law of England and of all the civilized States in the world has been developed.

It is known that the earlier Roman law grew up mainly through judicial commentaries on the text of the XII. Tables, those commentaries being concocted, not by the license of individual judges, but by the harmonizing spirit and tone of a long line of judicial magistrates, supported by the sympathetic co-operation of a constantly growing class of legal practitioners.

In England, the history of the common law is familiar to all. The earlier judges, to whom its development is due, sometimes spoke as though they were merely applying the rules of a lost written code, sometimes as though applying to practice a body of traditional maxims which had been handed down from one generation of judges to another. But in all cases their innovations on the imaginary code or maxims, or their interpretations of statutes, were guided not by individual discretion, but by rigid conformity to a logical method and to a legal instinct which had been formed and devised in the closely organized profession of the law. The same proposition is equally true of Continental countries, where "jurisprudence," or the study of "interpretative logic," as created by judges, plays so important a part in the practical application of the modern codes.

The true meaning for a French ear of the term *jurisprudence* cannot better be given than in the words of M. Portalis, in his "Preliminary Discourse," on the original "*projet*" of the civil code; and those words so precisely express the method of interpretation which is being described, and which is here alleged to have been, within larger or smaller limits, the most potent and beneficial instrument of legislation, that they are specially applicable in this place. M. Portalis writes, "In the " infinite diversity of subjects which fall under the control " of the civil law, and upon which a judgment in most " cases consists less in the application of a precise text " than in a combination of several texts, which *lead* to a " decision rather than contain it, *jurisprudence* is as in-

"dispensable as law. It is to *jurisprudence*, then, that the
"legislator must abandon those rare and extraordinary
"cases which cannot enter into the scheme of a rational
"legislation—the variable, unaccountable details which
"ought never to occupy the attention of the legislator
"—and all those objects which it would be in vain to
"attempt to foresee, and dangerous prematurely to avoid.
"Experience alone can fill up the void spaces which we
"must leave."

The breadth which M. Portalis accords to the discretionary power of the judge is greater than is needed for the purpose now being considered, which is merely the determination of the meaning of an obscure or ambiguous statute.

With respect to a selection between the main resources just indicated, and especially between that of deferring to and laboriously exploring the true intent of the legislator, and that of leaving all doubtful cases to be settled by the judge according to such methods as his judicial instinct accustoms him to employ, a difference will probably be established between the case of a more recent and a more ancient statute. In proportion to the antiquity of the statute, the actual intent of the legislator becomes at once more undecipherable and likely to be more repugnant to the policy of modern times. In proportion to the recency of a statute, the will of the legislature, if it be expressed at all, is more easy to gather from a vast variety of *indicia*; and a judicial superseding of it must seem to approach more nearly to an act of mere executive insubordination.

In all the above cases, however, a distinction has to be drawn between conscious or intentional, and unconscious or reluctant, legislation on the part of a judge. A judge consciously legislates when, either having no doubt about the meaning of the legislator, or being quite satisfied that there never was a meaning—that is, that no legislation took place—he is led to enunciate a new rule of law on the subject, professing at the same time that he is merely declaring the will of the legislator. The judge may do this with all honesty, and, indeed, with the benevolent view of preventing casual injustice or the success of malice and fraud. But, again, he may also do this in pursuit of some unworthy aim, as the support of class interests or the furtherance of the prerogative of the Crown. Conscious legislation of this sort is in the highest degree dangerous, and may easily become the source of the gravest corruptions.

There are, however, certain methods of unconscious legislation, through which a change is involuntarily made in the substance of the law while a genuine attempt is being made only to ascertain and apply it, which operate in other ways than through interpretation, properly so called. A description of some of these methods must shortly be proceeded with.

In the mean time it is necessary to allude to certain devices employed in modern statutes and codes for the purpose of avoiding the necessity for undisciplined interpretation. Such devices are "Definitions," "Interpretation Clauses," and "Illustrations." The purpose of all of these is to secure that words and sentences, having been used in one sense by the legislator, be strictly confined to that sense, and be rescued, as it were, from the perils of vacillation and uncertainty to which all language is naturally exposed. In English Acts of Parliament a somewhat reckless use is made of the "interpretation clauses," by which, instead of a word or a sentence being simply guarded against misapprehensions or abuse, the word or sentence is made to cover a number of artificial meanings which, in the absence of the clause, no interpreter would ever think of attaching to them.

A good specimen of the wise use of "Definitions" is afforded by the XVIth Title of the 50th book of the Digest, headed "DE VERBORUM SIGNIFICATIONE," in which a vast number of commonly recurrent terms and expressions have their rigid meaning defined and guarded. Another specimen of useful definition is presented by the new Anglo-Indian Consolidated Statutes or Codes, in which the simplest English is used, and all terms at all liable to perversion or abuse are severely circumscribed.

It is these last-mentioned bodies of law which also exhibit the happiest use of the method of taking precautions against misapprehension, by the use of "illustrative cases." These cases must be simple in structure, and neither too few nor too numerous; or else, instead of merely protecting the language against degeneration or erratic abuses, they will serve, like "leading cases," to restrict on all sides the import of the rule.

What has been hitherto said about *interpretation* applies especially, though not exclusively, to written law. It has been seen, however, that wherever a rule of law exists, whether it be written or unwritten, there is always a certainty of its undergoing modification in the course of its being applied in practice. The circumstances of the case which calls for its application are so frequently different from those which the obvious purport of the law comprehends, and yet those circumstances are near enough to those comprehended by the rule to suggest a modification of the rule in order to enclose them.

In written law this modification is effected by *interpretation* strictly so called, whether the legislation really involved by it be conscious or unconscious. The written language is either made to cover a larger meaning or a narrower meaning than that impressed upon it by the legislator. In the one case the interpretation is said to be *extensive*, in the other *restrictive*. The process of investigating the intention and will of the legislator must always commence in the first instance with an inquiry into the words he has used, and the meaning he intended them to bear. It is only when the words are ambiguous, and the meaning therefore uncertain, or when it is held undesirable, for some reason or other, to put the undoubted meaning upon the word, that other clues to the probable policy of the legislator can be made available. These may be supplied, in the way above described, by the general context as gathered from the language of neighbouring laws, or by a regard for the whole political situation at the time of legislation.

Interpretation resting upon a mere study of the words used in framing a law has been called *grammatical* interpretation, and that resting upon any other method, *logical*. These expressions are not very happily chosen, as grammar is only a part of logic, and the one cannot possibly be opposed to the other.

Apart, however, from any attempt, conscious or unconscious, to modify the character of written law by extensive or restrictive interpretation, written and unwritten law are both liable to decisive alteration at the hands of judges in a variety of ways. Such ways are (1), the gradual recognition and adoption of customs; (2), the incorporation of foreign law; (3), deference to the formulated opinions of text-book writers and commentators; (4), the framing of rules of procedure; (5), direct legislation under the cloak of conforming to a so-called " Law of Nature," " Natural Reason," " Natural Justice," " Common Sense," or " General Utility."

(1.) The original process, by which the spontaneous usages of the people became transmuted into true laws, is constantly being repeated throughout the whole history of a community, though, naturally, with greater facility and rapidity during the period in which a large mass of the law continues unwritten. The process, in the case of each custom so transmuted into law, commences with a cautious admission, within clearly-defined limits, of the custom as a rule binding on the parties who may be supposed to have contemplated its existence in their transactions with one another.

When a custom is found to exist, not among a very small group of men, but among all men engaged in certain occupations, and to be constantly observed in their common transactions; and if, furthermore, the custom be ancient, certain, and not counter to the general political and social welfare of the community, the admission of it as qualifying the ordinary legal rule becomes a fixed practice in courts of law. This admission in time acts back again on the rule, and gives it definiteness and solidity. In this way the custom becomes eventually binding on all men, and, in fact, indistinguishable from law itself. A very large part of the law of all countries is made in this way, and especially in matters relating to commerce. In England, the whole law of bills of exchange and promissory notes exhibits the completion of the absorbing process, and the general admission of the customs prevalent in the Stock Exchange and in agricultural tenures exhibits the earlier stages of it.

(2.) The incorporation of foreign law is another method through which law grows. The amount of this incorporation must depend on a variety of circumstances, and is likely to be less than elsewhere in an insular country like England, the laws of which reached a considerable degree of development before relations with foreign countries in times of peace became conspicuously active. The process is likely to be hastened by foreign conquest, or even by the introduction of large foreign populations, whose peculiar customs cannot fail to affect the administration of law. The prevalence of the Canon law throughout Europe (owing to the Ecclesiastical system, which, at one time or another, has dominated in all countries), and the language of International law (founded to so great an extent on that of the Roman law, and in use in the Admiralty and Prize courts of all countries), have together combined to infuse a very large tincture of what may be called foreign law into the systems even of the countries which, like England, have most obstinately resisted all external influences. More recently, however, the universal diffusion of codes founded on the type of the Code Napoléon, and the closer intercourse, both for social and for commercial purposes, of all the States of Europe, have been tending to make the foreign element in all European systems of law very considerable, so far as this element can be incorporated independently of express legislation.

(3.) A third, important, though silent and often ignored, mode of replenishing a legal system through judicial action alone, is the adoption of the opinions of eminent text-book writers and commentators. In the countries of the Continent where codes have been constructed, the works of text-book writers of repute, in commenting on the language of the codes, become scarcely less authoritative on the state of the law than the language of the codes themselves. In England this influence has been felt to a considerable extent, but mainly under very different classes of circumstances; such, for instance, as where the text-book writers are of considerable antiquity, so that the constant authority they have had seems to have gathered strength with every fresh race of judges who have been loyal to their sovereignty. The influence of such writers as Bracton,

Fortescue, and Coke may be explained as easily by reference to the uncertain and almost mystical sources to which the old common law was referred, as to the essential worth of those writers themselves.

The early beginnings, however, of the English common law were shrouded in such a mist of obscurity, and so many fictitious expressions had to be resorted to, to give it any substance or reality at all, that the writings of great judges, on the whole or on parts of the early law, could not but be welcomed as light shining in a very dark place. In later times a certain special deference has been accorded, in the law regulating land, to the custom or opinion of eminent conveyancers. The reason of this is that the mysteries attending the conveyance of land, the formal expressions essential to an effective deed for the purpose, and the rarity and close mutual connection of the men who devoted themselves to this branch of the art of law, all conspired to make conveyancers in some measure sharers with the judges in evoking the law relating to the peculiar branch of matters with which they had to deal.

(4.) The task of framing the rules of procedure is a task naturally and properly left by the legislator, within certain limits, to the judges who have to administer the law. It has already been seen that laws of procedure form the most ancient portion of every system of law, and it is only by slow and tentative efforts that material changes can be superinduced upon that part of the mechanism of the State which operates most immediately in the presence of the people, and to which they are, accordingly, the most tenaciously attached.

Nevertheless, occasions do arise, though almost unperceived by spectators, for the gradual introduction of new rules of procedure. The omission, at first accidental, of an accustomed formality, becomes habitual, and the judges no longer insist on the observance of it. What is at first an irregular variation from established usage, commending itself by its superior convenience, gradually becomes sanctioned as the only rule.

In this way the whole law regulating the conduct of trials, both criminal and civil, has in England been fashioned with the smallest possible help from legislation. A law of evidence, of the utmost degree of refinement, had been fully developed; the rules for the examination and cross-examination of witnesses had been reduced to a system of extreme precision; and the formalities to be observed before the trial by the parties to an action, for the purpose of ascertaining the true question to be brought before the court, had been so laboriously and so technically wrought out into a cumbrous method called "pleading," that only the pruning hand of the legislature was wanted to introduce a simple substitute adequate to the wants of modern times.

When any new jurisdiction is founded, or new court of justice instituted, or even when any decisive amendment of the constitution of any existing court is proceeded with, it is customary to leave the framing of rules of procedure, so far as they are not framed by anticipation by the legislature, to the general body of the judges who are most concerned with the administrative change.

It is to be observed that this function of framing rules of procedure is not, as it might appear, a merely formal and technical matter, having no important bearing on the substance of the law.

When the nature of the rights and duties arising from the law has been explained, it will be seen that they depend for their value and import upon the facility with which they can be made effectual in a court of justice Thus to facilitate procedure, in respect to any class of laws, is to give increased value to the rights and duties arising under that class. To complicate or embarrass procedure is to impair the validity of those rights and duties.

In this way the framing of rules of procedure becomes not the least important mode by which judges, in the very process of executing law, contribute to its substantive change or growth.

(5.) The last mode which it is worth while here to recount, by which judges supplement or modify a legal system, is by affecting to apply legal rules not made by the legislature and not alleged to be handed down from some traditionary authority in the past, but based upon certain large ethical, or so-called utilitarian, principles which, it must be thereby held, are presumptively part and parcel of the national law. Such principles are alluded to in such expressions as "Natural Law," "Natural Justice," "Natural Reason," "Common Sense," "General Utility," and the like.

That some universal ethical postulates are made in every system of law, and seem to be presupposed in the process of executing it, is not capable of being denied. But when once licence is given to judges to use these phrases when they choose, and to act upon them, the obvious consequence must be that the judge's interpretation of these expressions becomes the ready substitute for a rule of law. The "Law of Nature" may or may not be existent. In any way the judge's interpretation of that law may signally diverge from that of the legislator, and one judge's view may be wholly irreconcilable with that of another.

All these expressions have, indeed, very considerable significance, inasmuch as the terms of every law, whether written or unwritten, really connote, besides the ideas actually denoted by them, a number of ideas present to the mind of the legislator, and which need to be reproduced by the judge. Such ideas are sometimes formulated into very large and imposing proportions, called "legal maxims," which are said to underlie all parts of a legal system. They are constituent portions of every particular law, though their generality, and perhaps vagueness, need in turn an amount of judicial circumscription which is constantly narrowing their original purport.

But a vast number of ideas, presumably present to the mind of a legislator, and needing to be reproduced by the judge, are never formulated at all. To this class of ideas belongs the conception that the general aim of every law is to perfect the social constitution of mankind; and that, therefore, every operation of a law which seems to violate this constitution casts discredit upon the interpretation to which that operation is due.

The notion of a social constitution for mankind clothes itself in a variety of dresses, according as a prevalent philosophical or theological theory looks upon man either as spontaneously evolving a destiny for himself through the action of native and essential forces; or, as consciously reflecting upon and turning to account the tardy products of recorded observation and experience; or else, in the exercise of all the faculties which he finds himself to possess, as obediently submitting his impulses to the guidance of a Supreme Being who ever co-operates with the physical and moral nature of the creature He has formed, in pursuit of its true and only possible course of development. Whichever theory prevails, either in the world of thought or in the popular dialect, the language of the courts of law is likely to become consonant with it. Thus in some ages "nature," "justice," "reason," will severally express ideas which in other ages will be rendered by "sense," or even "utility." The same postulates, however, underlie each of these expressions,—to the effect that law is an instrument for the effecting of large purposes connected with the general welfare of the members of the State, and that no meaning of a law can be the true one which conflicts violently with this object.

The history of the French codes affords a curious illustration of the important place loose maxims of policy, morality, or even law, are apt to take, even in the compilations of law which affect to be most exact and exhaustive. By the 4th Article of the *Code Civil* it is laid down that "the judge who shall refuse to give a "decision—under pretext of the silence, obscurity, or "insufficiency of the law—can be sued as guilty of a "denial of justice." As subsidiary resources for helping a judge in such a dilemma, the following were suggested in the debates upon the Code, apparently by Napoleon himself: (1) *équité naturelle, loi naturelle;* (2) Roman law; (3) ancient customs; (4) *usages, exemples, décisions, jurisprudence;* (5) *droit commun;* (6) *principes généraux, maximes, doctrine, science.*"

Some part of the criticism of the Appellate Tribunal of Montpellier, to which, with the other Appellate Tribunals, the *projet* of the Code was submitted for review, is worth citing, as pointing out the peculiar dangers incident to a heedless use of legislative language not capable of severe circumscription. "What a juris-"prudence! having nothing better than an arbitary rule "to apply to the enormous range of objects that have to "be brought into harmonious combination under the new "system of legislation. . . . . What can be looked for "as likely to exercise a steady control over an unsym-"metrical jurisprudence which can only be constituted "by decisions subject to no appeal, inasmuch as, instead "of reposing on the firm basis of the law, they are made "to rest on the intermediate principles of 'equity,' or "vague 'usages,' on the ideas of logicians, and, in a word, "on what is merely arbitrary ? To an incomplete system "of legislation there is then added as a supplement a "jurisprudence full of defects."

It has thus been seen that, while the growth of law takes place in two main and parallel currents—the work of the legislator and that of the judge—yet these currents again admit of a great deal of subdivision. The various modes in which law experiences change in the hands of the judge who executes it have been successively commented upon.

It is no less necessary to notice that the conscious change in law by legislation is also effected in more ways than one. The legislature may either directly make its own laws, or may only create a subordinate authority with the requisite powers and capacity of making laws. Or, again, the legislative authority may, as it were, invite a subordinate authority to co-operate with itself, and initiate laws for the ulterior approval either of the whole or of some of the departments of the legislature; or it may construct the law, but leave a subordinate authority to put it in force only when occasion may suggest. These different methods are illustrated in the method of legislation pursued in England for the government of such of her colonies as have Parliamentary institutions; in the limited self-governing power conceded to municipal authorities, to railway companies, and to collegiate bodies; and in the schemes for the future constitution and regulation of endowed schools, made by the Endowed Schools Commissioners in compliance with an Act of Parliament, and which become law after lying for forty days unopposed upon the tables of both Houses of Parliament.

In the case of "codification," where the legislature consciously reconstructs and republishes the whole of a nation's laws, or a very large and important portion of them, there is, strictly speaking, no difference between the character of the law-making force and of that employed in the minutest legislative change. Whatever apparent difference there is lies in the subordination of the political to the legal purpose; or, in other words, the main object in view in making a code is to correct the anomalies and misgrowths that have attended the spontaneous development of law, and not to introduce substantial changes into the materials of the law.

All the various modes by which the growth of law is determined may, in accordance with the preceding observations and conclusions, be arranged as follows:—

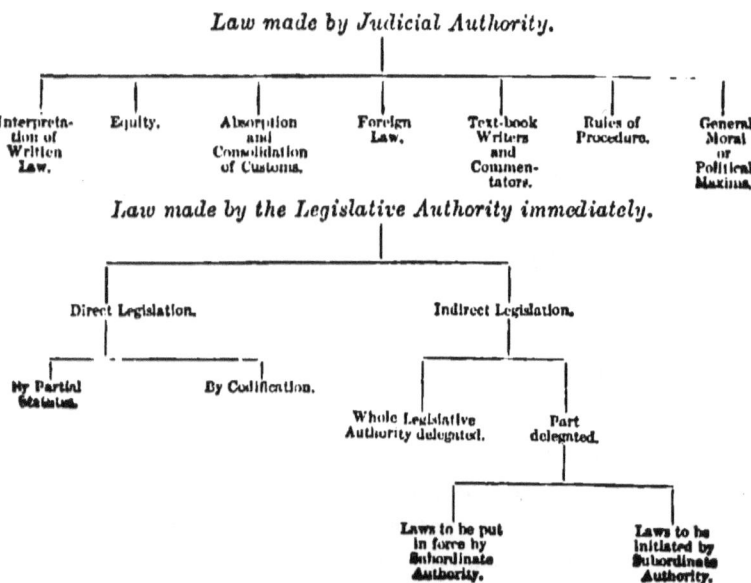

CHAPTER VI.

ELEMENTARY CONCEPTIONS AND TERMS.

Person and Thing.—Right and Duty.—Act and Event.—Will, Intention, Negligence, Fraud, Malice.—Imputability.

IN the study of a science dealing largely with moral conceptions, there are two characteristic difficulties, which tend to increase one another by their co-existence. One is that each leading conception presupposes a number of others, and it is always impossible to evolve fully any one without constantly anticipating the existence and use of all the rest. The second difficulty is that, inasmuch as all moral conceptions derive their meaning and validity from their universality, this very generally tends to impair their clearness, and to infect them with the obscurity of the various channels of human consciousness through which they have to pass. This obscurity is especially reflected in language, the looseness and indeterminateness of which, in all moral topics, is too notorious to need illustration.

The terms *good, evil, right, wrong, ought must, should, duty, conscience, obligation,* and the like, have each a different meaning in the mouth of every one who uses them, and in the ear of every one who hears them. The ethical and political history of law, as it has just been described, at once establishes how deeply from the very first, and through its whole process of development, the facts of law are implicated with the facts of the moral progress of individual and social man. The facts of law then suffer, as to their capacity for ready exposition, from all the cloudiness which hangs round the popular conceptions of the moral facts of life, and from all the ambiguities and flux to which the language expressing these conceptions is notoriously exposed. In order, then, to elucidate the facts, the expression and arrangement of which constitutes the Science of Law, it becomes necessary to clear them severally from their implication with the facts of ethical science, strictly so called, and to rescue the language expressing these facts from the indeterminateness it has contracted.

The primitive notions with which law deals are *persons* and *things*. The object for which the rules—at first spontaneous and casual, and afterwards regular and consciously invented—which constitute a nation's law are made, is the determining of the mutual relations of the human beings who form the community.

The whole community may be regarded as composed of an active crowd of multitudinous atoms, incessantly crossing one another's path, and interfering with one another's freedom of movement. The influence of family life and of the simpler forms of agricultural and industrial co-operation tend, of themselves, at the very birth of the State, to create within the realm of this confused atomic action an increasing number of fixed groups or centres of independent movement. About the same time another series of events is taking place, giving rise to the phenomena of law. These events are of a different description in different communities. Either the groups spontaneously enlarge themselves, and the village absorbs the family, or some one or more of the originally co-equal groups enlarge in numbers or increase in importance out of proportion to the rest. Or the whole community becomes subjugated to the sway or influence of some already organized State. Each of these classes of events has been exhibited in the early history of celebrated communities, and the researches on the subject are too well known to need to be more precisely referred to in this place. What is of importance, however, to notice is that, in every case, the final result is the adjustment of the limits of free movement of the various groups constituting the community, in respect of their capacity for disturbing each other.

As the groups break up and the organic whole of the family becomes resolved into the individual human beings composing it, the same beneficial result is experienced. The limits of free movement of all individual human beings in the community, so far as respects their capacity for disturbing one another, are adjusted by a series of rules, the binding force of which is generally recognized.

The next matter to be considered is, what is implied in "the capacity of the various human beings who constitute the community to disturb one another." This disturbance may obviously be effected in a variety of ways. It may be effected, for instance, by rude attempts to invade and break up the spontaneous groups of domestic and village life into which the originally barbaric elements organized themselves. The disturbance may be effected, again, by a violent interruption of the effort of members of the groups to cultivate the soil, to build houses, to store up the products of the ground, and to create the first beginnings of markets and merchandise. The disturbance, again, may be directed against the embryonic organ of Government from which the force of law itself is proceeding. The free movement of the conservator of the public peace, of the magistrate, the arbitrator, the judge, may be impeded, and, in this way, the growing progress of the community may be threatened in its most vital point.

It is to be noticed, then, that all these forms of mutual disturbance of members of the community by one another either touch human beings with respect to the outward physical substances (including the national territory), which exist in a community, or touch them independently of any reference to these objects. Both kinds of disturbance must be of the greatest importance, and the laws preventing and punishing them of equal importance. The life of the community, especially in its early days, can hardly be said to depend less on the security for ownership than on the security for life or for the integrity of the family. Personal security, ownership, family life, presuppose and imply one another; and, if one be permanently menaced, it is only a question of time when the ruin of the others is accomplished.

The result of the above analysis is that one broad class of oppositions is found to characterize the whole field of law; that is, the opposition between the human beings whose relations with one another are regulated, and the physical substances which are the occasion of great classes of these regulations. The former are styled *persons*, and the latter *things*. It is obvious that the distinction between persons and things is neither created nor first noticed by law. Its existence is deeply laid both in the natural and in the moral world. It underlies, indeed, the thoughts of every one, and no real confusion between a human being and the elements of the physical universe which he controls is possible.

It is the peculiarity of law, however, to import into the moral notions which it handles a sharpness of distinction and a clearness of limitation which is generally alien to the very nature of moral ideas. Thus, when law is addressed to human beings, it becomes essential to ascertain who the human beings are who are so addressed,—whether it is those alone who are resident in the territory of the State, or who were born in it,—whether it is those who through illness or physical pressure are unable to exercise any of their natural functions,—whether it extends to a corporate aggregation of human beings, such as a municipality, a school, a subject State.

A human being, or aggregate body of human beings, in this exact and limited use of the expression, is a legal "person,"—a term which, like other legal terms, on some sides covers more than is covered by the popular word, and on other sides covers less. A legal *person* is a human being, or aggregate body of human beings, looked upon as a subject of law. Not all human beings, then, are legal persons, those being persons in the popular sense who are not so in the legal; and there have been fictitious creations of the imagination to which, for legal reasons, the same term "person" has been applied.

This comes about in the following way:—A "*person*," in the narrower and more exact meaning of the term, is only known to the law as a centre round which a number of rights and duties gather, and who is, hypothetically, in possession of the moral and mental faculties needed to enjoy the rights and perform the duties. Under a condition of absolute slavery, such as has hardly ever been known in any civilized State in historical times, the unhappy human beings who are slaves are not persons in this legal sense. They are excluded from the benefit of all legal rights, and they are incapable of the voluntary performance of legal duties. Such advantages as they enjoy flow from the arbitrary and casual kindness of their masters, and such liabilities as they incur are imposed by their masters and not by law. But in the condition of slavery such as is presented in Roman historical times, and especially under the Emperors, and in the modern slavery of the western hemisphere, the slaves have always had a limited share of rights, as is shown by the penalties to which their masters were and are liable for cruelty or abuse; and they have been liable to duties, as is shown by the penalties to which they themselves were and are liable for offences against their masters or the State. Thus, in historical times, slaves have always been properly classed as legal *persons*, and never have properly belonged to the category of *things*.

It may happen, however, that though a human being is invested with rights and made liable to the performance of duties, yet he may, through infirmity, physical pressure, or other causes, be prevented from performing the legal duties cast upon him. He may, nevertheless, continue to be the object of the care and protection of the State. The integrity of his family relations is secured to him, his property is protected, and his personal independence and safety are strictly guaranteed. He is, at the same time, regarded as exempt from every legal duty, because he is unable to perform it. Special devices may, indeed, be resorted to, as by interposing trustees, guardians, and like persons, and by casting new and special duties upon them, with the view of making their acts a substitute for the defective or nugatory acts of the incapable person.

The rules for the creation and regulation of these classes of substitutive persons form a large and important branch of the law. The only reason for alluding to them at present is to notice that the fixed idea of "personality," as consisting in a capacity for enjoying rights and performing duties, is rigidly adhered to by law even in cases where, from the accidents or peculiar conditions of humanity, special devices have to be resorted to in order to make the assumed state an actual one

ARTIFICIAL OR FICTITIOUS "PERSONS."

But a similar train of fictions in a more palpable form accounts for a still larger use of the term *person* which has obtained in some systems of law. It was seen that the first conception of a legal person was the "being the centre of a group of rights and duties, and having the capacity to enjoy and perform them." It may, however, happen that an assemblage of rights and duties may group themselves together, and yet the particular person or persons who form the centre of them cannot be directly ascertained, or, for legal purposes, are shrouded in obscurity. The performance of such duties as may exist may be cast, as in the cases already mentioned, upon a definite number of persons or upon a class of State officials, whom the terms of appointment of the persons who are to enjoy the rights may not yet have designated; and the actual appointment may wait either for the happening of conditional events, or even for the arbitrary decision of a judge or executive officer.

It is natural enough, in cases like this, that the assemblage of rights and duties forming the group described should themselves acquire the legal aspect of personality, the circumstance being suppressed that the human beings who are the central objects for the advantage or disadvantage of whom the group exists are yet uncertain or undetermined. This line of thought explains the creation of a number of fictions in Roman law, which would otherwise be either inexplicable or inexcusable. Thus the *fiscus* (that is, the State viewed on its revenue or exchequer side), the corporate communities of cities or villages, the associated members of a trade (as the *collegia naviculariorum, pistorum*) were all severally treated as persons. In each of these cases the exact human beings who were the centres round which the rights and duties gathered were indefinite, or at least undetermined, though the rights and duties themselves were reduced to the greatest amount of precision.

The English "corporation sole," as a bishop—where the actual human beings contemplated by law are a number of persons living successively — affords an instance of a similar class of fictions. In a like way, by even a bolder application of the fiction, the *hæreditas jacens*, or aggregate rights and duties of a deceased person previous to acquisition by his successor, pious or charitable institutions (*piæ causæ*), and even lands looked upon as subject to servitudes or entitled to the benefit of them (*prædium serviens sive dominans*), were, for some purpose, treated as legal *persons*. In other words, judicial attention was fixed upon the rights and duties assembled together or particularized, and, for the moment, the actual human beings interested were kept in abeyance, the reality of their existence somewhere and at some time being nevertheless implied throughout.

The purpose of this investigation is to establish that the only conception of a *person* known to law is that of a human being looked upon in reference to his rights and duties; that, in modern times, the class of legal persons is exactly co-extensive with that of all the members of the community, that is, the subjects of the State; that, in ancient times, there may have been presented conditions of such absolute slavery that the class of legal persons comprised all persons in the community excepting slaves; lastly, that for legal and judicial convenience, it has been found expedient to extend the use of the term *person* in certain directions, in cases in which there are reasons for treating an assemblage of rights and duties with the same unity of method as that with which they would be treated if they centred in a single human being, and that the special form which this device has assumed has been sometimes that of treating an indefinite number of human beings as if they were definite, and sometimes that of treating indeterminate, future, or hypothetical human beings as if they were determinate, present, and actual.

The true opposite of a *person* is a *thing*. It is natural that a similar series of devices should have been practised upon the latter term as upon the former. The term *thing* ought strictly to be limited to all those physical substances, or detached portions of the material world, which form the subject of that incessant competition which it is one main purpose of law to arrest. For it is one of the chief ends of law to ascertain and settle the relations of persons to one another in respect of their rival claims to appropriate the material products of nature or of art. These material products need to be expressed by a legal term as definite and precise as the legal term *person*. The term *thing*, which covers, in popular speech, the whole of these products, might with advantage, for legal purposes, be strictly confined to them. But this term has, in fact, suffered, even in its legal uses, certain extensions and deflections, the history of which must be described.

The term *thing*, and the closely corresponding Latin term *res*, have been employed to cover not only tangible objects, but also those which are intangible. These intangible objects are certain assemblages of rights and duties which relate to *things* in the strict sense. Such were, in Roman law, an inheritance, an obligation, an action. A fiction was resorted to similar to that already described as employed in extending the legal use of the term *person*. Attention was concentrated upon the rights and duties, though it was true that the centre round which these rights and duties grouped themselves was a tangible object or assemblage of tangible objects.

Thus, though an inheritance consists of a multitudinous number of physical products and materials, the only unity collecting them together is found in the combination of rights and duties existing in him who is the past or future incumbent. So with an obligation. The subject matter of the legal bond implied in an "obligation" is frequently, though by no means always, a *thing* in the popular sense. But attention is withdrawn from these physical objects, which may, in any one case, be extremely numerous and diversified, and is fixed on the aggregate of rights and duties which constitute the legal relationship. Similarly with an action. In each of these cases, the quality of physical unity is, as it were, imparted to the transaction, claim, or interest concerned.

This extensive use of the term *thing* has been practised in English law, and also in the "Code Napoléon." In England, the class of "incorporeal things" is a large and important one, including such objects as annuities, easements, tithes, commons, and franchises. The sort of justification which is given of this use of the term *thing* may be gathered from the following extract from a well-known English text-book (Smith's "Real and Personal Property"):—

"An annuity, for instance, is an *incorporeal thing*;
"for, although the money which is the fruit or product of
"the annuity is of a corporeal nature, yet the annuity
"itself which produces that money is a thing invisible,
"and has only a mental existence. The term *incorporeal*
"hereditaments is sometimes applied to remainders and
"reversions; but it would seem more accurate to treat
"of them rather as interests in things, than as things or
"subjects of property themselves."

It is not easy to see how an annuity has a better claim to be included in the class of "incorporeal things" than a remainder or a reversion. Surely an annuity is equally with these, only an interest in a corporeal thing, and remainders and reversions, equally with annuities, have only a mental existence.

The use of the word *chose* in France may be understood from the following extract from M. Rogron's "Commentary on the second Book of the Code Napoléon":—

"On entend par *choses* tout ce qui existe physique-"ment *ou moralement*, excepté l'homme, si ce n'est dans "les pays où l'homme est esclave; car les esclaves étaient "et sont encore considérés comme des choses."

This extension of the term *chose* to all that "exists morally" is, in fact, a confession that the term needs to have some larger and vaguer meaning impressed upon it than that of strictly physical substance. The expression "morally" might allow of the term being used to express whatever the writer pleased. This mode is still more dangerous than that familiar to the Roman and English lawyers.

It is to be observed that, for the special purpose of a legal argument, or in order to look at a group of rights and duties from a special point of view, that which is usually treated as a *person* may, provisionally, be treated as a *thing*. Thus when a father or master brings an action for the detention of, or for injuries inflicted upon, his child or apprentice, or when a husband sues for injuries inflicted upon his wife, the child, apprentice, and wife are in fact held to be *things*. The action is not brought in pursuance of the legal rights of the child, apprentice, or wife. For the purposes of the action, they might as well be criminals, slaves, or beasts of burden.

The action is brought in pursuance of the rights of the master, father, or husband. The persons who directly suffer from the injury are, for the purpose in hand, and solely to the extent needed for this purpose,—treated as if they were things, the understood ownership of which law engages to protect. The person who injures the child, apprentice, or wife might, under some systems of law, have to incur the risk of two sorts of actions—one, in which the father, master, or husband is the plaintiff; and the other in which the person directly injured is the plaintiff. In the former case, the person injured is treated as a thing; but, of course, not so in the latter case.

It is worth while also to notice that the father, master, or husband has two classes of rights in respect of those severally dependent upon him. He has a right (*jus in rem*) "against all the world," as it is said, for the maintenance of which he is entitled to bring an action against persons who injure those so dependent upon him; and he also has a special right (*jus in personam*) against those persons themselves, with respect to the due performance of the duties involved in the several relationships.

From this investigation it will appear that the terms *person* and *thing*, when used in a strictly legal sense, by no means tally with the corresponding terms as popularly employed. The modifications of the meanings of the legal terms are, nevertheless, determined by strict logical principle, and have a definite ethical and etymological history.

It has been impossible to discuss the legal use of the terms *person* and *thing* without anticipating again and again the legal use of the terms *right* and *duty*. Such anticipations, however, are unavoidable, in expounding the principles of a complex science in which each conception and term implies and connotes all the rest. The only remedy is to wait till every conception and term has been investigated, and then to study the whole subject afresh from the commencement.

The term *right* is the central term at once of the

Science of Law, and of the Science of Morality. A complete understanding of the term, as it is used in the exposition of each science, carries with it a complete understanding of the nature of science itself. The difficulty of treating the subject, especially for purposes of international communication, is all the greater because the English *right*, the Latin *jus*, the German *recht*, and the French *droit*, are no two of them exactly co-extensive in range of meaning. For this reason it is all the more important to bring into distinct relief the latent conceptions which underlie the more important and essential meanings of these terms in the several languages. The accidental meanings of the terms, whether supplementary to or modifying of the rest, can then easily be evolved.

As the State is gradually being formed, out of the initial family groups which constitute the primitive community, the claims of the individual being to an independent existence become progessively manifested in a variety of ways. These claims are enforced, partly by the growing moral sentiments of the bulk of the community, as these spontaneously develop themselves under the fostering influences of domestic life and industrial occupations, partly by the organized force of the whole community expressed in law. At first, the personal claims of each member of the community are the mere outward form in which the tendency to individualistic, as contrasted with corporate, existence clothes itself. The individual member of the community can only exist as such if space is allowed him for the free movement of his muscles directed by the free action of his mental faculties. So far as this free movement is restricted, so far are the possibilities of individual existence reduced; and when this movement is fettered on every side, these possibilities become annihilated. In other words, the life of the human being loses its essential characteristics and becomes attenuated to a mere phase of physical life.

It is necessary here, however, to interpose a caution. At the first birth of a nation the growth of individual liberty is the only test of the possibility of moral and social life. Yet when the conception of liberty has been definitely framed, and the enjoyment of it has once been so largely diffused as to secure the permanence of the State, then the occasional loss of liberty in the case of individual citizens is not only compatible with the highest moral attainment in them, but may prove the condition for their loftiest development. Even here, however, the loss of liberty, to the extent to which it exists, implies a degradation of the State, and, if persisted in, can only lead to its dissolution.

It may, then, be opined that the vital energy of the primitive State is exhibited more in the growth of personal liberty than in anything else. It is only in a condition of liberty that industrial occupations can be pursued; that commercial enterprises can be undertaken; that family ties can be cherished; that social bonds can be gradually and slowly matured; and that leisure can be found for the gradual culture of the various sentiments, emotions, and aspirations, on the mutual play of which, throughout the whole community, the complex life of the State depends.

"Liberty," indeed, is in itself only a negative term, and denotes the absence of restraint. But it also connotes a positive condition of the most momentous sort. It implies rest, meditation, imagination, slow and steady culture of the faculties, combinations and associations for all sorts of purposes, and especially that slowly-formed belief in the certain power of carrying resolutions into action, on which so much of human strength and greatness depends. "Liberty," then, on its positive side, denotes the fulness of individual existence. On its negative side it denotes the necessary restraint on all which is needed to promote the greatest possible amount of liberty for each.

Apart from all thought of the artificial creations of law, there is no doubt some definite amount of qualification of the positive freedom of each man, which presents exactly the condition most favourable, at a given period, to the welfare of all. This amount of qualification may be impossible to assign for all periods and for all nations, and it will differ from period to period and from State to State. The amount of it actually existing is likely to err sometimes by excess, sometimes by defect. It will be determined, like other moral growths, partly by an almost purely instinctive grasp of the only conditions in which human life is possible; partly by the gradually and spontaneously recorded dictates of human experience; partly by the conscious reflections of sages or statesmen.

The generic expression which denotes, for any age and country, the exact measure of personal liberty for every man which supplies the most favourable conditions for the highest possible development of the moral existence of all, is "rights." The correlative liabilities of every man to respect the liberty so limited is expressed by the term "duties."

It appears at once, then, that, though some classes of rights are universally recognized, and seem to be appropriate to all stages of human society, yet it can hardly be said that there are any "rights of man" as such, or that there are any modes of liberty or of restraint to be universally described as essentials of the State in all countries.

Where such expressions as "human rights" or "rights of man" are resorted to for the purpose of popular argument, they are often extremely useful, enclosing, as they do, a logic peculiar to themselves, though not always of the kind intended by the speaker. The real value of these terms is that they remind the violators and corrupters of society that there is a standard of liberty and justice different from that set by their own self-interest and passions; that the value of this standard has been stamped by the general experience of mankind in all ages; and that it is fortified by the deepest associations which have been progressively fashioned in the mental constitution of all civilized men.

While the purely moral conception of *rights* and *duties* is making its way in the strivings after liberty witnessed by primitive times, the solidifying influences of law are at the same time giving fixity to the existing conceptions, and constantly introducing modifications into them.

As the practice of marriage grows into a custom of marriage, and the custom into a law, the liberty of the husband and wife in respect of one another and in respect of their children becomes gradually surrounded with more and more determinately fixed limits, and the liberty of all others in respect of the integrity of the said marriage-tie becomes also suitably restrained. The rights and duties of the husband, the wife, the children, and of all other persons become closely marked out and defined. The form and evidence of the marriage become matter of urgent concern and strict description. The grounds, if any, of the dissolution of the marriage-tie, and of the abrogation of the rights and duties thereby existing, demand also the most accurate demarcation. The formal methods for the protection of the rights and the enforcement of the duties incident to marriage become matter of precise definition. Not, indeed, that this order of events is chronologically the true one. In fact, the rights and duties seldom come into clear relief at all till they have been adjudicated upon, and thus procedure and rules for the regulation of procedure form the initial stage in the development of true legal rights.

Nor is it correct, except by way of illustration, to isolate the rights and duties appertaining to family life, as though they ever existed previously to, and independently of, other large classes of rights and duties. The rights to personal security, as the topic of criminal law, are naturally among the earliest appreciated by a rising State. Not, indeed, that human life itself is regarded as having any especial value, but the need for reliance upon the good faith of others and the horror of particular forms of crime, especially any partaking of impiety, are felt sufficiently keenly to generate a prevailing disposition to punish those offences by which personal security is most obviously menaced.

Ownership, again, as a fact, instantly gives rise to the conception of rights of ownership, and to corresponding duties, lying upon all members of the community, to abstain from interfering with what belongs to recognized owners. The recognition of this class of rights and duties calls for a description of what things may be appropriated, and what may not; of the acts or events which shall be taken as signs that rights of ownership have attached; of the provisions for distributing things owned on the death of an owner; and of the methods for making the rights of ownership available by the direct interposition of courts of law or otherwise.

When the next stage of social development is reached, at which rights under contracts come to be recognized, a certain modification in the conception of a right is attained. In the case of the former class of rights—those appertaining to family life, to personal security, and to ownership—the liberty of one or even of a few persons is enlarged, and the liberty of all other persons in the community is narrowed. In the case of *contract*, on the other hand, the liberty of one person is narrowed, the liberty of another proportionately enlarged, or the liberty of each of two persons is enlarged in some respects and narrowed in others. The liberty of the other persons in the community is left just as it was.

A similar class of rights is presented in the case of persons who are held liable by law to make compensation for the invasion of rights of the general class first alluded to. The person who has suffered has a right to compensation against the injurer alone. The injurer's liberty is thus narrowed; that of the person injured is enlarged. This circumstance has given rise to a celebrated division of rights recognized in Roman law, and, more especially, by the commentators upon that law. According to this division, all rights either imply duties lying upon all members of the community whatever, other than the person vested with the right; or else they imply duties lying upon one person or a few persons only. To the former class belong all rights of ownership, rights to personal security, and certain of the rights ensuing from family relationship. To the latter class belong the rights ensuing from contract, or wrong, and certain other of the rights arising from family relationship; such, for instance, as the rights and duties of husband and wife, father and child, in respect to one another, and irrespective of their relations to the outer world (*jus in rem* and *jus in personam*).

It will, however, have been seen that the general effect of the sharp limitation which law gives to rights and duties results not only in distributing the field of free action among all members of the community, but in distributing that field in the most definite, and, as it may happen, in the most artificial way. The particular way in which the liberty of one shall be sacrificed to that of another must depend upon the discretion of the legislature, and it is likely enough that the greatest mistakes will be made from time to time by way both of excess and defect. It is a main purpose of a wise legislature to correct these errors of the past in both directions.

It has been noticed by the best German writers that the general effect of law is to enlarge man's empire over the outward world of men and things. By family law, the limit of his power of control over the wills of his family is ascertained. By the law of ownership, the limits of his power of control over all persons whatever, in respect of things, are ascertained. By the law of contract, the limit of his power of control over special persons is ascertained. Through the operation of all these laws generally, much of the uncertainty of the future is banished; the capriciousness of the human will and the undulations of human passion are removed out of the calculation, and man can base his projects upon elements possessing an amount of certainty and definiteness which, in the absence of laws of the nature here described, would be wholly impossible.

The above investigation prepares the way for a more exact analysis and definition of a legal *right* and *duty*. A legal *right* is seen, first of all, to draw all its validity from the direct interference of the State. It may or may not correspond with a co-existent or antecedent *moral* right. It may be more or less extensive than such a right. But, in all cases, it arises purely from the energy of the law itself, as expressing the will of the supreme political authority, and its validity must be judged from a political, and not from a moral, stand-point,—if ever these two can be opposed to one another.

When the State thus imparts a right, it concedes to one of its number a limited amount of its own indefinite power of control over all its subjects. Instead of directly infringing (as it has power to do) the liberty of certain of its citizens, it concedes or delegates to certain others of its citizens the capacity of infringing that liberty. The State, strictly speaking, operates by both methods. It sometimes, indeed, infringes or restrains liberty directly by its own immediate act, in imposing duties without making any rights co-extensive with them; or, at the least, where the rights thereby accorded to private persons are treated as of subordinate importance.

This is the real test of what is a "crime." A crime is an act which the State, for purposes of its own, resolves absolutely to prevent, and to prevent which it resorts to such measures as, without respect to any other considerations, seem most likely to be effective. A crime is, indeed, generally, an undue use of the liberty of one person at the expense of the proper liberty of others. But it may imply no invasion whatever of the liberty of another; as in the case of coining, cheating the revenue, and some sorts of treason. Nevertheless, the State uses all its energy to prevent it, and directly restrains the liberty of all persons so far as that liberty would imply the opportunity to commit the acts it designates as crimes.

But the State also acts by another method, and parts with some of its controlling power to the persons to whom it concedes rights. It marks out their realm of free action, and the corresponding limits upon the free action of others. The State promises the aid of all its machinery of justice and police (though sometimes illogically, on condition of payment for its use) for the support of the liberty it concedes, that is, of the rights of the persons who are thus favoured by the State to the immediate disparagement of the rest. These rights may have regard to family relationship, ownership, contract, or personal security and reputation. Some of them may derive additional support from the criminal law, and from the direct duties it imposes. But, whether or not re-inforced from this quarter, the nature and mode of protection of all these classes of rights is, in general outline, identical.

In consequence of the existence of the right, one man can do more and another less than he could in the absence of it. The right in every case comes directly from the State, and owes its continuing validity to the State. The law expresses in detail the nature and limit of the right, the mode in which it accrues, the circumstances through which it may be lost, and the modes of its protection or of obtaining compensation for its violation.

A right, then, is *a measure of control delegated by the supreme political authority of a State to persons said to be thereby invested with the right over the acts of other persons said to be thereby made liable to the performance of a duty.*

The above investigation, ethical and historical, leads to a consideration of two topics which have each been largely handled by political writers, and the careless treatment of which in popular discourse has often been attended with injurious consequences. One of these topics is the true nature of *political liberty*, and the other, the *possibility of the State having legal rights against its own subjects*.

It follows at once, from the above inquiry into the nature and history of legal rights, that all rights accorded to one man imply a restriction upon the freedom of others. The region of one man's untrammelled action is narrowed as the region of another man's untrammelled action is extended. This result cannot be avoided by any political artifice. If one man is allowed to appropriate, all other men are commanded to abstain from interfering with his use of the thing appropriated. If one man has a certain freedom of locomotion and of speech conceded to him, the same law which concedes this freedom does, by its very terms, restrict the freedom of those who might desire to interrupt the locomotion or the speech.

The problem for the legislator is to discover what amount of restriction upon the liberty of each tends to secure the greatest aggregate amount of liberty for all. It need not be said that this is the hardest of all political problems, and, even in the absence of tyrannical intentions or gross abuses, the best and wisest legislators have made, and still continue to make, the most flagrant mistakes in their endeavours to solve the problem.

It has thus come about that liberty is an earnest political cry, as though there might be a condition of society in which no man's actions were restrained in any direction whatever. The true meaning and deep intent of the cry is that no man's liberty ought to be restrained except for the purpose of indirectly enlarging the liberty of all men, including himself; and that the progressive influence of good laws, combined with other moral forces, is to train men so effectually to the promotion of the general good, that the very impulses to trespass beyond the proper region of free action are not only controlled, but exterminated.

This may be expressed in another way by saying that the ultimate aim of legislation is then most near to being achieved when the *legal* rights and duties of all persons in the community are so happily distributed and adjusted that the most favourable conditions are attained for the recognition and enforcement of the *moral* rights and duties of all.

The other topic adverted to is that of the possibility of a State having rights against its own subjects. That the State, through its representative,—the supreme political authority of the day,—can own land and other things, make contracts with its subjects, bring actions against its subjects, and, generally, appear in courts of justice in exactly the same guise as any other corporate body, is sufficiently notorious. But the question has been properly propounded as to whether, in these and like cases, the claims asserted on behalf of the State are, strictly speaking, *legal rights*, or are only analogous to such rights.

The latter view would seem the correct one, because the State is the sole origin and fountain of all rights, and the very nature of a right implies that it emanates from some authority other than the person in whom it is vested. The State, then, cannot be regarded as conceding rights to itself, and therefore its claims of the nature of rights of ownership, of rights under contracts, of rights of action, and the like, are only nominally *rights*. It is for the public convenience that the legal principles, as recognized in courts of justice, applicable to the determination of claims of this nature, should be the same as those applicable when the legal rights of private citizens come into controversy.

These observations, of course, only refer to the claims of the State itself, and not to those of any constituent portion of its supreme political authority, such as the rights of ownership or of contract belonging to the English Sovereign in her personal capacity. These rights are, obviously, rights in the severest sense, though it may happen that, owing to the peculiar situation of the person in whom they vest, some special principles, probably of antique origin, apply to their enforcement in courts of justice.

The purpose which law has in creating rights and duties is that of controlling the *acts* of the members of the community in their intercourse with one another. The term *act*, in ordinary usage, has a number of different meanings, and the context amidst which the term is used is in most cases sufficiently clear to prevent ambiguity. But, for purposes of law, the quick sensibilities of men in a conversational mood cannot be relied upon to secure fixity, or at least certainty, of meaning, and it is these very sensibilities which become sources of error in interpreting and applying law.

In common speech the term *act* is sometimes applied to what is purely internal, when an act of the will, or of the conscience, or of the imaginative faculty, is spoken of. Sometimes, again, the term is limited to the muscular motions of a human being, when these muscular motions are *voluntary*—a qualifying term which, together with *will* itself, needs precise definition.

At other times, again, the term *act* denotes the voluntary muscular motions of a human being attended with some few of their immediate consequences, as in speaking of a good act or a bad act, an act of charity, or an act of violence.

Lastly, the word is occasionally used to cover the complex actions of a number of individual persons, and also a long train of complex consequences. Thus the beheading of Charles I. would be called the *act*, not only of the executioner or of the regicides, but of a number of other persons, and attention would not be fixed only upon the muscular effort by which the head was severed from the body, but upon the general consequences and political significance of what was done. So the Indian mutiny; the insurrection of the Southern States of America; the passing of the Bill for the disestablishment of the English Church in Ireland; are each frequently designated as single and indivisible *acts*.

Thus law, in availing itself of the term *act*, must have

recourse to some one of these popular meanings, and when it has selected one, it must adhere to it without deviation. The only one which is at all adapted to its purposes is that of *voluntary muscular motion*. The application of the term *act* to resolutions of the will or the conscience is unsuitable for law, because law is directly concerned only with that part of men's conduct which is exposed to the judgment of the senses. Whatever inquiry it directs to be made into states of mind and feeling is wholly subordinate and auxiliary to the inquiry into the probable consequences, and, therefore, into the true nature, of *voluntary muscular motions.*

Acts, then, in the eye of law are such muscular motions as are preceded by the peculiar phenomenon entitled *will.* All other outward movements—whether occasioned by the merely animal energy of organized life or by other physical forces, and whether exhibited in a changed situation of persons towards each other, of things towards each other, or of persons towards things—are denominated, for purposes of law, *events.*

Law, then, classifies all the possible outward movements, the aggregate of which constitutes the whole sum of human life and of physical activity, under one or other of the two great categories of *acts* or *events*. The possibility of the separation between these two categories is, in many instances, matter of the most urgent concern for the lawgiver. The question of imputability and liability to punishment must constantly depend for its correct answer upon whether an alleged or proved muscular motion was or was not preceded by the phenomenon styled *will*—whether, in fact, it was an *act* or an *event.*

The term *will* is thus seen to have its meaning presupposed in the use of the term *act.* It happens, indeed, that even a still looser use, in popular phraseology, has been made of *will* than of *act*. In fixing upon a definite use of the term for purposes of law, special care has to be taken that no psychological theory is propounded by that use. It is never to be forgotten that law is directly addressed to the coarser needs and conditions of human nature, and not to the finer; and that it seeks, in the process of its execution, for the sympathetic co-operation of the casual bystander and of the well-intentioned though common crowd of superficial observers. Furthermore, law, in determining the rules of its own application, registers not the speculations and conjectures of the man of science, but the everyday results of vulgar experience.

For these reasons, law embodies the practical conclusion of all men,—and the firm persuasion of most men,—that, within limits at all events, men can be deterred from courses of conduct by the influence of *motives*, that is, by an expectation of the consequences of their conduct. This implies that men have the choice of directing their conduct in one way or in another, as seems to them good.

The first outward element in what is called conduct is muscular motion, whether of the hands, tongue, face, or limbs generally. It is assumed that, before this motion takes place, the consequences of it are pondered, however rapidly, instinctively, or almost unconsciously.

Between these moments of pondering and the moments of muscular motion, there is held to intervene a moment of resolution or decision, of such an energetic and peculiar nature as, under average conditions of physical health, and in the absence of outward restraint, is invariably followed by the muscular motion resolved upon. It is this mental resolution or final determining effort which, for the purposes of law, constitutes *will*. It is the presence or absence of this which, in cases where the muscular motions are identical, distinguishes between a true *act* and an *event*.

It imposes an unceasing strain upon the acuteness of the judge to ascertain, in certain cases of disease or violent interference from without, whether the conditions of the normal operations of the will were truly present, and therefore an alleged act can be properly imputed to the person whose muscles certainly moved in such a way as to occasion suffering to another. There are cases of disease in which a person cannot control the movements of his muscles. There are conceivable cases of physical pressure, where one person has, as it were, brought under his own control the muscular system of another in such a way that that other becomes, for the moment, the mere passive instrument of the person controlling him. In both these classes of cases *will* is absent, and there is no true act.

It will be seen that it is acts *with their consequences*, and not acts themselves in their isolation, which are the true objects of judicial investigations. It is the events which immediately follow upon a voluntary muscular motion which give it its true character and description. The same voluntary muscular motion may precede a deed of kindness and a deed of cruelty; may result in a theft or a martyrdom. It is upon the immediate consequences of acts that law fixes its eye; and the degree of imputability of an offence depends upon the correctness of foresight, at the moment of action, which can be attributed to the person acting. This foresight, or this attitude of mind, of a person about to act, towards the immediate consequences of his act, is denominated *intention*.

It may be said that it is impossible to draw the line between the immediate and the remoter consequences, and that therefore it must be necessary to explore the condition of the mind of the person who acts, in reference to all the consequences of the act, however long and involved the train of them be. But the supposition of this difficulty affords a good instance of the practical mode in which law cuts knots which are inexplicable to psychology. It is found that, though, in numerous cases, the remote and immediate consequences cannot be severed, yet that in the vast majority of cases a very real and practical line is drawn, by common observers, between one class of consequences and the other.

The immediateness of consequences, for purposes of this common observation, depends upon a variety of different elements, of which juxtaposition in point of time or of space, and probability of sequence, are the most considerable. Thus the act of handling a deadly weapon may have a number of consequences of a varied nature, though some of them will at once be classed, by ordinary observers, as immediate, and the remainder as remote.

Among the immediate consequences are striking a person with it, causing his death thereby, and then committing suicide with the same weapon. Among the same class of consequences would also be reckoned the wresting the weapon from the hands of some one about to do injury with it, or the turning it to its proper purpose as an instrument of war, of industry, or of mechanical application. Among the remoter consequences, on the other hand, of handling the same weapon may be the robbery of the person killed, the appropriation of the value of his life-insurance policy, the disappointment of justice—or, in the other imagined case, the prevention of a crime.

Now, it is neither the act alone, nor the act with its immediate consequences alone, which it is the policy of the law to prevent. Yet the only safe general presumption that can be made is that, in the absence of special obstacles, men foresee, at the moment of action, the immediate consequences of their acts, and accordingly as they hold those consequences to be desirable or otherwise (whether as ends in themselves or as means to ulterior ends), they seek to avoid them by acting or by abstaining from action.

Whether, in a particular case, a man actually has foreseen the immediate consequences of his act, becomes often the most perplexed topic for the application of the judicial criterion. A variety of circumstances may tend to rebut the general presumption that men foresee the immediate consequences of their acts. Some of these are general in their nature, and affect all men at certain periods in their lives or under certain common conditions. Others are temporary, local, or accidental in their nature; and the presence of these has to be established, not, as with the former, by the force of general presumptions, but by that of special evidence.

To the former more general class of circumstances, the effect of which is to prevent the immediate consequences of an act being correctly apprehended, and so to qualify *intention*, the most familiar are those arising from Age. In early infancy a child voluntarily moves its muscles in all sorts of directions, and brandishes in a variety of ways every implement within its reach. The actual immediate consequences of this playfulness may occasionally be serious, bringing detriment to things and persons. But, during the first years of infancy, no one supposes it possible that the child could have foreseen what would happen, and therefore law, in all countries, credits an infant child with an absolute incapacity of doing a wrongful act. Where compensation is awarded to sufferers, it must be exacted from the parents or guardians of the child, who might have foreseen and provided against the damage, just as the owner of a dangerous animal, or of a slave in Roman times, would be responsible for injuries inflicted by them.

The absolute incapacity of forming an *intention* attributed in all cases to the early years of infancy, is extended, in all systems of law, to a later age in respect of the generality of the more unfrequent acts, of which nothing but time and experience could teach the immediate consequences; and even to the time of early manhood in respect of all those acts to which an extremely complex condition of civilization has annexed consequences in all respects artificial and arbitrary.

What shall be the age at which the several periods of exemption from responsibility shall terminate must be positively settled by the law of each country. It will vary with the climate, the mode of education, and the manners of each particular country, and of the same country at different epochs. It will be made to vary again in respect of the sort of transactions contemplated, a greater and earlier formed capacity of foresight being anticipated as to acts the doing of which is discouraged by universal custom and by widely diffused moral sentiments, than as to acts which are only discountenanced by the positive rules of law.

It is upon this principle, as will be explained more fully in a later chapter, that, in England, criminal irresponsibility ceases at an earlier age than civil, while an absolute presumption of irresponsibility in respect to crime is only admitted for the first seven years of human life.

Besides, however, such general circumstances as impair the capacity of all men, at certain periods, for forming an intention, there may be local or temporary circumstances, the presence of which, when judicially established, is presumed to have a similar effect. The most remarkable of these circumstances is insanity, of which congenital idiocy, and inebriety voluntarily brought about, are, in fact, only specific cases.

Insanity, in the largest sense of the term, as used for legal purposes, is a temporary or permanent disorder of the relations between the mental and physical functions of man, of such a nature as to destroy the value of the current presumptions, founded on those relations as existing in a condition of health.

It will be noticed that in this description of insanity, not a word is said which implies the truth or falsehood of any physiological or psychological theory. All that the lawyer and the judge, within their own province, know about *insanity* is that the case is from time to time presented to their notice of a person having done an act, of which a person in an average condition of health would be properly presumed to know the immediate consequences, yet of which he certainly did not know the immediate consequences.

Medical evidence on the subject says that the case presented belongs to a typical form of disease. The same evidence varies a good deal as to the nature and history of the disease, and as to whether it attacks the mental faculties directly, or only indirectly through the medium of the body; or even as to whether the mental faculties and the bodily can, for scientific purposes, be contemplated apart. Medical evidence, again, is found to differ largely as to the possible extent and operation of the disease; as to the way in which it assaults the moral susceptibilities, confusing the notions of right and wrong; and as to the way it impairs free action as well as correct judgment, generating irresistible impulses, or hindering action when on the verge of performance.

This notorious conflict and hesitation of medical opinion would be extremely perplexing to the judge, did he allow himself for a moment to be diverted from a purely legal view of the matter. The most that medical evidence can do is to lift the case out of that class for which the ordinary presumptions, applicable under conditions of average health, may universally serve, and, by calling the judge's attention to the general phenomena observable in cases like the one under consideration, to construct a new class of presumptions, by which the circumstances of this particular case may be tested.

Thus, for judicial purposes, insanity is merely a term to cover a certain class of exceptions from the current presumptions as to persons of a certain age, who are, other circumstances being favourable, competent to foresee the consequences of their acts.

It may be indeed that the person whose acts are being judicially weighed had no capacity of willing, and so the alleged *act* was only an event. A presumption in favour of this, operating against the ordinary presumption that the voluntary muscles are moved in obedience to the will, and not otherwise, may also be raised by medical evidence, such as that adduced in proof of *insanity*.

According to this view of the matter, which will undoubtedly be found to be the true one, insanity, as a characteristic and well-ascertained physical condition, affords no general excuse for the commission of crimes or for disobedience to law. Its actual presence in any given case destroys, modifies, or suspends, the general presumption as to the voluntariness of muscular motions, or as to the intention preceding the act. It may even go so far as, under the general aspects of the case, and in conformity to medical experience, to raise presumptions directly the reverse of those customary under conditions of health.

But the utmost that general medical evidence can do

is to qualify subsisting, or to introduce new, classes of presumptions. The circumstances of the particular case must be investigated for themselves, in the light of the presumptions finally made, and the particular condition of the mind of the actor at the exact moment under consideration must be keenly scrutinized.

English law supplies an exact illustration of the working of this distinction between the provinces of the judge and the physician. According to the principles of this law, no amount of general or even lifelong insanity can excuse a person so afflicted from having a crime, alleged to have been committed by him, judicially investigated just as if he were sane; nor, if he made a will during a lucid interval, would his constant insanity afford a conclusive presumption against its validity. In both cases the constant persistence of the disease and its carefully recorded general effects upon the mind and body remove the circumstances from among those to which alone the current presumptions are applicable, and even raise a presumption unfavourable to the supposition of mental restoration. But this last presumption only guides a particular investigation, and does not dispense with it.

The cases of *drunkenness* and of that violent sort of anger, which, in some of its aspects, is scarcely distinguishable from insanity, stand on peculiar grounds of their own, inasmuch as, though the effect on intention, and even on the voluntariness of muscular motion, resembles that resulting from insanity, yet they are conditions for which the person suffering under them is directly accountable. These states are the immediate consequences of voluntary indulgence, and these consequences may properly be assumed to be foreseen. Thus, strictly speaking, all the disastrous results that often follow from indulgence in drink or in unbridled passion, are properly imputable to him who voluntarily puts himself into a state from which these results would possibly, as he might have known, spring.

Nevertheless, where a distinct perception of the nature and immediate consequences of an act forms the very essence of its legal validity or imputability—as in the case of making a contract or a will, or joining in a conspiracy to do an illegal act—the state of mind implied in drunkenness and in excessive passion is generally held to repel the presumptions of voluntariness and intention. In other cases, again,—as in murder and robberies with violence,—where it is the general mental condition, rather than a clear and precise conception of fine results, that gives the character to the intention, drunkenness and passion are held, it is true, in English law, to afford no excuse,—though, in fact, they often operate by way of mitigation of the penalty, through the intervention either of the judge or of the Crown.

There are other great classes of facts which, when they are present under special circumstances, are universally taken into account by courts of justice as qualifying the intention of persons affected by them. Such are *ignorance, accident,* and *fraud.* The general sort of ignorance which besets every one during the first years of life has already been adverted to. But, besides this, there is what may be called a special sort of ignorance, which is liable to befall every one in respect of the multitudinous transactions in which he is called to take his share. This ignorance may be of the most varied sorts and degrees, and the diffusion and multiplicity of it render it an extremely difficult element to provide for in the administration of justice.

One source of ignorance is what has sometimes been called "rusticity," which especially befalls the poorer and least educated section of the community, so often as they are called to take part in the negotiations of civil life. Some particular classes of persons, such as soldiers and sailors, are, from their occupations, peculiarly exposed to ignorance of this sort; and some systems of law, in view of this, have directed certain special presumptions to be made in their favour.

The most frequent form of ignorance that may be expected to present itself is ignorance of the state of the law. This ignorance may be displayed either in a general want of acquaintance with the rules of law, or in a special want of acquaintance with the modes in which those rules operate as affecting a person's own rights and duties. Thus a person may either not know that a certain rule of law exists; or he may not know that he ought to do certain acts which the law commands him to do, or to abstain from certain acts which the law commands him to abstain from. This difficulty seems, on the face of it, to be very great, and it is likely to be increased, by the impediments to the providing of evidence as to the actual condition of a person's knowledge on matters so intricate as laws, rights, and duties. If ignorance of the law were readily accepted as an excuse for disobedience to law, it would seem to be impossible to close the innumerable openings thus afforded to fraudulent impositions on courts of justice.

The practical method that has been adopted in the most celebrated legal systems, in order to obviate this inconvenience, is the following:—A general presumption is made that every one is acquainted with the state of the law, and with the nature and extent of his own rights and duties. This presumption is for the most part not allowed to be rebutted, though the injustice that might follow from an unswerving application of it is partially modified by certain devices. Thus exceptional favour, as has been already shown, is sometimes accorded to certain classes of persons, who, from their special situation, seem to need the peculiar protection of law; and, just as the consequences of their general ignorance are indulgently provided against on the principles already stated, so these same principles are made applicable to their ignorance of law. To these classes of persons belong, in some or in all countries, women, the young, soldiers, and sailors.

Another device for diminishing the harshness of the general maxim, that every one knows the law, is that of derogating from the presumption itself in cases where the principle of law is so generally understood throughout the community that ignorance of it in a special case leads to the supposition that the person establishing his ignorance has been in a peculiarly unfavourable situation, or has been subjected to misrepresentation or imposition on the part of others, and, on either ground, deserves extraordinary indulgence.

Lastly, the operation of the maxim may be controlled by diminishing or wholly relaxing the penalty which the breach of the law involves, in cases where the moral culpability seems to be more or less reduced in amount by varying degrees of ignorance as to the state of the law.

There is a third class of occasions in which ignorance of facts may so alter a person's situation that he may, for certain purposes, be unable to form that accurate judgment, as to the immediate consequences of his acts, which the general presumption of law supposes every one capable of forming. These occasions may arise from the intervention of fortuitous impediments, or of the intentional acts of other persons; in other words, from *accident* or from *fraud*.

It is quite possible that, though a person has every reason to believe certain immediate consequences will follow from his acts, yet, owing to the operation of causes he had no opportunity of taking into account, these consequences may not follow, and very different conse quences may follow in their stead. Thus it may be that a person gives to an invalid what he believes to be an innocent draught of medicine, not knowing that the bottle he takes from the usual place had been changed by some one else, and that the draught he actually gives is a deleterious mixture or a dangerous poison. Or a person may tear up a document which he erroneously supposes to be an insignificant one, or the copy of his will, while, owing to some one else having shifted the position of his papers, what he really tears up is the original will itself, and consequently, apart from special provision for his case, he dies intestate.

For these cases of ignorance, as affecting intention, it is less difficult to provide a remedy than for those previously considered. In the case of those the ignorance attached to widespread classes of society, and there was a danger lest, in showing promiscuous indulgence to every alleged case of ignorance, general anarchy might result. In the case, however, of ignorance brought about by special accidents, these must always be rare and exceptional, and no harm can follow from making the special relief no more than exactly co-extensive with the need.

Thus, according to English law, as applied to the above selected illustration, if the person giving the draught which causes the death of another had no knowledge that the probable immediate consequence of giving it would either be the death of the other person, or would be the introduction of a train of causes which would result in that death, he would be exempt from all liability. The question of possible negligence, which perhaps might be involved, will come under consideration lower down. In the other illustrative case an effectual remedy would be given by allowing evidence of the contents of the destroyed will to be produced from other quarters. This was allowed at Rome, as it is in England.

The most important cause, however, of dislocated intention is that sort of wilful interference on the part of others which is styled *fraud*. The essence of fraud is that one person induces another to do an act under the supposition that its immediate consequences will be of a sort he would either desire or not object to, while, owing to some deception practised upon the actor, the real consequences are of a kind probably beneficial, indeed, to the person perpetrating the fraud, but either the reverse of beneficial to, or, at least, of a nature wholly unexpected by, the person who is the victim of it.

This is the simplest and most elementary form of fraud, though its actual forms are of almost infinite diversity. They will all, however, be found in some way or other to trifle with the intention of the person upon whom they are practised. He is induced to do an act, or to assent to another person's doing an act, the consequences of which he thinks he distinctly foresees, but owing to some trick practised upon him—whether by verbal misrepresentation; by the secret substitution of one document for another; by the writing of the name of a non-existent person as though he were existent; by the imitation of another's handwriting; or by the mere suppression of material facts—the consequences he anticipates do not follow. He has acted in ignorance, and therefore his act was not intentional.

A test of the vigour and vitality of a legal system is the measure of its success in providing a remedy for the wrong and suffering caused by fraud. In a very early state of society, the main violations of social order are effected through overt assaults upon that order, rather than through the silent and insidious instrumentality of fraud. It also happens that, in the early social condition, the attention of law-makers and judges is directed far more to outward and visible acts than to those mental phenomena which have been gathered up under the term *intention*. Thus, just as frauds begin to get frequent, the improved instrumentality in the hands of judges is ready for the discouragement of those frauds.

The Prætor at Rome and the Chancellor in England have been the main judicial organs in the two countries by whom, as it were, a special faculty has been elaborated for the sole purpose of disappointing the machinations of fraud. The devices of fraud, however, contrive to keep pace with the means employed for thwarting them, and the enormous growth of one large part of the law is determined by nothing else than by the ever new and unexpected manifestations of forms of eluding both the clearest language of the law and the most vigilant watch kept by those who administer it.

In speaking of *intention*, it is necessary to notice that *intention* itself—that is, the attitude of the mind in view of the immediate consequences of acts—is subject to a certain amount of legal control. Law prescribes in all countries, a certain *minimum* of mental alacrity and assiduity to be exhibited by all persons in the community under various circumstances; and for some persons, under some circumstances, prescribes a special amount of such alacrity and assiduity, very far exceeding the *minimum*. Such a prescription is absolutely needed in order to secure the common advantages of civil intercourse; for, in default of such a prescription, every one's personal security, reputation, and health would be at the mercy of every other person who might choose to indulge himself in thoughtless and reckless intrusion upon his neighbours.

Thus, in each condition and situation of life, law supposes that every subject of the State will watch carefully that his acts do not interfere with the enjoyment of rights which, in that condition and situation, are vested in others. The amount of watchfulness that is needed will be determined by the extent of the right under the particular circumstances. But, whatever the extent of the right, the violator of it will not only be responsible for his act in cases where he took no care at all to prevent the injury, but also in cases where he did not take all the care exactly defined by law as needed to be shown under the circumstances.

The absence of this variable amount of care, so demanded by law, is called *negligence*. The presence of it is styled *diligence*. In all systems of law the amount of diligence required under different circumstances must vary extremely; and it will, in fact, be exactly measured by the extent of the rights of the person towards whom it has to be exhibited. A person, for instance, has a larger right to personal security in circumstances in which the law leads him to expect the presence of greater appliances for his protection. Thus, furious driving would be forbidden in a metropolis, but perhaps allowable in a country lane. A person equally injured would have a remedy on the ground of negligence in the former case, but might not have it in the latter.

CHAPTER VII.

LAW IN RELATION TO (1) THE STATE, (2) THE FAMILY, (3) THE OTHER CONSTITUENT ELEMENTS OF THE STATE.

HITHERTO the subject-matter with which law is conversant has only been incidentally alluded to in order to assist the inquiry into the true nature of law, and to explain the circumstances under which it becomes fully developed in a community. It is now time to map out with precision the department which law occupies in the organization of a State, and to review the general classes of objects which a legislator proposes to himself in the enactment of laws.

These objects may be described, in general terms, as twofold: the conservation of the State, and the adequate accomplishment of the purposes for which it exists. The first class of these objects may be said to be "statical," and the second, "dynamical." The former are, in kind or quality, the same for the State at every period of its existence, while the latter undergo incessant variations, of which the limit can hardly be, at present, conjectured. Not, indeed, that it is always possible to draw a sharp line between the forces which conduce to keep a State in existence and those which promote its ulterior progress; inasmuch as a condition of stagnation is nearly akin to one of decay, and there is reason to believe that, in politics at least, not to go forward is to go backward.

Nevertheless, it will appear that in every State there

are some institutions and conditions which are permanent and essential, while others seem to take a variety of forms and colours at different stages of political advancement, and, in some measure, to determine the rate of that advancement. It is thus a natural and convenient mode of distributing the purposes of laws, to denominate one class as "statical" and the other as "dynamical."

The value of an inquiry into the purposes of law, as conducive to the maintenance and the progress of the "State," must depend upon an accurate notion being obtained of what the term *State* denotes. This term is so largely employed in popular conversation and loose political discussion that it has contracted, like most other leading political terms, an indecision and ambiguity of meaning from which it is next to impossible to liberate it.

Thus, at one time, and for one class of debaters, the *State* is nothing more than the "supreme political authority," or the legislature, of the nation. At another time, and for another class of debaters, the *State* is the Executive, or the "Government" in the English sense, that is, the persons selected from the preponderant political party of the day to discharge the executive functions of the Crown. Sometimes, again, the *State* means nothing more than the nation, or the aggregate body of persons connected together by certain common ties of blood, of language, of historical vicissitudes, or of territorial habitation. Lastly, the *State* sometimes means the ever-renewed population of a country, as contrasted with their Government at any particular time.

Now, though, provided the persons who use the term *State* in any of these senses are consistent in their use of it, it is not possible to say that any of these uses are wrong, it may yet be said that some of these meanings are more convenient to adhere to than others, and that the best meaning that could be put upon the term would be that which reflected as many, and lost as few, of the popular meanings as possible. In order to reach such a meaning, the radical conception which underlies most of the uses of the word State must be further investigated.

It is a conclusion based upon the results of experience and observation, as illustrated by the application of strict deductive reasoning, founded on truths universally acknowledged, that the social development of mankind can only proceed through the multiplication of groups and through unity of contribution.

In other words, humanity is threatened by two hostile tendencies, one of which prevents its initial growth out of animalism, and the other thrusts it back into animalism again. The first tendency is that expressed in barbarism, which is a multiplication of small groups without contribution. The second tendency may be designated, for the sake of brevity, as imperialism, which implies an intense unity of contribution, but an annihilation of independent groups.

Where either of these tendencies prevails, the chief faculties of man's nature are stunted in their growth or rendered abortive. It is obvious that this must be so. All man's warmest and most active emotions must be called into exercise by that which is near at hand, and present to his senses and to his constant thought. At the same time he needs the utmost variety of object, of situation, and of opportunity, to stimulate and call into existence his manifold faculties of thought, feeling, and action. This proximity and variety in the objects which solicit the affections, and impel to action, is supplied by what has above been called the multiplication of groups. These groups may be larger or smaller, and according to their magnitude and to the closeness of their coherence will the advantages here indicated be attained.

In the most barbarous condition of society possible, the family, however strangely constituted, is always tending to form the basis of a true national grouping; while the associations for warlike purposes, however desultory, have a similar tendency of a more artificial kind. The feebleness, however, in the constitution of society at this stage, is due to the narrowness of the area in point of space, and to the limitation of vision in point of time, by which the activity of the individual members of the community is restricted. In this sort of society there can be no effective solicitude for the welfare of families beyond the immediate neighbourhood; no distinct concern for the fortunes of the next generation, and, still less, of posterity; no conscious identification of the present with the past and the future life of the community, and, thereby, no prevalent sentiment of the duty of self-sacrifice for principles not immediately connected with obvious facts.

The best description that can be given of the State, in its innermost conception, is that it is the living and actual exponent of a condition of society in which all the elements needed to supplement the organization of a barbaric community, as above sketched, are supplied.

Where there is a State, the groups indeed remain the same as before, with all their independent energy, activity, and capacity for mutual inter-action; but, in the place of waste and abortiveness, they all contribute (however tentatively at first) to the accomplishment of a common aim, and to the general support of a rich, because common, life. The common aim and life is not merely ideal and delusive, but that which intimately concerns the well-being of every atomic member of the community.

A new and vast, though silently operating, educational process takes place throughout the whole people. The records of the past begin to be gathered up and treasured:

the opinion of posterity becomes an incitement or a warning; a sentiment of willingness to give up individual life itself in defence of the integrity of the national life becomes predominant over all poorer and more selfish inclinations; and feelings of national pride and brotherhood,—and, at first, of rivalry or antipathy towards all other communities similarly situated,—become inseparable elements of the national consciousness.

The State is then completely formed. What are the forces that have formed it in any given case—or that form it in all cases—may furnish occasion for endless debate. It may be the cogent necessities of defence against a foreign foe; it may be the accidental introduction of a new form of religious worship; it may be the appearance of a gifted statesman or poet, or the introduction of a body of foreign laws. Whatever the originating cause, the final results are much the same. The world is the gainer by a new centre of civilization and progress; that is, by the birth of a new *State*.

It is easy to see that the effect of what has been called Imperialism—or the extension of the physical power of a single dynasty over an extent of territory, limited only by physical obstacles, and not by the moral demands of the subjected population—is the reversal of this process. It is the negation of the true State; the result being the paralysis of all the independent groups, coupled with the necessity of forcible contribution towards the material support of the tyrannical dominion. In this way, again, all care for the future, all self-identification with the prosperity of a corporate whole, all thought of the past, all pride in national successes, all spirit of brotherhood, gradually die out. Each part of the empire is vicariously tyrannized over by the deputies of the Sovereign, and corruption of every sort eats deeply into the vitals of the whole community.

History and existing facts combine to testify to the truthfulness of the picture.

It is to be noticed that in every nation, at each moment of its history, the practical problem of preserving the State and resisting its annihilation through "over-government" has to be encountered. Every law that is made should tend to effect one or other of these objects, and therefore it is of the utmost consequence to ascertain what are the essential elements in the true State, the preservation and development of which it should be the aim of all laws to favour and not to impede.

The two main ingredients introduced into barbaric society by the conception of the State may be said to be *organization* and *government*. Organization implies a relation on the part of each constituent group (or component element of the community) with every other group and with the whole, as an integral body. This relation is of such a nature that each group contributes to the efficiency of every other group and of the whole; and the whole, strengthened by such general contribution, increases the efficiency of every separate group. Government implies the conscious superintendence of the fortunes of the community, both present and future, and involves the manipulation of the physical strength latent in all parts of the community, for the purposes both of controlling recalcitrant members of the community, and of protecting the community from assailants from without. The main instrumentality by which Government operates is *law*, or bodies of general rules declaring the acts which members of the community are to do and not to do in order to facilitate the accomplishment of the general purposes for which the Government exists.

It has thus appeared that the State is an aggregate portion of the human race, preserving its ideal integrity inviolate in spite of the death of successive generations of the actual representatives of it from time to time; of dimensions suitable to the fullest possible development of the resources of human nature; and having its modes of occasional action determined by "Government." It is then the preservation and development of this entirety, the "State," that is the purpose of law as a subordinate agency of Government, and it remains to consider what are the distinct objects to which, in pursuit of this general purpose, laws are, and must be, addressed. It is to be borne in mind, in the course of the inquiry, that the province of law in this matter is severely limited,—first, because Government is by no means the only, or even the chief, agency employed for the development of the State; and, secondly, because law is only one out of a variety of means employed by the supreme political authority in carrying out the ends of Government.

The primary object, then, which law has to keep in view, is the support of the integrity of those original groups on the continued vitality of which, as has been seen, the whole structure of the society depends. These groups are such as families, villages, towns, parishes, and the like, according to the situation or ethical peculiarities of the particular country under consideration.

The preservation and description of the Family as an integral atomic group, out of an assemblage of which groups the State is formed, is one of the most momentous of the objects on behalf of which laws exist. Even in conditions of society a long way removed, as yet, from the era of the foundation of the true State, marriage (however strangely diversified in its circumstances) is fenced about by customs as rigid and tenacious as the most mature laws. The true nature of the family group, and the amount of interference with the process of its spontaneous construction which law may properly exert, present problems which can only be satisfactorily solved by experience, and in the attempted solution of which it is likely that the most unhappy mistakes will long be persisted in. These problems are of the following sorts—first, as to the conditions and forms of marriage, and the possibility and conditions of divorce; secondly, as to the extent and comprehensiveness of the family group; thirdly, as to the amount of interference justifiable on the part of the State with the independent activity of the constituent members of the family.

First, as to the conditions and forms of Marriage, it is to be remembered that the purpose of law is not to constitute those groups, from the multiplication and organization of which the State derives its existence; but to define the limits of them, and to ascertain their relations to one another, as well as to contribute to their stability. In respect of the constitution of the State, marriage must be viewed as an *act* which determines the creation of a new family group, and from which act a number of relations, actual and possible, moral and legal, spring; relations which, taken in their aggregate, constitute marriage as a *status*. It is obvious that the determination of the moment at which a new family group takes its rise is of the utmost concern to the State; and, furthermore, the importance of keeping distinct from one another the different groups is of scarcely inferior concern. It is in view of this last object that rules for the prevention of intermarriages between blood relations and certain others, based as they often are, at first, upon curious superstitions or questionable physiological theories, are finally adopted and enforced by law.

With respect to the form of the marriage, the two main considerations must be *certainty* and *publicity*; though, even to the partial sacrifice of these considerations, it is often held expedient for law to recognize the forms of marriage already spontaneously adopted by custom. Nevertheless, the tendency in all advancing nations is to secure certainty and publicity by better guarantees than those afforded by popular practices, and thus the anomaly is often presented of two sorts of marriage ceremony co-existing in the same State,—the one reflecting and preserving the ancient usages of the people; the other, the creation of positive law as based upon carefully weighed considerations of public convenience.

The question of Divorce is perhaps the one which the conscious lawgiver encounters with the greatest reluctance, inasmuch as the arguments which carry weight with himself are peculiarly liable to misapprehension by the people generally, and are, indeed, from their nature, hard to state in a strictly theoretical form. To grant indefinite facility for divorce seems to deny the indissolubility of marriage, and to that extent to menace the integrity and permanence of every family group, thereby seriously affecting the interests of all the constituent members of the family, and so far impairing, as has been seen, the essential structure of the State itself. To grant a divorce in no case whatever, on the other hand, leads to the consequence, in numberless cases—few though they be in comparison with the remaining cases of marriage—of bringing irreparable suffering upon innocent persons, and, indeed, of favouring the growth of another set of fresh family groups wholly beyond the recognition and protection of law. To grant a certain, but not an excessive, amount of facility for divorce, again, is likely to lead to a number of frauds upon public justice, to investigations in a high degree detrimental to public manners and morals, and to the concession of a discretionary faculty to judges which, in some states of society, might be fraught with the utmost danger.

Such are the problems before the legislator, in the

matter of divorce, stated in their most general form. The actual aspect of those problems in any given epoch in a given country will depend upon the traditions and habits of the country, the existing standard of public morality, and the prevalent character of the judges. The solution belongs rather to the statesman than to the scientific theorist, though the latter may usefully remind the former how much of the question belongs to the region of law and how much to that of morality.

As to the rights and duties of the husband and wife in respect of each other and of the children of the marriage, one main consideration underlies all the rest; that is, the attitude of preponderance or of equality which the husband and wife shall assume in respect of one another. The matter, indeed, is closely connected with the larger one as to the legal relations of men and women throughout the community in respect of ownership, industrial and professional occupations, and political rights. The principles upon which these legal relations in all States are or may be determined may conveniently be considered in this place.

It is admitted by reasonable disputants on both sides of the controversy with respect to the relative legal claims of men and women that, whatever may be the case in primitive times before the foundation of the true State, the whole tendency of civilization is to place man or woman, for all purposes of moral and social advantage, on an exactly equal footing. The excessive division of labour, the diffusion of education, the prevalent doctrines of personal liberty and of the dignity of the human being, as well as the vicissitudes of wealth and poverty, all tend to render impossible a condition of society in which all men have fixed and permanent advantages, physical, moral, and social, over all women. This is so transparent, that the argument in favour of different laws for men and for women, based upon any imagined inferiority of position or of moral claim on the part of women, is now nearly deserted in favour of one far more plausible and far better adapted to the actual facts of modern society.

It is said that though there is no imaginable inequality between men and women in respect either of moral dignity or of legal claim, yet the differences between men and women are so wide-reaching and radical, that all hope of assimilation of laws affecting the two must be delusive, as any attempted assimilation could only be pernicious. The premises of this argument would appear to be true, though not wholly in the way implied by the arguers, but the conclusion based upon them certainly does not properly follow.

To one casting an eye on the continuous history of a political society, the following is the sort of panorama that would be exhibited in the matter now under consideration.

The first stage of society would exhibit women as being of little account, except for their obvious services in contributing to maintain the existence of the society, and in ministering to the physical needs of the men, whose prowess in the field defends the nascent society against its assailants.

The second stage would exhibit men and women co-operating together in providing for the necessities of the whole community, the strength and prowess of the men being of little more account and little more in demand than the patience and acuteness of vision found among the women. Nevertheless, the memory of the former stage would not have faded away, while the actual and necessary peculiarity of some part of the duties and occupations of many women would tend to prop up the notion that women existed, not as integral elements of the whole society, but as subordinate ministers to the well-being of men.

A third stage of society, however, presents a new scene. The idea has gained ground that the life and success of the whole community depend neither upon an equality in its integral elements nor upon the subordination of some to the rest. This idea expresses itself in a variety of forms in the case of men. All permanent restrictions which have hampered the development of individual men are gradually abolished as anachronisms. Political rights, once the privileges of a few, become the common inheritance of all. Monopolies are discarded, and the only obstacles to general emancipation and free self-enrichment which remain are those held to be implied in the constitution of society itself, and are not the creation of theories of natural inequalities between man and man.

But the vitality of the same idea is found to extend itself to women in their relation to men. Here too there may be, and are, differences fixed by nature, and which laws can neither make nor change. On inquiry, however, it is found that laws have been made not merely to maintain these differences (for if the differences were natural and immutable they needed no such factitious support), but to aggravate and to extend them. It becomes obvious that women have suffered even more than men from the domination of monopolies, exclusive theories, and tyrannical usurpation.

The true differences between men and women are indeed more marked and peculiar than those between men and men, and advantage has been taken of this to exaggerate all the evils which inequality has inflicted on men. But if the usurpation has been grosser, the social loss to the State has been greater. It is these very differences which, when properly developed, become the source of all the fine reactions and reciprocal emotions which supply the main energy of the State's life. These differences can only be expressed in their full natural strength and exuberance under conditions of perfect freedom. Any attempt to force is as vicious as an attempt to cramp; and, in fact, the one has the same result as the other.

It thus comes about that, if modern States are to proceed to the next onward stage, the differences between men and women, whatever their kind and amount, must be left to exhibit themselves spontaneously, without being fostered, and so thwarted, by ignorant legislators. The same course of legislation must be pursued with respect to the abolition of legal distinctions between men and women as between men and men. This is not a question of policy, but of moral necessity, and it will sooner or later be recognized to be so.

The second class of problems which it was said lie before the legislator with respect to the maintenance of the family group, is that concerned with the extent of that group. The problem is at this day a far easier one than in past times, owing to the operation of the class of facts which have just been adverted to. In England and in the United States, marriage, divorce, and guardianship are the only topics with which law, as supporting the integrity of the family group, is concerned. But in ancient Rome, and, to a certain extent, in the continental countries which have based their laws on the Roman and the Canon law, the "family" appears as a small society, every member of which has his place assigned by law, and his rights and duties in respect of every other member carefully determined.

In the Roman law, again, the slave was also a member of the family group, and, in fact, the natural conception of the family, as based upon marriage and blood relationship, gave place, for a time, to a secondary conception of the family, according to which the children of the married persons ceased to belong to the family by "emancipation," and the children of other persons became members of the family by "adoption."

The history of these usages is a curious illustration of the dominion that legal conceptions can obtain over even the most fixed and powerful of all associations of thought; while the gradual decline of them, first under the jurisdiction of the prætors, and then, under the legislation of the emperors, points out how enduring is the conception of the natural family, as the integral group out of which the State grows, even in the face of the dominant conceptions of law. The "Patria Potestas" in Roman law, surviving to some extent on the continent at this day, affords a striking instance of the energy with which the main forces of the State may be converted to doing no more than support the harmony and integrity of the family group.

The third class of problems before the lawgiver, in reference to the bearing of law upon the maintenance of the elementary groups of which the State, as an entirety, consists, concerns the permissible amount of political interference with the individual persons composing the several groups. It is only in very primitive society that the head of the family, as representing every member of it, is the only person known to the law, whether as owner, or contractor, or as solely responsible for the wrongful acts of those under his control.

There are historical facts which seem to indicate that there is a stage of political life in which the group is everything, and the individual member of it nothing. But even at this stage, the group is a group of human beings; and, in the last resort, it must be definite and distinct human beings who feel the pressure of law. At a later stage, the group gradually fades into greater and greater indistinctness, though (as has been seen) the description of its limits always continues a prominent topic of law, while the attention of the lawgiver seem wholly fixed upon the responsibilities of individual men and women.

The family is the most conspicuous and momentous, as it is the original, of the groups which it is one main purpose of law to circumscribe and to defend. But it is by no means the only group of the kind, and in advanced communities there are a variety of other groups, the combination and mutual relations of which are of urgent concern to the well-being of the State. It has recently been pointed out by one after another of the explorers into primitive conditions of society that, in all Aryan communities at any rate, an organization into villages succeeds, while it incorporates, the earlier and simpler organization into families.

This new mode of organization is brought about by a number of causes, such as the extension of families through the fiction of "adoption;" the accidental pre-eminence of particular families, leading to a certain union of subordination among the rest; casual combinations for purposes of mutual defence or co-operation; and the general influences of neighbourhood and of the sentiments of relationship and friendship to which neighbourhood gives rise. When such an organization is fully formed, of which living examples are presented in India at this day, a new field is opened for the operation of law. In order to support the integrity of the whole State, it becomes the purpose of law to define the relations of the several villages to one another, and to ascertain their obligations to the State itself, which represents them all. But law is also concerned with maintaining their internal structure; with mapping out the regions of independent action for the constituent families; with distributing the produce resulting from joint efforts; and with ascertaining the liabilities incumbent upon each for the general benefit of all. This internal law grows up, at first, in the shape of mere customary usages, which have commended themselves by their transparent utility, or have been the mere expression of actual and persistent facts.

This village group, though, from its generality and its antiquity, it seems to merit especial attention, is, in fact, in no different relation to the whole State from that of the modern groups of the parish, the county, and the borough. With respect to each of these, the same class of problems lies before the legislator. Internal laws have to be devised (if they have not spontaneously developed themselves) for the preservation of the essential structure and character of the group. External laws have to be devised for the purpose of bringing the several groups into relation to one another, and enabling or compelling them to minister to the general support of the whole State.

The inquiry how much belongs to one class of these laws, and how much to the other, is one of the most arduous problems of modern statesmanship. An error in one direction or in the other is almost equally perilous. There is the danger, one way, of fostering a number of independent communities without strength, patriotism, or permanent vitality. There is the danger, the other way, of enervating the groups by external interference, and, while seeming to magnify the State, of actually attenuating and destroying it.

In modern politics, the difficulty is to a certain extent reduced in magnitude by the use of a number of devices for promoting the free and sympathetic interaction of local and central government, apart from the application of two rival bodies of law. Among such devices are the representation, in the central legislature, of the several more prominent groups; the combination of the jury system with that of travelling judges of assize; and, more especially, the constant control exercised over local legislation by such central bodies as Government offices, the English Privy Council Boards, and, in some cases, the two Houses of Parliament. The success of these devices must turn upon a number of conditions, which may render them not applicable under all circumstances. Thus mere physical distance, variations in language, or diversities of race and traditions, may render even the most plausibly devised system of Government incapable of binding together into a true State communities too widely separated in space or alien in sentiment from one another. If the attempt be made, in the face of insuperable obstacles, anarchy or paralysis must be the sole result.

These considerations, if thoroughly weighed, may serve to explain the causes of the disintegration of the Roman Empire; the debility of the modern Asiatic kingdoms; the conditions of interdependence between the States of the North American Union; and the true relations which England must establish between herself and her colonies, if she is even nominally to retain her hold upon them.

There is one peculiar group, if such it can be named, to which law, in all ages since the Christian era, has been called to lend its aid in the name of the interest which the State is alleged to have in its vitality and perpetuity. This is the group founded upon a community of religious belief and worship. The phenomenon of law regulating the internal structure, and prescribing the mutual relations of groups of this class is entirely novel, because it is only in comparatively recent times that more than one considerable religious body has existed within the limits of a State at one time. The ancient and mediæval notion of religion was that the confines of religious belief and worship were exactly co-terminous with those of the State itself, and that, if any individual persons happened to dissent from the dogmas generally adhered to, they were of no more account, and were not less obnoxious, than political traitors or rebels.

A number of events, to which, for the present purpose, it is not necessary to do more than allude, have combined to introduce in all the countries of modern Europe a marked change in this respect. Religion is still a powerful—and perhaps, on the whole, the most powerful —influence, both in the conduct of the life of individual persons and in the construction of corporate societies which are highly organized in themselves, and possess all the solidity and strength derivable from intense intellectual convictions and highly-wrought emotional fervour. But these associated bodies of persons are in many States numerous; and in no modern State are they capable of being reduced to one or two. Thus, admitting that groups of this sort, like the other groups already alluded to, are natural elements in the composition of the State, it is still a difficult problem to decide the exact measure of support and control they should severally meet with at the hands of law.

In some important respects these religious bodies differ from the other groups—family, village, parochial, county, and borough—which have been previously adverted to as affording subject-matter for law. Religious bodies almost invariably co-exist only by forced efforts of mutual toleration, while all the other bodies co-exist apart from all necessary thought of rivalry or antipathy. The existence of any single family, village, or county, presupposes, almost as of necessity, the existence of a number of others. Everything is prepared for mutual help and co-operation, and these only lack the stimulating presence of law to discover for each its true relations to all the rest, and to the State.

Religious bodies, on the contrary, for the most part, subsist, in theory, by the exclusion of one another. Their mutual condemnation of each other's opinions and practices may be smoothed over in practical life, through the personal virtues of members or pre-eminent leaders of the several societies. But toleration, at the best, can only be looked for as a precious growth requiring the most anxious culture, and by no means as an essential and natural condition.

If these religious societies have to be brought into that relation with the State into which it is the peculiar function of law to bring all the groups into which the members of the community spontaneously organize themselves, there are only a limited number of courses to be adopted, between which a selection must be made. Thus, law may select for its peculiar patronage a certain number of these societies, according to their respective claims as grounded on the number and wealth of their adherents, on the antiquity of their pretensions, or on the apparent usefulness and truthfulness of their tenets. This patronage may be exhibited in conceding exemptions from general civil burdens to the ministers of the religious body favoured; in supplementing the salaries of the ministers from public funds; or in according a peculiar amount of protection to the property vested in the body.

Or, again, law may select for its peculiar patronage one body out of all the rest, such body being chosen on the ground of its past history in relation to the general history of the country,—the selection of it being, presumptively, justified by its present size and influence.

The patronage in this last case is likely to assume a more decided form than in the former cases, and those phenomena are produced which are exhibited in England at this day in respect of the Established Church. The Queen or King must necessarily be a member of this Church. All the chief ministers of this Church are members of one branch of the legislature. All the formularies of public worship are fixed by Act of Parliament. All breaches of ecclesiastical duty are cognizable in special courts of justice constituted by the State for this purpose. All the chief ministers of the Church, and a vast number of the subordinate ministers, are appointed by the executive Government of the day. This is what is meant by saying that the Church of England is "established." It is obvious that "establishment" will have a different meaning for every country, and for the same country at different epochs in its history.

A third method that law may adopt is to show complete neutrality with respect to all religious bodies, only treating them in the same way as other corporate bodies which are organized for any purely secular purpose. In this way, their rights of ownership would be fully protected, and the mutual liabilities of their ministers and congregations defined by the general law of contract. Certain supplementary laws, again, may provide for the special registration of bodies fulfilling certain conditions, the result of which will be the concession of privileges to their ministers for the performance of certain important public ceremonials, as marriages, and for the assurance of quiet and order in the performance of public worship.

Which of these methods a State will adopt, for the

strengthening and regulation of the religious bodies which assist in its own composition, will depend as much upon the actual condition of the country as determined by its previous history, as upon conceptions of ideal perfection or even of immediate expediency.

Besides the groups which have hitherto been described as the subject-matter of law in the discharge of its main and characteristic function of maintaining and developing the structure of the State, there are, in modern times, a number of other temporarily or permanently associated bodies which, on behalf of the services they affect to render to the whole community, solicit the special protection, as they demand the regulation, of law. One class of these bodies is that the purpose of which is to make special and extraordinary provision for the current, or for the exceptional, needs of mankind, whether physical or mental. To this class belong hospitals, asylums, and universities or schools.

The origin and regulative principle of these bodies is the devotion of funds accumulated in one generation, or accumulating from generation to generation, to the accomplishment in all future time of the objects contemplated. The care and administration of the fund is committed to the charge of certain persons either designated by the person devoting the fund, or nominated, from time to time, by public officials, or determined by some mode implying a union of both sorts of appointment. It is obvious that the advantages or disadvantages to the State of recognizing such a permanent consecration of the material wealth of the country to such ends as are here indicated, and in the fashion described, must depend upon a number of considerations of which the statesman must take full account. Whatever be the special demands due to the peculiar circumstances of the country at a given time, laws must be devised for the purpose of maintaining the existence of the bodies of persons from time to time entrusted with the task of administering the several funds; of determining their modes of action; and of fixing the degree of their public responsibility.

The peculiar dangers to which the institution of these so-called "endowments" is exposed are of the following kind. In the first place, though the main objects on behalf of which the wealth of one generation may be beneficially applied to the use of future generations, may be easily described under the general heading of unavoidable accident, remediable or even irremediable disease—bodily or mental—and education; yet, even within such general terms, there is large room left for the play of mere eccentric disposition. To confine strictly the class of permissible endowments within any language capable of being comprised in the terms of a law would seem to be almost impossible.

Some writers have urged the political expediency of allowing the largest conceivable license to settlers and testators in the matter of the objects to which they wish their accumulated wealth to be devoted, provided that at some future time, however distant, the wealth either lapse afresh into the treasury of the State, or be diverted to objects approved as beneficial by the supreme political authority of the day. The question is wholly one of comparative expediency, and the answer to it for any particular country must depend upon the motives which in that country seem to be the most favourable to the accumulation of wealth, when considered in the light of the necessary inconvenience flowing from the arrest of the circulation in land and money, which is the necessary result of endowments. It is probable that a security that their funds will be wisely employed, in all future time, in accordance with the demands of that time, will stimulate to make gifts to charitable objects quite as many persons as will be deterred by a knowledge that their own design may hereafter be reconstructed.

Secondly, another difficulty is experienced in regulating endowments by law on the ground that while, at every moment, the administration of the funds must be regulated by definite persons, the nomination of these persons is a matter demanding a peculiar degree of discretion, and their constant supervision equally calls for the most unresting vigilance.

In the case of the innumerable endowments which the superstition or well-meant eccentricity of past ages have handed on as perplexing heirlooms to succeeding ages, the making and regulating nominations to trusteeships with the requisite amount of circumspection, and the control of the conduct of trustees, in every case involves an omnipresence and omniscience on the part of the administrators of law which clearly cannot be looked for. The mode in which this sort of difficulty is encountered in England is by the appointment of temporary or even permanent commissions, with power to investigate the circumstances of certain classes of endowed charities; and either simply to report upon the manner in which the funds are administered with a view to legislative reform, or to take the management of them to some extent into their own hands, with such aid from the legislature as they may from time to time receive or require.

But such devices are very desultory in their operation, and even the most inquisitorial of commissions seldom succeed in touching more than the more important and conspicuous classes of endowments; while, even as to these, the remedy afforded is, without incessant aid from the legislature, only momentary, if not wholly inefficacious.

The only true remedy for the difficulties experienced by law in the process of making endowments subserve the general interests of the State, and not conflict with those interests, is to ascertain clearly the true principles upon which alone the privilege of diverting for ever the general wealth of the community to special ends dictated by the caprice or even passion of private persons can be permitted; and then to provide fearlessly for the gradual suppression or reform of all existing endowments not in conformity with these principles.

Much difference of opinion, indeed, may exist as to the exact nature of these principles, as with respect to the expediency of admitting an indefinite latitude to the fancy or the seemingly irrational prejudices of donors; or of importing into the mode of applying them variations which reproduce in no sense the original conception of those donors. But no difference of opinion can exist as to the inexpediency of letting the funds be wasted or applied to objects which universal experience has condemned as pernicious and destructive to the State; and even still less can exist as to the vigilance that must be exerted to provide against the fraud and incompetence of those in whose hands the funds may from time to time be vested.

The topic of "endowments," viewed as a subject-matter of law—and, more especially, as furnishing a succession of groups of persons, the maintenance and control of which groups is closely bound up with the prosperity, if not with the existence, of the State—introduces another topic of even still greater moment, because of its near connection with all the other topics already passed in review. This topic is "trusteeship"; and, though "trustees" can hardly be called "groups" of persons either naturally or artificially associated together in the political sense here impressed upon the term "group," yet, inasmuch as one main method by which law regulates the essential groups is through the intervention of persons denominated *trustees*, the consideration of "trusteeship" properly belongs to this place.

The actual history of "trusteeship" in England is well known to every one tolerably well acquainted with the social and legal history of the country. It is here of importance only to look at what is essential and likely to be permanent in the institution, neglecting, as far as possible, what is accidental or peculiar to the course of development of any particular country.

The necessity for the institution of "trusteeship" arises from the fact that vast numbers of persons in the community who are invested with rights are unsuitable persons, for a variety of reasons real or presumed, to do all those acts which are needed in order to make the rights available; to defend them if menaced; or to discharge the duties the performance of which cannot be wholly dissociated from enjoying the advantage of the rights. The grounds of this unsuitability may be very various, as also the modes of providing substituted persons in the stead of those believed to be unsuitable.

Among the classes of persons in this predicament of unfitness to do the acts pre-supposed in the enjoyment of rights, and essential to their maintenance, are obviously all those persons who have not yet come to years of discretion, this period being fixed either by law or by the will of other persons competent to give directions in this respect. There are those, again, who by reason of mental infirmity, either congenital or superinduced in later life, are in the same position as children; that is, they can enjoy the advantages of rights, but can neither do the acts needed to render the rights effective, nor discharge the duties incumbent upon them in respect of those rights.

With reference to these classes of persons, the institution of "trusteeship" under some name or other is an obvious necessity; and, indeed, the nature of the institution, in all its most essential characteristics, is much the same in all countries.

But there are other classes of persons, with respect to whom the institution is far more artificial, and indeed implies a considerable advance in the pliancy of political and legal methods. Such are persons who are so numerous and so indefinite, that, though, as they become individually determined, they are quite capable of enjoying the advantages derivable from rights, yet great inconvenience to themselves and others would follow from regarding any one of them capable by himself of doing solemn acts, and discharging multifarious duties; while any prospect of getting all the persons to combine in doing such acts and discharging such duties must be abandoned as chimerical.

This difficulty is at once met by interposing capable persons, upon whom the administrators of law have their constant eye, and whose duty it is to use the utmost vigilance in guarding the interests and discharging the duties of persons who, from their dispersion and indeterminateness, are treated as incompetent to the task themselves.

There is yet another class of persons who may be treated as standing in still greater need of the assistance of others for the protection of their rights, and that is, the unborn. In the case of every endowment the unborn interested persons are of at least quite as great importance in the eye of the law as those actually in being. It may be said, indeed, to be the peculiar characteristic of the State, as a permanent body, that posterity is as much in its thoughts as the present generation; and though it may properly hesitate to encumber coming generations with liabilities and responsibilities devised by those who must be ignorant of future needs and claims, yet when once the rights of a future generation are recognized, provision will be made for rendering these rights in all ways efficacious. The State does this most obviously in the case of endowments, when it watches, with all the jealousy it can, the mode of appointment of the persons who from time to time have to guard the rights both of those living and of those yet to live. But the State exhibits the same care for those not yet in being when it recognizes rights conveyed by will to children yet unborn, or allows land to be entailed for the benefit of distant generations. In this last case each holder is, in fact, a trustee for future holders, whether called so or not, and would be compelled to do all the acts essential to the support of the rights in which others, yet undetermined, have as great a concern as he has himself.

The modes of appointment of trustees may be very various, and the State is tempted to vacillate between two opposite lines of policy. It is possible to leave the appointment of trustees to those who are most immediately concerned in the performance of the acts and duties in respect of which the appointment needs to be made. A private person can acquire a more accurate knowledge of the character, trustworthiness, and capacity of a given man who is near at hand, and whom he has known all his life, than is attainable by public officials or administrators of law at a distance, and involved in a mass of other concerns equally demanding attention. On the other hand, if the trust extends over a considerable time, the original trustees die, or fail in one way or another, and new trustees have to be supplied, the question is presented as to the principle upon which the appointment ought to take place.

The other mode of appointment is to nominate certain

permanent officials, who shall be charged with all the duties appertaining to trusteeship, and the employment of whom shall involve a certain regulated charge upon the estate. This method would certainly be suitable, if only as an alternative one, in the case of all private trusts; while in the case of public endowments, municipal corporations, ecclesiastical and religious bodies of all sorts, special classes of trustees, suitable to the peculiar circumstances of the trust, as well as to its special history, might conveniently be introduced,—provision being made, in all cases, for the due admixture in the body of trustees of official trustees, local as well as central. It is probable that the grossest abuses, both positive and negative, attending the discharge of public trusts in modern States, would, in this way, be most effectually provided against.

It is not necessary in this place to proceed further with the examination of the leading groups of persons for the composition and mutual relations of which it is among the main functions of law to provide. It is important, however, to notice that, though originally, and even finally, men are regarded, for purposes of law, as members of small communities and associations, the aggregate body of which constitutes the State, yet, in the immediate action of law, it is individual men and women, and not associated bodies of them, who are addressed.

It may be, indeed, as happens at some epochs, that individual persons are only addressed by law as representing or personating groups. But this fact does not affect the operation of law, because the groups so represented are, as it were, cast into the shade by the person who stands in front of them, and it is with his rights and duties alone that the law concerns itself. In time, however, as Sir H. Maine and others have established, the

LAW IN RELATION TO THE STATE.

earlier groups, whether of the family or the village, undergo a sort of spontaneous dissolution, in the course of which the old group is gradually lost sight of, or becomes of subordinate importance, and new groups, constructed on a more artificial type, gradually emerge. Then, again, the same phenomena recur. The newly-associated bodies form the true units of which the State is composed. The individual men and women become again subordinate in importance to the small societies to which, for various purposes, they belong; and yet it is of necessity to these men and women that the law immediately addresses itself.

Thus, though the ultimate purpose of law is the development of the whole State life—that is, of the corporate life of all the men and women who are, or, in any future ages, shall be members of the State, and not alone the welfare of the particular men and women now in existence—yet it can only be through the agency of these particular men and women that the higher and ulterior aim can be reached. It thus comes about that a large part of the subject-matter of law is concerned with what may be called private rights and private duties; that is, rights in which the personal advantage of one or a few persons seems to be (though it is not) the primary object of law, and duties, the immediate or sole object of the imposition of which seems to be the maintenance of those rights.

A grave misapprehension of the objects and purpose of law, in the aspects here described, has led to the most mischievous results in the region of practical politics. If once it be held that the limiting value of a law is the amount of personal advantage it secures to an ascertainable number of existing men and women, it follows, as an inexorable consequence, that the desires and passions of the majority must always be allowed to prevail over the remonstrances of the minority. The field of politics becomes a mere scene of scrambling among a rabble of contentious self-seekers. Every nostrum, economical, medical, or social, advocated by the most impudent charlatans, finds its supporters in the legislative body, and, as a result of a compromise among competing advocates, has a chance of being, at least provisionally, adopted. The only test of the expediency of a proposed law becomes that supplied by statistics; the very mention of political, or even of moral, principle is scouted as an irrelevant anachronism; and in the vaunted pursuit of the greatest amount of happiness, the community suddenly wakes up to find itself plunged into an abyss of the deepest degradation and slavery.

The only prevention and cure of this disastrous condition of things is to be sought in a keen and deeply-inwrought appreciation of the truth that the whole is before the parts, and that individual well-being is to be sought, not directly from law, but from all the innumerable influences of which the State is a chief and immediate minister. Law upholds the State, and the State upholds its members.

The functions of the State are performed through very various instrumentalities; some of them taking the form of organized municipal associations; some that of educational, artistic, or scientific guilds; some that of appeals to the historical imagination, by way of figuring the past of the nation and preserving a sense of its continuity; and only a few that of direct compulsion, through the medium of law and the executive Government.

Thus the individual man is placed, as it were, between two competing, though, on the whole, harmonious streams of force—the law which supports the State and the groups of which the State consists, pressing upon him on one side; and the direct influence of the State itself operating partly through law, pressing upon him on the other. In this way it happens that every person's rights and duties are of a twofold nature, some of them lying in a narrower circuit, and only connecting him with his fellows in the immediate neighbourhood; others connecting him with the State itself, in all its aggregate power and sublimity.

Some consciousness of this distinction gave rise to the celebrated opposition of public and private law,—an opposition which, undoubtedly, is not without an important meaning, though devoid of the precision necessary to give it value. Private law, however, may be said broadly to be that kind of law which seeks the advantage of the whole through the intermediate advantage of the parts, and includes large portions of the law of ownership, of contract, and of special classes of persons (as of husband and wife). Public law, on the other hand, seeks only the advantage of the whole without any overt reference to the advantage of the parts. Constitutional law, criminal law, and, to some extent, laws of procedure, are thus generally included in Public law.

Having thus pointed out the general function of law in supporting the structure of the State, it remains to investigate the mode in which it actually affects the individual men and women to whom it is addressed. This introduces the consideration of laws of ownership, of contract, and of crime.

CHAPTER VIII.

LAWS OF OWNERSHIP OR PROPERTY.

It has been seen, from the considerations urged in the last chapter, that the subject-matter of law may be compendiously described to be, first, the definition, and, secondly, the support, of the various groups, natural and artificial, of which the State is composed, and in the mutual action and reaction of which upon each other the appropriate activity of the State consists. But law attains its purposes in two different and, in some respects, opposite ways. It operates directly upon the groups, and it operates on the individual persons whose union and mutual relationships constitute the groups. One part of a whole system of national law is concerned with one of these species of operation, and the other part with the other species, though with respect to some important classes of laws it is difficult to say to which part they properly belong.

Thus all that portion of the law which is called "Constitutional Law" has little reference to the rights and duties of private persons, those rights and duties being only incidentally described so far as they are instrumental in achieving the main and ostensible purpose of this whole branch of law—that is, the description, limitation, and invigoration of those great groups of persons who discharge the legislative and executive functions of Government.

So, again, the portion of law which ascertains the solemnities and legal consequences of marriage and parentage,—personal as it must be in its direct application,—nevertheless treats, from first to last, the interest of the individual person as subordinated to the importance of maintaining unimpaired the integrity of the significant groups to which he or she belongs.

The same remarks apply, though in a less degree, to laws providing for the support of permanent institutions taking the form of corporate societies, whether for educational, sanitary, charitable, or mere exceptional purposes. The interest of existing individual persons cannot be, and is not, left out of account, but it is manifestly, or almost obtrusively, treated as means to an end, and readily sacrificed so soon as the attainment of this end would seem otherwise in peril. It is true that, in fact, individual and momentary interests are always tending to conflict with the general and lasting interest of the group; but the possibility of this is always lamented, and when it occurs, it is treated as a corruption and disease.

But there are other vast portions of every legal system in which the group, and even the State itself, would seem to be neglected as objects of political concern, and in which the individual interests of particular persons, or the general and common interests of all persons, without any reference to their associated character in smaller or larger groups, is the end to which law is addressed. To this portion belong laws of ownership, of contract, and of (so called) civil injuries and crimes. It will be convenient to consider these several topics in succession, commencing with the laws of ownership.

It is generally recognized, in the present day, that

laws of ownership have, historically, undergone a progressive change in their import and nature,—at all events, for those portions of the human family which have most advanced the attainment of modern civilization. In primitive times, such laws of ownership as existed were the main or sole instrument of maintaining the integrity of the family group. The formation of the family group seems to have corresponded chronologically with the desertion of purely nomad habits and with the practice of an agricultural or, at the least, of a regulated pastoral life.

At this stage, the protection of the integrity of family ownership, the guardianship of such claims as were or might be founded on recognized possession by a family, was, in fact, the protection or guardianship of family life itself. The pasture meadow, the wells, the sheltering trees, and, in time, the arable field, changeable as they might be in accordance with the demands of fresh physical wants, were, in fact, the incarnate embodiment of the mass of associations on which the sentiment of the indivisible unity of the family was based.

No doubt these associations were inherently weak and brittle, infinitely more so than in the next stage, when associated families gave birth to village communities, and to the institution of common fields with regulated modes of culture. But the degree of the strength of the notion of primitive ownership is not so much here insisted upon as the fact that the notion, whatever it was, and however strong or weak it was, was not distinguishable from the notion of the permanence and unity of the family itself.

Thus, early laws of ownership, based, as they necessarily were, on the notions and customs existing antecedently to the period of true law,—that is, of the foundation of the State,—were, so far as they existed at all, among the most material and essential conditions of social existence. How far the era of village communities and the anomalous, or as some say, the normal, era of feudalization, contributed to enforce this view of laws of ownership, is obvious without further elucidation.

It may be laid down as a general proposition, that for those countries which have given rise to the most exuberant and civilized bodies of law, laws of ownership were, at the first, a large portion of that part of the law the main purpose of which is to define and to strengthen the primitive groups from the ulterior association of which the State derives its existence and character.

To this stage, however, another one gradually succeeds. The fact or institution of ownership is such an indispensable condition of any material or social progress that, even throughout the period during which the attention of law is concentrated upon family and village ownership, the ownership, on the part of individual persons, of those things which are needed for the sustenance of physical life, becomes increasingly recognized as a possibility or necessity.

One of the most important steps out of savagery into civilization is marked by the fact that security of tenure depends upon some further condition than the mere circumstance of possession.

The use of the products of the earth, and, still more, the manufacture of them into novel substances, consists, generally, of continuous processes, extending over a length of time during which the watchful attention of the worker can only be intermittently fixed upon all the several points and stages. The methods of agriculture and of grazing, as well as the simplest applications of the principle of "division of labour," similarly presuppose the repeated absence of the farmer or mechanic from one part of his work while he is bestowing undistracted toil upon another part; or else entire absorption in one class of work, coupled with a steady reliance that another class of work, of equal importance to himself, is the object of corresponding exertion on the part of others.

In all these cases, the mere fact of physical holding, or *possession*, in the narrowest sense, is no test whatever of the interests or claims of persons in the things by which they are surrounded. The exact modes in which such interests or claims become recognized in early society have often been a topic of curious, but generally futile, speculation. The inconvenience and barbarity of protecting no one in the use of the things around him except him who is actually using the things, and during the time he is using them, are so palpable, that a very slight and tentative social experience might seem sufficient to introduce the true notion of ownership.

But, in fact, there can be no doubt that, as with all other leading moral experiences, the institution of ownership does, from merely accidental circumstances of a favourable nature, reach a considerable pitch of development before the possibility of such an institution not being in existence so much as suggests itself to the imagination. Indeed, the popular imagination which could distinctly picture to itself a condition of society divested, of every fact implying ownership, could only be found in a condition of society in which ownership, as a fact, was already familiar.

The true order of evolution of all such leading notions is that, under certain peculiarly and accidentally favourable conditions, a practice is actually introduced,— generally as an anomalous exception from the current usages. The influence of the practice spreads gradually by the mere effect of its conformability to human well-being. A rapidly operating association of ideas makes the practice at once familiar and cherished. After a time, and at repeated intervals, a disruption of the practice is attempted from one quarter or another, and with more or fewer circumstances of violence. The thought and feeling of the community are roused to conscious activity. The fact of the prevalence of the practice, the true nature of it, and the extent of it are submitted to examination. For the first time, also, the ethical or material value of the practice, and the true modes of testing that value, are also called in question. All these critical processes are, indeed, very gradual ones; and while they are, at first, accompanied by the most hesitating and almost awestruck reluctance, they continue to be executed with increasing vigour and self-confidence throughout the whole life of the nation, till the nature, limits, and value of the moral idea or institution are finally limned out in the clearest possible shape.

There has been here sketched the mode of evolution of the fact or idea of ownership. But the mode is identically the same in the case of government, marriage, contract, crime, and such more abstract notions as liberty, justice, patriotism, and even the primary ideas of right and wrong. These are ideas, practices, institutions, and facts, bearing such a definite relation to the physical, intellectual, and ethical constitution of man's nature, that the absence of them is incompatible with the existence and progress of human society. Nevertheless, they are not consciously created from the first by sapient men in order to promote the ends of that society. Nor, indeed, is their texture such that the mere fiat of the lawgiver, attended by all the array of penalties at his command, can call them into being, or even largely promote their growth.

They take their rise, at the first, from exceptionably

favourable facts, or, in other words, from the accidental absence, in certain times and places, of common impediments. Under continuously favourable conditions, these ideas and facts become rooted and familiar in the popular mind. The ways and habits of the people are fashioned upon the hypothesis of their existence. Early poetry and song take notice of them. The occasional invasion of their sanctity gives rise to sentiments, often desultory enough, of mingled awe and abhorrence. The practical rules in which they must needs express themselves call, from time to time, for the interposition of wise and trusted men to rescue them from ambiguity, to ascertain their validity, and to prescribe the special mode of their application in particular circumstances. They thus assume much of the character of true laws, needing only the final institution of the State, and of courts of justice as the instruments of the State, to perfect that character.

It may be that the course is precipitated by the frequently recurring phenomenon of an early code,— that is, a published body of customary rules, generally extracted by the force of popular clamour from the secret treasure-house of an aristocracy or a priesthood (see Maine's *Ancient Law*). Any way, the path (though tardily enough pursued) is from this epoch cleared for full investigation, criticism, social disputation, philosophical controversy, forensic struggle, and legislative debate. The idea or fact is thenceforward firmly established in all its transparent clearness and true proportions.

The fact of ownership and the laws of ownership have, up to this point, been regarded in two aspects. One aspect is that of the place they occupy in maintaining the primordial elements of the State in their unmutilated integrity, and in giving to the early family and village group their substantial framework, projected, as it were, into the world of physical things. In this aspect, laws of ownership originally present themselves as historical facts; and at the epoch at which they so present themselves they are, strictly speaking, part of the constitutional law of the country, their public purposes taking precedence, at every point, of the advantages they claim to confer on individual persons.

Another aspect in which the facts of ownership and of laws of ownership have been exhibited is that of the modes in which they conduce to the material well-being of the State, or, rather, that in which they supply the indispensable conditions for the attainment of that well-being. In this latter aspect men are regarded less as possessed of capacities for forming themselves, and for being formed, into small groups from an assemblage of which the State is constructed, than as individually endowed with a physical and moral constitution which expresses itself in a variety of definite wants, desires, hopes, and tendencies. So far as these latter are of a purely material sort, it has been seen that ownership, as an institution and as a ground of law, is one of the most important instruments in satisfying them.

But it is yet to be shown that it is not material wants, hopes, desires, and tendencies alone to which ownership lends its aid as a potent instrument of satisfaction and even development. The moral aspirations and needs of individual man are scarcely less signally sustained and gratified by ownership than the material. And this gives rise to yet a third aspect in which the fact of ownership and laws of ownership admit of being presented.

It is obvious that, apart from the possibility of ownership, the position of man, as a moral being, is pitiable and even contemptible in the extreme. He keeps for himself and for his own uses just so much as he is able to retain hold of, and for just so long a time as he can retain such hold of it. His energies must be wholly engaged in the exercise of vigilant retention. His hand is against every man's, because every man's hand is against him. There is no room or opportunity for speculation about the future uses to which he shall turn his possessions, nor even about any but the most obvious and simple immediate uses. There can be no play for the imagination as to the effect of protracted or carefully planned labour upon the things about him, and still less as to the consequences of regulated co-operation with his fellows. Suspicion, fear, self-indulgence, an instinctive sense of the wisdom of immediate consumption, and of trusting as little as possible to the morrow, are the habits of mind generated under such circumstances, and which, in fact, represent an almost ideally savage state.

Nor is it merely that the absence of ownership prevents the most precious qualities and elements of human nature from being properly cultured and developed. It prevents those qualities and elements from so much as existing at all. A faith in the future, a faith in others, habits of self-reliance and of forming far-sighted, deliberate, and complicated plans, are very hard to call into being, as they need the utmost possible stimulus of all sorts to develop them highly. But it is ownership and, ultimately, laws of ownership which perform the main function in both creating and stimulating these qualities and habits.

If a man *owns*, and not merely possesses, his imagination centres round the object of ownership, and through the medium of it he is brought into permanent and incessant contact with other persons about him; with his own future life and his modes of conducting it; with his children and successors; with all the institutions, social or political, with the validity and integrity of which his own rights of ownership are indissolubly connected. This is most especially true in the case of the ownership of land and immovables; and one of the main political arguments in favour of a system of peasant proprietorship is based upon a recognition of these facts. But it is also true in respect of all ownership whatever. The recognition of ownership implies the existence of a society, however small or feebly organized; and what might be supposed to be a mere tribute to, and expression of, natural selfishness becomes the most remarkable aid in educating men into unselfishness.

From the above considerations it will be seen what is the meaning of the favourite view of the great school of German jurists, to the effect that ownership increases man's power (*vermögen*) or physical and moral capacity. As an owner, actual or possible, man is a more worthy and capable being than he would be otherwise. One large portion of human life, even under favourable circumstances of climate, production, manufacturing skill, and mechanical invention, must be concerned with processes of turning to human uses the things of the earth. The might, physical and moral, of any particular man must be largely measured by the control of human labour, present and prospective, which he can exert, or by the quantity of past labour of the product of which he is able to avail himself. In a highly organized society the poorest member shares in this physical and moral grandeur with the richest. That he is not actually starving; that the possibility of work and recompense yet await him; that others, at least, are richer than himself, and therefore able to help him; or, at the worst, that he can attribute his poverty either to exceptional calamity or to personal shortcomings of his own, are momentous facts which tend to raise even the most worthless beggar immeasurably in the scale of humanity as a dignified member of the race.

This last aspect, however, of ownership, as an essential instrument in the culture of large and valuable elements of human nature, gradually leads on, in a very advanced condition of civilization, to a yet higher conception. A sentiment grows that, just as each workman can elaborate from the fruits and products of the earth far more than is needed for his own personal consumption, and just as a person with a large command of labour has an enormous surplus over and above what he can employ in procuring the most luxurious advantages for himself and his family, there must be some appropriate end to which the product of things owned, and the benefits of ownership, ought to be directed, other than that implied in the satisfaction, even to the full, of the owner's own wants. The unequal division of the things of the earth, which no scheme of laws of ownership can obviate, however much it may mitigate it, makes ever increasingly pressing the problem as to the use to which, morally, the surplus profits of things owned ought to be turned.

There may be an advantage in the concentration of wealth, and in the unity and economy of management which it brings with it; but there can be no general advantage in favouring a state of society in which the few are surfeited with excessive riches, and the many are scarcely able to obtain the necessaries of life. It is for the moralist and the politician, enlightened by the teaching of the political economist, to solve this problem. It is only necessary here to state that the true aspect in which ownership is to be regarded is that of a trust for the general benefit of all. The idea may or may not express itself in the form of law. If it do so express itself, it will take the form of Communism of one species or another.

It is a very unfair charge to make against those who advocate the introduction of a Communistic type of society to allege that they design to abolish *property*. They wish to change the existing laws of property, and to have enacted in their stead other and (as they think) better laws. Some of them may even go so far as to be willing to disappoint the expectations of existing owners, and to supplant them by bringing in a new race of owners. The morality or expediency of any such policy must, in every case, be judged on its own grounds, in view of all the circumstances. But the advocates of Communism, as such, can never be charged with the attempt to abolish ownership or property in itself. So far are they from this, that they are of all men the most zealous to define minutely the rules under which individual ownership, when once accrued, shall be respected, the fruits and products of common things shall be distributed, and every member of the community secured against the consequences of caprice or accident of any sort. Indeed, every Communistic theory involves a most complicated law of property.

Having ascertained what are the ethical and material antecedents of ownership, and of laws of ownership, and what are the circumstances and ideas to which laws of ownership are indebted for their growth and development, it remains to analyze a law of ownership into its constituent parts, and to investigate the logical nature and historical fortunes of each of those parts.

A law of ownership has, for its immediate object, to ascertain the relations of persons towards each other in respect of the possession or use of things. The possession or use is, in itself, a mere physical fact. The effect of a law of ownership is to bring this possession or use under the control, as it were, of social reason; to determine under what conditions it shall or shall not be protected; to name the things in respect of which possession shall be recognized at all; to define the limits of time and space over which the possession shall be allowed to extend; and to ascertain the persons who, in respect of any given thing, at any given time, shall be entitled to the possession or use of it. When once the rightful possessor is, in respect of a given thing, at a given time, ascertained, he has vested in him legal rights against all other persons whatsoever. The extent of these rights may be small and limited, or be large and indefinite; and this, both in respect of the time during which the rights have to last, and of the variety of the uses to which the thing possessed may be turned. So, again, there may be a multitude of ways which the law may select for denoting that these rights have become vested in a particular person, and the law may interfere to a greater or less extent with the freedom of individual choice in recognizing a right of ownership as vesting in one person rather than in another.

Thus the elements in a completely developed law of ownership may be arranged in some such way as the following:—First (1) of all, the *things* as to which ownership is possible have to be determined. Secondly (2), the quality and extent of the *rights* recognized by law have to be precisely described. Thirdly (3), the *modes* in which those rights become vested have to be described and enumerated. These are the main essential parts of every law of ownership.

For purposes of codification, or for a convenient classificatory exhibition of the whole law, it may be desirable, and it is customary, to make the divisions more numerous. Thus "*persons* who own" will generally be found to form a distinct head of the whole subject. But, in modern States, there are no persons whatever,—except perhaps the numerically insignificant class of outlaws and felons,—who are wholly destitute of all capacity of being owners, though, for one purpose or another, a variety of limitations, temporary or permanent, are frequently imposed upon important classes of persons in respect to the actual exercise of rights of ownership.

These limitations do in practice reduce the value of the right itself, because a right cannot be separated in thought (however much it is in legal language) from the exercise of it. The effect of these limitations, however,—as applied, for instance, to lunatics, children, and in some cases to married women,—is to impose on other persons, in respect of the incapacitated persons, duties which shall, hypothetically, put them in the same advantageous position they would hold if they were capable of exercising, or were allowed to exercise, rights of ownership to the fullest extent. The expediency of constructing these anomalous classes is not here in question. With respect to lunatics and children, that expediency is not likely to be disputed. With respect to married women, the matter is closely related to the whole topic of the legal protection or oppression of women, and a rapid change of view on the topic generally is making itself apparent both in this and in other countries.

Other subdivisions generally to be found in the enumeration of the chief heads of a law of ownership are "modes in which rights of ownership are terminated," and "modes of protecting rights of ownership." The matter falling under the first of these heads is, partly, expounded, as of necessity, in treating of modes in which rights become vested; because it often, if not universally, happens that rights vest in one person only because they have ceased to vest in another,—as in the case of an ordinary succession on death, or of a conveyance by sale. Again, the exact description in time, nature, and extent of a right carries with it a description of the mode in which it is terminated, because it is terminated only because, by its original nature and limits, it cannot last longer.

"Modes of protecting rights of ownership" have in themselves a superior claim to be counted among the essential elements of a law of ownership. But it is better to treat the protection of rights generally as a distinct topic of equal applicability to all kinds of rights' whatsoever. In all the best known systems of law, it is customary to treat laws of ownership under three different departments of the legal system: first, under laws of ownership proper, in which the substantive rights of owners and the modes of acquiring those rights are described; secondly, under the law of civil injuries and criminal law, where all the distinct modes of violating rights of ownership are enumerated, and the subject generally treated from the point of view of duties rather than rights; thirdly, under laws of procedure, where the remedies for the actual or threatened breach of laws of ownership, among other laws, are described and enumerated, and all the steps unfolded by which an injured owner is to seek compensation, or to guard himself against future injury.

According to the distribution above suggested as most convenient for the present purpose, the first (1) topic with which it has been seen that a law of ownership has to deal is that of the things in respect to which ownership is permissible. It is not in respect of every physical object that, at any given time, the law cares to exercise control, and to prescribe rules and conditions of appropriation. The purpose of the law's interference is to arrest interminable competitions, and to promote security by regulating distribution. But it depends upon the actual circumstances of a community, and upon the stage of its social progress, whether certain classes of things are or are not comprehended in the list of things as to which ownership is possible. For instance, in very primitive times, whether the community be pastoral or agricultural, the economical value of land is so extremely small, that it is only when family life has already become highly organized that land is a topic of laws of ownership. Indeed, so long as the population is small, the needs of it limited, and the quantity and choice of land indefinitely large, it is not possible that any idea of appropriation sufficiently fixed to afford a basis for law can, by possibility, exist.

It is true that the rise of the genuine family, the development of agriculture, and the formation of the village community, are so nearly contemporaneous with the first appearance of embryonic law, that the hypothesis of land being excluded from an enumeration of the possible subjects of ownership is a violent and unnatural one, except for the mere purpose of illustration. Apart, however, from this extreme case, it is obvious that, in a small population with simple habits of life, land occupies a very different position, in respect of importance and dignity for legal purposes, from that which it occupies where the population is densely crowded and the quantity of land available for agricultural, pastoral, building, productive, and residential uses is severely restricted. In early Roman law, land only ranked with cattle and slaves as a serviceable instrument of economical existence, and as only one out of a few such instruments; whereas in modern systems, the laws relating to land are regarded as of the utmost political importance, and those around which the most vehement political passions may be expected more and more decisively to gather.

If, however, in a primitive community, land exists in tolerable plenty, it may be said that other things scarcely exist at all, and therefore it is long before they are recognized as subjects of legal ownership. The fortunes of *res nec mancipi* in Roman law and of *personal property* in English law, as contrasted with those of *res mancipi* and *real property*, are now sufficiently familiar to all. A general account of their history may be given by saying that, in very early times, only a very few specific things are regarded as possible subjects of legal ownership, and that these things are those which are of the most obvious practical utility to a primitive community. Among such things stand pre-eminent land and immovables generally.

As the community progresses, as manufactures and commerce are developed, and wealth assumes a vast variety of forms, movable property calls for the interposition of law, first to recognize it as a subject of ownership, and then to place it on a footing of equal dignity and importance with that of immovable property. Inasmuch as general intelligence grew after the time that immovable things were the chief or sole possible subject of ownership, it was to be expected that the legal rules applicable to the ownership of the newer kinds of property should be more simple, as well as artistic, than the rude and complicated rules applicable to the older kinds.

The last stage of the progress—that which is now proceeding in the leading countries of Europe—is the rapid assimilation of the laws of ownership applicable to the older classes of things owned to the laws applicable to the newer class. Sir Henry Maine has described the course of this evolution more at length in his "Ancient Law," and for the present purpose it is sufficient thus briefly to allude to it by way of showing how the class of things capable of ownership is originally formed.

There are, furthermore, in all States, a number of other

classes of things which, for one reason or another, are, either temporarily or permanently, excepted from the category of things of which appropriation is possible. Such are things devoted to the uses of religion; things employed in the actual administration of the State; things regarded as belonging, in a sense, to every one, though managed and, in fact, owned by public officials, in order to secure the greatest benefit of all, by affording protection against spoliation or encroachment on the part of any one. To the last class belong the shores of navigable rivers, public harbours and docks, public paths, and (if they do not fall under the previous class) streets, roads, and museums, or public institutions for the culture of science and art. Under the second class fall Government buildings, palaces, dockyards, arsenals, and materials and implements appertaining to them of every kind.

The first class—that is, things devoted to the use of religion—will depend for its description, in some measure, upon the existence or not of the institution of a National Church. Apart, however, from the fact of such an institution, the practice of recognizing endowments, that is, the permanent consecration of land and other things to definite ends regarded as not inconsistent with the well-being of the State, operates so as to remove certain specific things out of the class of things capable of appropriation. They are not, strictly speaking, appropriated by the occasional persons who, from time to time, are called to administer them. Nor are they appropriated by the occasional persons who, from time to time, reap the benefit of them. Nor are they appropriated by the State itself. They, in fact, are artificially and provisionally placed in a class of things which are incapable of being owned.

Things which belong to the class of things as to which ownership is impossible may cease to belong to that class, either by separation from it, or by the arbitrary enactment of law. Such effects are produced when a college is allowed to exchange its lands, or when Government sells its military or naval stores.

Land, as a subject of ownership, might indeed be treated as belonging to the class of things set apart for the service of the State, though in the earlier stages of the development of the community the quantity of land, and the limited number of uses to which it is capable of being turned, combined to keep this aspect of it out of sight. Yet, in fact, the relation of a State to its territory, which in modern times enters into the essential conception of the State, implies that the land cannot be looked upon, even provisionally, as a true subject of permanent individual appropriation. This view obviously commends itself from the mere facts that the land is the only indestructible commodity in the country having an existence co-extensive in duration with that of the State itself; and that the culture and produce of the national soil must always be a matter of urgent State concern, quite independently of all considerations of the classes of persons to whom, from time to time, the task of labouring on the soil is, as it were, delegated.

A period may, however, arrive when the density of the population and the fixed limits of the national soil make this view of the essentially political character of the land not only plausible but irresistible. If the land is looked upon as susceptible of permanent appropriation by some persons, other persons must, by the same theory, be regarded as possibly excluded from it,—that is, banished from the territory of the State. Before reaching such a crisis as this, States are usually arrested by an imperious appeal to review the conditions and tendencies of their land laws. The State is brought face to face with the fact that the spurious notion of the possible appropriation for ever of the national soil by private persons has made alarming progress both in popular theory and practice. The cure is to be sought through a variety of changes in the laws of ownership, as well as through more direct Governmental action—such as is exhibited in the imposition of land taxes, the preservation of commons, and the facilitation of purchases of small plots of land by other persons than those who, by the mere force of their wealth, are absorbing the whole soil.

The political influence, moreover, of large landowners is of itself a sufficient ground for a watchful jealousy on the part of the State. Whatever be the issue of the controversy as to the economical and social advantages of large and small farms, and however undoubted is the importance of security of tenure to the cultivators, still the paramount dominion of the State over every part of its territory is a fact which, in a high condition of social progress, cannot be emphasized too strongly, or made to be felt too universally and really.

In most systems of law, and pre-eminently in those of Rome and of England, the word *thing* when used of a object of ownership has undergone a peculiar process of expansion, which is manifested in the expression "incorporeal things." The original use of the word "thing," or "*res*," in law would seem to limit the meaning of the words to visible objects, detached portions of the material universe. The very necessity of applying the epithet "incorporeal" seems to imply that but for the addition of the epithet, it would be assumed that a "thing" was "corporeal." On the other hand, the word "*res*" might properly be translated "that which can be an object of *thought*;" and the Roman lawyers undoubtedly employed the word *res* in a still wider sense than the English lawyers have ever affixed to the word *thing*.

It was, in fact, discovered—so soon as lawyers began to reflect, either for judicial or political purposes, upon their own system of law with the view of organizing and digesting it—that certain rights had, as it were, become solidified into so compact and distinct a body that they presented themselves to the imagination almost in the light of tangible objects. It was thus with an "obligation" in Roman law. An "obligation" was the sum of the duties that arose upon the making of a contract or the commission of an injury. The history of the term seems to show (as Sir H. S. Maine has explained) that the meaning of it at one time included all those duties and *all the corresponding rights;* but that this latter part of the denotation soon slipped away, and the term *obligatio* had, in the best days of Roman law, only reference to duties. But these duties were of a definite and precise nature, bringing to the person in whose favour they were to be performed corresponding advantages or rights of an equally definite and precise nature. The duties or the rights could pass from one person to another in certain clearly ascertained ways. They could under certain conditions become the subjects of engagements and contracts. In fact, these duties and the corresponding rights which were gathered up in the term *obligatio* were capable of being figured to the mind as external objects which were proper matter of legal interference for the regulation of their succession or transfer. In this way they were styled *res;* and in the same way an *hæreditas*, or sum of all the rights and duties to which an heir succeeds, and a "right of action," were equally called *res.* It is by just the same order of thought that the English class of *incorporeal things* has been created, of which a "copyright" may be taken as

A *copyright* is a right of a peculiar kind, and corresponds with duties lying upon all persons whatever, other than the person in whom the right vests, to abstain from certain acts, such as the printing and publishing certain determinate matter. A copyright cannot be strictly called a right of ownership, because there is no physical substance in respect of which the right is exercised; but in many points it is analogous to a right of ownership. It is held against all the world; it carries with it material advantages of a very intelligible and marketable kind; it is usually subjected to many of the identical legal incidents as to succession and transfer which appertain to rights of ownership. It is not surprising, then, that this anomalous sort of right, instead of being treated by itself as an exceptional topic of law and requiring exceptional provisions, should be first denominated a *thing*, that is, an "incorporeal thing," and then be artificially included among the things to which laws of ownership properly apply. The same account may be given of the other matters, which, in English law, are included in the class of incorporeal things. Such are easements—as rights of way, and rights of common—and also rights to tithe.

It will be noted that legal classifications of things in respect of ownership may be founded upon two different principles of discrimination. These are, the physical character of the things, and their artificial legal attributes. It would be more convenient if one principle alone were adopted, as is attempted in such modern codes as first divide all things into those which are movable and those which are immovable, and then lay down arbitrary legal definitions for all those things the physical mobility of which is uncertain, or which, for political purposes, it is held expedient to treat sometimes as movable, and, at other times, as immovable. The only purpose of classification of this sort is to express compendiously the legal rules applicable to certain sorts of things by enclosing them under a common name. This common name may be furnished in a variety of ways; or, owing to the varying situation in which certain things are found, it may be impossible to include them under any common name, and they must be arbitrarily classed, sometimes under one name and sometimes under another.

The second (2) main topic treated under the head of "Laws of Ownership" is the description of Rights of Ownership. A right of ownership, in itself, however minute it is, carries with it a legally supported claim to use a definite thing, for certain more or less definite purposes, and for a definite or indefinite time. The meaning of this claim, or right, is that all other persons whatever are forbidden to interfere with the owner in the exercise of his power in respect of the thing owned, up to the point to which the limits of that power reach. Thus, in ascertaining the description of a given right of ownership, the main points to be attended to are the number and quality of the uses to which the thing owned may be turned, and the length of time during which the enjoyment of the right lasts.

Another point sometimes also insisted upon is the capacity of transferring the right to another. But a distinction has here to be made between the relevancy of this topic to the description of the right from a purely legal point of view, and its relevancy to the limitation of the right from a political point of view. If a person has a complete capacity to transfer a right, this is a reason, politically speaking, for rendering that right more extended and unqualified than if he had no such capacity. Indeed, the extension of a right follows, almost as of necessity, from the enlargement of the powers of transfer. But this is a political, and not a legal, consequence. It is expedient that, if a person has the power of conveying his land to whom he will, he should be more free to cultivate and improve his land as he pleases than if his successor was determined by law. But this consideration does not touch the essential character of the right itself. The right to convey belongs to a peculiar class of rights, and undoubtedly enhances largely the value direct and indirect of a right of ownership; but the consideration of it rather belongs to the next head, that of "Modes in which Rights of Ownership are Acquired" than to the present one.

It is obvious that the length of time during which a right of ownership lasts is likely to have an important influence on the uses to which the thing owned may be turned. If the time is definite and short, those uses will be strictly defined and will be few and narrow. If the time is long, or indefinite—whether long or short—the uses are more likely to be numerous and multifarious. A peculiar phenomenon is produced when several owners, or at least two or more, have different rights of ownership in the same thing, that is, are entitled to turn the same thing to different sorts of account. A common instance of this is presented by the case of a field let on lease by the proprietor to a farmer, and over which the occupier of a neighbouring farm has a right of way. Here the right of the proprietor may be entirely in suspense, having, as its substitute, a right arising out of the lease against the farmer alone. The right of the neighbouring occupier is a right to use a portion of the field for a very definite and restricted purpose. This last has been called a "fractional" right, or has been said to be "carved" out of the greater right.

All so-called "easements" or "servitudes" are, strictly speaking, of exactly this same nature. The person or persons in whose favour the easement exists have a right to detract from the extent of another person's right to use a certain thing. This detraction may take two different forms. It may either imply an active intrusion on the part of the person enjoying the easement, as in the case of a right of way, of pasture, of drawing water, and the like; or it may only imply an enforced abstinence on the part of the person against whom the easement is exercised to do all the acts he would, but for the easement, be entitled to do.

The latter species of easement is illustrated by the case of a right to light or to air, that is, a right that an adjoining proprietor shall not raise any buildings so high as to interfere with the light or air to which the occupier of a neighbouring house has been customarily entitled. This species of easement has been called *negative*, and the other *positive* or *affirmative*. One main difference between the two is that the latter is unintermittently exercised, and the former only occasionally. Hence, in cases where the actual and continuous exercise of a right is needed in order to sustain it, as in preventing the right of another accruing through what is called "usurpation" or "prescription," mere non-user of a right for long intervals of time may be no evidence of relinquishing the right in the case of a positive easement, whereas, even where the time is very much shorter, the non-user of a negative easement, that is, passive acquiescence in its violation, may be satisfactory evidence of its relinquishment.

Easements and servitudes are, in fact, only species of joint proprietorship, having, however, this characteristic, that the person in whom the easement vests is denoted solely by the circumstance of his occupying, owning, or residing upon, some adjoining place. In Roman law a certain vacillation was exhibited in the use of this definition; and a class of merely personal rights, however the person in whom they vested might be determined, were sometimes ranked with "servitudes," and designated "personal servitudes." In the modern codes which are based upon the Roman law, these are usually classed by themselves, as they are in Justinian's Institutes (differing as these do in this point from the Digest), under such special names as *Ususfructus, Usus,* and *Habitatio;* and the relation they bear to true servitudes is only to be judged of by their proximity to them in a code.

It has been already incidentally noticed that not only must the extent of a right of ownership be measured in some degree by its duration, but that its duration is likely to determine largely its actual extent while it lasts. He who owns for his life is generally allowed a fuller use of the thing owned than he who owns for a year or a week; and he who owns subject to the possibility of his right being determined at any moment by another is likely to be very much more restricted in his use of what he owns, than is one who owns for a determinate time. Thus, in estimating the value of a right of ownership, it is of considerable importance to ascertain whether the time for which it lasts is definite or indefinite; whether it is determined by some event which may never happen, as the fulfilment of some difficult condition; whether by one which must happen sooner or later, as the close of one or more lives; or whether by the voluntary act of persons other than him in whom the right vests. These different contingencies, coupled with greater or less powers of transfer, give rise to all the varieties of absolute ownership, estates upon condition, life estates, estates for years, and estates at will.

The third (3) topic of Laws of Ownership is that of the Mode in which Rights of Ownership accrue. It is obviously of the very essence of the policy by which laws of ownership are enacted that as little doubt as possible should adhere to the question as to how rights of ownership come into being. It is not only desirable that actual competition should be arrested, but that the very notion of competitive claims should, as far as possible, be excluded at the outset. This result can only be secured by rendering as familiar as possible to the popular mind the legal principles upon which rights of ownership come into being or are passed on from one person to another. It will be all the more possible to render them thus familiar if the legal principles themselves are based on natural tendencies or spontaneously adopted practices, the law only interposing to give to these practices certainty and increased validity.

Notwithstanding this important aim, the law which determines the conditions upon which rights of ownership shall accrue is likely also to be framed in accordance with a general policy, whether wise or not. Such a policy will determine how far it is desirable to favour the accumulation of land or other things in a few hands, or to withdraw certain things for long periods of time from the general market; how far it is desirable to encourage inventors and authors by granting them temporary monopolies or other advantages; how far it is well to recognize the claims of immediate and of distant relatives in the distribution of estates upon the death of an owner; and how far, and in what way, the practice of making a Will is to be encouraged and provided for.

Thus the State has to reconcile several different aims in constructing that part of its law of ownership which determines the modes in which rights of ownership accrue. It has to comply, as far as possible, with well-rooted and spontaneous practices or maxims; it has to select such simple and intelligible methods as shall easily be established in the popular memory, and become part of the national consciousness; it has to carry out its own policy in respect of the distribution of the land and other things, as based upon experience, observation, and general political foresight.

The State has three main problems to solve; one, as to the mode in which rights of ownership shall come into being for the first time, that is, with respect to things which were never owned before; another, as to the extent of freedom for the individual will in transferring rights of ownership; another, as to the proper mode of legal interposition in restricting the possible extent of such right. The general policy which all States agree to pursue in respect of the solution of these several problems will best be understood by a consideration of what is the difficulty it has to meet in all the several cases. This difficulty may be described as that of undisciplined competition. There is a competition for the possession of everything whatsoever, so soon as the exclusive possession of it is discovered to be of value. There is a fresh competition for the same thing, so soon as the owner—that is, a person whose possession is recognized and generally supported—has, voluntarily or involuntarily, surrendered possession. And, lastly, there is an endless competition among the owners of different things with respect to the amount of interference with each other allowable in the course of turning to account the things they severally own.

Ownership is always a regulated possession, though it is commonly much beside. Indeed, this description is of itself wholly inadequate, as there are innumerable cases in which the owner of a thing neither has the possession nor any claim or right to the immediate possession of the thing. Nevertheless, it is only through the medium of "possession" that the idea of ownership can obtain any precision at all, and, in fact, ownership must almost always have direct reference to possession, whether present or future. It is important, then, to investigate the real nature of *possession*.

The true order of ideas is the following:—In ordinary speech, and apart from any legal significance attaching to the word, the possession of a thing is the merely holding or grasping it. If the thing be too large to hold, possession means the being able at any moment to turn it to all its possible uses or, at the least, to detain it so effectually as to prevent any one else turning it to any possible use. Thus, according to the illustrations so constantly given, he who has the key of a cellar and can open it when he pleases, is the possessor of the wine in it. He who has the key of a stable and can take the horse out when he pleases, or can prevent any one else taking it out, is the possessor of the horse. This has been called "natural possession," and has in itself no legal idea attached to it whatever.

It is clear that there may be good reason for protecting a person in simple possession of this nature, and for giving a certain amount of legal validity or provisional legal validity to claims based on nothing more than possession of this sort. But legal recognition involves definition, and obviously some possessors of the sort above described demand and deserve protection in a far higher degree than others do; while some, as the thief or robber, do not deserve it at all. Thus, when once law interferes to protect and regulate possession, a number of other ideas besides that of merely physical detention are necessarily introduced.

One such idea is the mode in which the possession began, whether by violent extrusion of another, by secret tampering, or by voluntary gift,—or even by mere discovery, invention, or original creation (*justus titulus*)

Another idea is the state of mind of the possessor, whether he believes himself to be in the right; or suspects, or knows, himself to be in the wrong; whether he believed that the person who gave him possession was entitled to give it, or knew him not to be so entitled (*bonâ fides*). A third idea is the duration of the possession; whether it is quite recent, so that no expectations could, from lapse of time alone, be reasonably grounded upon it; or whether so long a period of undisturbed possession has elapsed that great inconvenience and even practical injustice would ensue from disturbing the possessor in the peaceable retention of that which he has so long held.

Two main occasions occur for the protection which, in one way or another, law accords to possession; and as one or the other of these occasions is in view, one or more of the above subsidiary ideas becomes the important element in discerning the true character of the possession in question. One occasion is the defence of the possessor in his possession for the purely provisional purpose of ascertaining, by a judicial process, his legal and moral claims to be further or even constantly so protected. The object of the law is invariably to arrest competition, and most of all forcible violence. But in matters of possession, extending as they do over so vast a field so closely connected with human wants, feelings, and passions, the probabilities of conflict arising out of questions of disputed possession are incessant and enormous. A mode of preventing such conflicts is to remove them from the arena of physical force to the arena of law, and while according provisional protection to the person actually in possession, and even reinstating him if dislodged with violence, to secure that the merits of the rival claims be judicially investigated without loss of time (*possessio ad interdicta*).

The other occasion for recognizing possession is when it has endured a long time, under circumstances in which it seems more conducive to the general welfare to support it permanently than to reinstate a former possessor who has (it may be, through no fault of his own) lost his possession. In these cases the length of time that must elapse, the degree of *bonâ fides* needed in the present possessor, and, possibly, the mode in which the possession must have begun, are all relevant to the enquiry, and will be definitely fixed by the general Law (*possessio ad usucapionem*).

The position, then, of a person thus permanently protected in his possession is the following :—He is treated henceforward not merely as an actual possessor, and as deserving of mere provisional protection and reinstatement in case of his being violently extruded, but he is now able to establish a claim to lasting possession against any one else whosoever. He not only has what has been called the "right of possession," or the casual right to have claims which are founded on the mere fact of possession—if not merely violent and forcible—judicially and peaceably investigated, but he has the "right to possess." This, of course, is a right of a much higher and ampler kind, and it is a right of this sort which, at the earliest stage of legal progress, is exactly co-extensive with a right of ownership, or, in other words, with "property" or *dominium*, two terms which are frequently opposed to the term *possession*.

It happens, however, in the course of time, owing to economical and social incidents, that a person who is recognized by the State as having a right to possess finds he can turn the thing to which his right relates to better account by putting some one else in possession of it than by possessing it himself. For instance, he may "own" or have a right to possess, a greater number of fields than he is able to cultivate by his own unaided exertions. He may either pay other persons, as his servants or labourers, to cultivate some of the fields on his behalf; or he may allow some other person or persons to cultivate the fields on their own behalf, merely paying him a certain sum for the privilege. If a bargain of this last kind is made and recognized by law, henceforth the actual cultivator alone has the right to possess, and not the person through whom he claims. So if the owner of a thing hands it over as a security for money borrowed, and an engagement of the sort is recognized by the law, it is the lender, and not the borrower, of the money who henceforth, for a time, has the right to possess the thing which is given as a security for it.

Nevertheless, in both these typical cases, though the original owner parts for a time with his right to immediate possession, yet he retains his right to possession at some time or other; and the arrival of this time may, through a private arrangement, be determined by the happening of all kinds of events, certain or uncertain. In this way the notion of ownership, though it always relates to possession at some time or other, becomes detached from that of immediate possession, and, in popular speech, is often contrasted with it.

But it may happen that a lessee or pledgee, in the instances above cited, who has acquired from the owner a right to immediate possession, may part with or accidentally lose this right; and that not in favour of the owner, but of some third person. In such a case it is the third person who may be recognized in law as having the right to immediate possession; while the person through whom the possession has come to him may have, at the most, a right to future possession only; and the original owner a right to possession only at a period still further removed. It is conceivable, again, that from a variety of causes and transactions, even the third person may, in his turn, part with or lose the right to possess, and only retain, at the most, a right to possession at some time or other.

The series of tenants and prospective tenants of the same thing may, indeed, chance to be an indefinitely long one; it being true, however, at any given moment, that there is only one person, or assemblage of persons, who has a right to immediate possession; and that there is one person to whom the right of immediate possession will ultimately revert, after the possession of every one else has come to an end. This last person might be styled, and is sometimes styled, the "owner;" though, whether he chances to be called so or not, in popular speech, will depend upon such circumstances as whether he derives present benefit from the possession on the part of others or whether there is a probability of his coming into possession himself within a limited time.

The ground landlord of a street in London who receives an enormous rent from the tenants immediately holding under him, is held to be none the less the owner because the time is indefinitely remote at which he or his descendants will have a right to immediate possession, supposing the rent continues to be regularly paid, and the other conditions of tenure to be fulfilled. On the other hand, the Crown, from whom lands are sometimes held on a tenure involving nothing more than the performance of some ancient service, is not considered as owner of the lands, although, in default of the service being rendered, the Crown might have a right to immediate possession. It would rather be said that the owner had, by his remissness, forfeited his lands.

The results of this investigation are that ownership or property always has reference to possession, either immediate or prospective; that the notions of actual possession, of a right to immediate possession, and of a right to future possession, are perfectly clear and distinct; but that,—inasmuch as the rights of an owner (in the primitive sense) often become, in the progress of civilization, distributed among a hierarchy of successive persons,—the notion of ownership is only made clear and distinct when it is treated as equivalent to the right to possess at some time or other, according to which sense of the expression there may be several contemporaneous owners of the same thing. What is lost, however, by want of conformity to popular speech is abundantly gained in legal precision. Hence ownership must be taken to mean a right to possession, guaranteed and protected—as all other rights are—by the State, whether the possession be immediate or future; and any person who has such a right to possession might, if it be not doing great violence to common language, conveniently be called an owner, it being understood that, in this sense, there may be many owners of the same thing at the same time.

The difficulty of nomenclature is really brought about by the fact that, with respect to large classes of things, as land, houses, farming stock, plant for manufactures, negotiable instruments, and furniture, a distribution of the rights included in ownership is far more common than unity of ownership. In primitive society, unity of ownership is for all things almost the only form of ownership known. The only right competing with the owner's is that of a casual possessor who has accidentally come into possession, or who has bought the right from a presumptive owner who had no power to deal with it. The opposition of owner to possessor is here distinct and valuable. The same is the case with respect to many movable things in civilized countries at this day. As to articles of personal wear, or decoration, or things of a very perishable nature, the owner still remains clearly distinguishable from the possessor. But with respect to most other things, as has been seen, it is not so. There is generally a series, and sometimes a long series, of persons who severally have rights to possession immediate, future, or more or less qualified by conditions. It may thus happen that the person popularly designated as the *owner* has the least valuable right of all. Thus, in order to ensure precision of meaning, either a new term must be substituted for the term *owner*, or a new meaning put upon this term.

Hitherto it has been assumed that the only way in which a person having a right to possess can deal with that right is to confer upon another person the right to immediate possession, while he reserves to himself the right to future possession, the time and conditions of such future possession being determined by considerations of mutual convenience between the parties. But it may happen that the original owner (for he may be called so for the present) wishes to make a marketable commodity of his whole right to possession, both immediate and future. The State may or may not recognize transactions of this kind, and in primitive times it has often happened, from one cause and another, that such transactions are unknown rather than unrecognized. But, supposing the transaction is recognized or is beginning to be recognized, the State will probably conceive that, with respect to the things of the greatest public importance in the country, especially land, it has a claim that the transaction shall be as public and notorious as possible; so that every one may know who it is who has a right to possess, and that the State itself may know who it is who is henceforth to be called upon to discharge such public burdens as accompany the acknowledged ownership of certain classes of things. These considerations are enforced by the desirability of obtaining the best and most conspicuous proof of the reality of the transaction and of the good faith of the parties, in case a contest should ultimately take place in a court of law. On all these grounds it will be found that a great part of the history of the law of ownership in all countries, and a great portion of the law itself, is concerned with the formalities of making voluntary transfers.

A fresh problem is presented (though it really solves itself by spontaneous practices long before it is consciously presented) when the person who has a right to possess dies, or contemplates the imminent fact of his own death. This subject is connected with the whole matter of intestate succession and testamentary disposition, and has a relation to it similar to that connecting it with contract law and the law regulating family rights.

Sir H. S. Maine has pointed out how the original notion of the unity and perpetuity of the family, as an undying corporation, explains much of ancient law relative to the treatment of rights on the death of the last person in whom they vested. They pass on, as of course, to the next surviving representative of the family, because they are, in fact, vested in the family as a whole, and not in any single member of it. The *paterfamilias* acquires in course of time the right to sell his rights present and future; but he is bound to do so with solemn formalities, in the presence, and with the assent, of his clan, who would (in the case of the family failing) have the ultimate right to succeed to the possession. When the notion of voluntary disposition, however cumbrous and troublesome the modes of it be, has once become familiar, the transition is easy to a simplification of the forms, to partial secrecy, and to perfect, or nearly perfect, freedom of alienation in life and of testamentary bequest.

These practices of succession to members of the family,

in the absence of a Will, are so conducive to the attainment of a number of important moral and political ends, that it is not surprising they are so universal and have undergone such extensive developments. The practices are, above all, strictly promotive of what have been pointed out as the chief objects of law, that is, the sustenance of natural groups, and the promotion of internal cohesiveness and mutual reciprocity of action in those groups. Death is a fact that menaces the existence of the State by disappointing personal expectations, by bringing about discontinuity and breach in family and social relationships, and generally, by rendering the future uncertain and incalculable. Law, as well as religion, strives its uttermost to triumph over death, and in doing so displays its most signal power. Testimonies to the extent of this power might be gathered from the extraordinary empire over the imagination possessed by the institution of the *hæreditas* at Rome and, in a less degree, of executors and administrators in England. Through the means of such devices as these, the inconvenience caused by the disappearance from the midst of the State of one of its members is reduced to the smallest possible.

Possession has hitherto been looked upon as of the simplest possible kind, and as including nothing more than simple detention of a thing, whether that detention is or is not accompanied by certain mental circumstances or antecedents. But as, in course of time, the notion of possession of this elementary sort becomes familiar, it becomes also apparent that something more than simple detention must be included in it. The very same political grounds that entitle a bare detainer or holder of a thing to protection by the State also entitle to similar protection one who holds a thing in a particular way, that is, turns it to certain determinate uses.

Thus a pawnbroker may be said to be in possession of that which he simply keeps locked away and can turn to no use at all. A lessee of land is equally said to be in possession, when he enjoys all the freedom to cultivate, and even to sub-let, which his landlord or the original owner has. Similarly, two or three persons may be said to be jointly in possession of the same thing or piece of land, though obviously the freedom of use enjoyed by each must be limited by that of the rest, and must be very different in extent from what it would be if he alone were in possession. Thus when possession is spoken of as a fact, it must always be explained and defined with reference to the special circumstances of the case. The same thing may be possessed by several persons either in the same or in different ways.

It is obvious that so soon as possession of these varied sorts becomes protected by law and rendered either provisionally or permanently secure—in other words, when possession becomes converted into ownership—it results that the rights which arise are of very different kinds and degrees. They depend for their character and value, partly, upon the number and quality of the uses to which the thing to which they relate may be put; partly, upon the duration of time for which they will continue; partly, upon the probability or certainty of their actually accruing, if still only matters of future expectation. The number and quality of the uses to which a thing may be put will often be found to be (to use one mathematical expression) a function of, or (to use another) to vary proportionately with, the length of time during which the right will last. This results from the general principle that the natural limit of the right of one person is that supplied by the rights of others. Thus a weekly tenant is less free to use his apartments, or to injure them, than a tenant for years or for life is; and where the reversionary interest is extremely remote and uncertain, the freedom of use enjoyed by one or more of the tenants is scarcely distinguishable from that which would be enjoyed by the reversioners, or by the ultimate owner himself.

The most general restrictions on the extent of all rights of ownership are those supplied, first, by the co-existing rights of surrounding owners, and secondly, by the general interests of the whole State. The former class of restrictions are illustrated by the generally recognized legal duty of not interfering with the light, air, and other healthful conditions which are essential to the enjoyment by a neighbour of his own rights. By the well-known principle of "servitudes" or "easements," a special right even to invasion of the rights of others in these and some other respects may be acquired. The principle universally applied to ascertain the existence and extent of such exceptional rights is that of prior possession. The evidence of such possession is derived from such facts as lapse of time, absence of dispute and litigation, or else positive consent on the part of the owner whose rights are presumptively encroached upon. Some of these acts of encroachment cannot so well be called injuries to the rights of others as mere diminutions of them, or as they have sometimes been called "fractional rights." Such are the great class of rustic servitudes in Roman law, taking the various forms of rights of way, rights of making or using water-courses and aqueducts, and rights of pasturing cattle. Each of these rights is a good illustration of the various forms which possession takes as society progresses, as well as the fruitfulness of the fact of possession in founding and guarding rights of ownership.

The subject of the division of easements or servitudes has been already treated. It was seen that they have been divided into two classes. One includes those rights in which the burden on the adjoining owner consists in his own free action being simply impeded, without the right of the other being positively extended. Such rights were "urban servitudes," as those which prevent the adjoining owner raising his chimneys beyond a certain height, or otherwise building obstructions to his neighbour's light or view, or setting up a business likely to be noxious to his neighbour's health. The other class of fractional rights includes those in which the person in whom the right vests is thereby enabled aggressively to invade his neighbour's premises and to do acts there which, but for that right, it would not be permissible for him to do. Such rights are the "rustic servitudes" already mentioned. These two classes of servitudes have been termed (as was said in another connection) *negative* and *affirmative* respectively.

It was seen that the evidence of that continuous possession which alone can ground the right must, in the case of negative servitudes (in which possession goes on without any succession of acts manifesting it) be of a different character from that needed in the case of affirmative servitudes, where the possession is in itself a continuously repeated act, and therefore this repetition is, as it were, its own and its only evidence. Thus mere non-user of an affirmative servitude for a great length of time might be very insufficient evidence that the possession was intentionally relinquished and would not be resumed, because interruptions in the continuity of possession form an essential characteristic of this sort of servitude. Whereas, in the case of non-user of a negative servitude, the mere omission to use it, if accompanied by knowledge on the part of the owner interested in disputing it,—such knowledge being testified by adverse acts inconsistent with the continuance of the right—might in itself be quite sufficient to prove its loss or abandonment or to disprove the alleged fact of its acquisition.

The limitation of rights of ownership above noticed as due to the interests of the State, takes the form, partly, of general principles forbidding the use of things in certain modes proved by experience to be publicly noxious; as, for instance, the carrying on dangerous trades and occupations without due precautions, the building houses of a style not conducive to public health or to the ornamentation of a town, the keeping and dealing in housebreaking tools or explosive weapons, the using houses for immoral purposes and the like: partly, of restrictions and deductions occasioned by the necessities of the revenue, as in the case of periodical taxation, excise, and regulations for the prevention of coining and of fraud by pawnbrokers, money-lenders, bankers, stock-brokers and like persons standing in a quasi-public capacity; partly, of the constant liability to which every owner is exposed to have his goods or lands either confiscated for the public good or, at the best, exchanged for other things of an equal market value but of a different quality.

It has thus been seen that ownership is a form of regulated and secure possession either present or prospective, and that the essential character of the legal interference which converts possession into ownership is the creation and maintenance of rights. The maintenance of rights of ownership, when once called into being, is naturally a most important part of the activity of the State; the more so, as, historically speaking, it is through this activity in the judicial department that the reality of the rights themselves first becomes matter of distinct consciousness.

The modes which the maintenance of rights of ownership takes may be addressed either to preventing probable infractions of rights, or to punishing and obtaining compensation for actual infractions. Or again, they may be addressed to the protection of the forms and solemnities by which rights of ownership are susceptible of being conveyed from one person to another either in life or on death. Then again, special machinery may be devised for the prevention of an injury to a right of ownership immediately the injury has begun and before it has proceeded far. The Roman Interdict and the English Injunction, as applied in some cases, are illustrations of this last variety of procedure.

Lastly, the proceedings may be either civil or criminal or both, according as the injury seems to belong to a class in which the interest of the owner is more immediately concerned than the interest and good order of the State, or the latter more than the former, or both seem equally concerned. Then the remedy may either take the form of actual restitution, where that is possible, or of compensation by payment of money, or of mere punishment with or without compensation.

CHAPTER IX.

LAW OF CONTRACT.

THE purpose of the Law of Contract is to impart stability and security to certain temporary relationships with one another which men spontaneously frame for themselves. The relationship between two contractors differs from the relationship of family life in the spontaneity which originates it, and in the freedom which the parties enjoy for the purpose either of describing and modifying its terms or of annulling it altogether. Thus the essential quality of the relationship implied in Contract is freedom in respect of its original creation; in respect of the description of its nature and of its terms; and in respect of the mode and period of its conclusion. The real policy which dictates a law of contract is that of giving the same reality and consistency to the groups which evolve themselves through the play of social and economic life as primitive law gives, in the manner already described, to those groups, of which the gradual formation is the indispensable condition precedent to the very existence of national life.

It happens, indeed, that—though the essential characteristics of these new, or, as they may be called, voluntary groups, is freedom—law cannot affect to regulate their construction and watch over their fortunes without, to a certain extent, impairing that freedom. A law of contract commences by restricting the practice of contract, though its influence, in the long run, is vastly to extend that practice. Similarly, at constantly recurring stages, law is called upon to put fresh obstacles in the way of contractors, and yet the result and sole justification of these obstacles is an indefinitely increased confidence in the making of contracts.

The fact of contract, as looked at, for a moment, quite independently of law, is due to the natural conditions of social and economic life. A moderately developed social existence cannot be attained without accumulation of wealth, and wealth cannot be accumulated without co-operation, division of labour, and mutual reliance. Mutual reliance implies a steady belief in the future conduct of others; and also in the future conduct of oneself, that is self-reliance. It is only by long experience that the possibility of such mutual reliance can become a familiar notion, and the social and economic value of it be profoundly appreciated. In the actual history of a State it will probably happen that the notions of truth, of trustfulness, and of good faith, are evolved, not only through progressive experience of their social fruitfulness, but still more through the more or less elevated doctrines of religious teachers, the denunciations of prophets, the calm, warning voice of philosophic sages.

But the force of this last class of influences is really due to the fact of the absolute harmony between good faith and the constitution of man as a social being. It is to dim glimpses of this fact, both in the seer who exhorts and in the populace who listen, that the actual efficiency of the lesson is really due. Man commences by practically trusting his fellow man; he goes on by finding it is good and useful, as well as safe to trust him; he hears the voice of his best teachers telling him that he was born to trust and to be trustworthy; and at every step he takes in trusting others and in showing himself worthy of trust, he becomes increasingly conscious of an enlargement and satisfaction of his nature, which, to him at least, is unmistakable evidence of trustfulness being that to which his true constitution adapts and calls him.

In every case of a contract between two persons, one of them, at the least, binds his acts in the future, and the other knows that he does so and directs his own conduct in accordance with that knowledge. For the person so relying upon the other's future action, so much at least of the cloud of uncertainty that ever hangs over the future is lifted. For the vacillation and changeableness of human action and will, the certainty of a sequence of physical nature is substituted. The person who thus engages to bind his own future acts may be induced to do so by a variety of different considerations. He may be induced to make the engagement by way of reward for a service already rendered him, or by way of reciprocity, as the price of some service done or gift presented at the time, or as the price of some service to be done in the future. In the last case each of the persons binds his future acts, and, though the transaction is one, both the rights and the duties arising from it are twofold.

Such is the transaction termed "contract," in its essence, and in the absence of law. The result of every contract is to create (as has been already intimated) a group of persons wholly apart from all similarly formed groups, and having their mutual relations determined by a rule which has been voluntarily evoked. Such groups, only in a less degree than the natural domestic groups, are of extreme importance to the vitality and development of the nation; and yet, like those groups, when standing alone and unprotected, they are, from their very minuteness and isolation, peculiarly exposed to catastrophes.

Sir H. S. Maine, in his "Ancient Law," has described how laboriously and almost painfully the habit of making the commonest contracts is built up in early society. A notion of the frailty of the engagement seems to hang round every stage of it, and nothing but the most resolute efforts of the whole society can give it even the appearance of enduring validity. These efforts take the form of a necessity for a number of witnesses, for cumbrous ceremonies, for punctilious and exactly performed gestures. If an error is made in the formalities, the obligation is gone.

Thus it is not so much that law interferes with the making of contracts because of their imperfect security when only dependent on moral sanctions, as that the same state of society which gives birth to primitive contract does at the same time, and from like causes, give birth to that legal circumscription of contracts which alone renders them, in such social circumstances, even so much as possible. Historically speaking, there could have been no period at which contract existed and yet a law of contract did not; because, at the era of society in which alone the engagements implied in making contracts are possible, legal rules and institutions are the only cementing bonds which keep the society together, and the notion of a twofold system of moral and legal rules side by side is wholly alien to that stage of civilization.

It is true, however, that, throughout the whole course of national development, the relations to each other of the moral and the legal aspects of contract are undergoing incessant change, and sometimes curious alternations. In the first stage, as has been seen, the moral and the legal contract are not separable from one another. In the next stage, the moral contract has disengaged itself from the legal contract, and law either singles out a number of common contracts which it converts into legal contracts—so making them available in courts of justice—or it is ready to convert all contracts into legal contracts, only excepting a few, on the grounds of it being impolitic to give them encouragement. The former of these methods is that which was adopted at Rome, and the latter is that adopted in England. At a stage still further on, the legal notion of contract encroaches more and more on the moral one, to such an extent indeed as almost to produce a parallel with the earliest stage of all, when the legal surroundings were of far greater moment than the moral and mental condition of the parties. At this last stage, the proved frequency of frauds and the excessive multiplication of contracts, in a condition of active commercial intercourse, enforce the necessity of prescribing formalities with increased rigour and of punishing the neglect of them with nullity. This is, in effect, going a great way towards completely substituting the legal conception of contract for the moral one.

The general relation of a legal to a moral contract being ascertained both from a scientific and from an historical point of view, the next question that presents itself relates to the necessary elements of which a legal contract is composed.

It has been seen that, apart from all considerations of law, a contract or agreement, in the least exact sense, involves the presence of two persons, one of whom binds his future acts in a definite way, and the other confidently relies upon his doing so. The acts may be of a more or less determinate number and kind, covering, indeed, almost all the transactions in which it is possible for human beings to be engaged; and the future period to which the acts relate may be either near at hand or very far removed, or may be recurrent at stated intervals of time, or may be made to depend upon the contingent occurrence of future events, which are either certain to happen some time, or may possibly never happen at all.

Hence the first task that occupies the law-giver in taking contracts under his control is to determine whether any restriction whatever shall be put upon the kinds of future acts as to which persons shall be permitted, with the sanction of law, to bind themselves. The solution of this question must partly depend upon the solution of another, what restrictions (if any) ought to be put upon the quality of the persons who are permitted to bind themselves. Though these two questions, however, are on some sides of them, closely related to each other, they are none the less capable of being treated distinctly.

This mode of treatment has generated two great branches of the law of contract, as exhibited in all advanced States, the one containing an enumeration of the *persons* who may or may not bind themselves by legal contracts, and the other dealing with the principle upon which, in any particular State, persons are not allowed to invoke the sanction of law, in binding themselves to do or not to do certain specified or generally described acts. What particular acts or forbearances happen to be excluded from being the possible subject matter of legal contract may, for a long course of time before the prevalence of conscious legislation, depend mostly on accident, or on what seems to be such. But experience gradually dictates the sort of acts and engagements which alone can usefully be recognized by the State when it betakes itself to enforce the agreements which men make with each other for their mutual convenience.

The sole ground and justification of such State interference is to correct the bad or disastrous consequences that follow from an occasional breach of faith in a condition of society in which good faith is universally expected and relied upon. It is monstrous to suppose that the habitual observance of legal contracts is solely or mainly due to the legal penalties which attend non-observance. A nation of habitual contract-breakers could not have sufficient coherence to organize or to enforce a law of contract and, like Montesquieu's "Troglodytes," in the utter absence of mutual respect or self-respect, they must all perish miserably. Nevertheless it is true that a law of contract largely contributes towards the maintenance of good faith in the keeping of contracts in many other ways than by the penalties it inflicts, or by the compensation it exacts. Law does for the region of contract what it does for that of family life, of property, and of Government. It imparts definiteness and objective reality to what otherwise is latent, desultory, and intermittent. It arrests attention, and publicly addresses the individual conscience with a voice which the din of daily life cannot smother. It gives precision to action, and, while checking unreasonable expectations, gives calmness and security to those that are well founded.

But it is obvious that law would only defeat its own ends by supporting contracts or agreements of certain kinds. It is no doubt a critical and perilous task for law to venture upon, to attempt to distinguish a moral from an immoral object, or to determine what sorts of contracts are, in the long run, prejudicial to the truest interests of the State. Legislators have at all times committed the grossest errors in attempting legal distinctions of this nature, and their best excuse is that they have faithfully reflected the ignorance and the prejudices of their age. Even now, when slave-purchasing and slave-holding are illegal by the law of England, it is judicially doubted whether a contract for the purchase of slaves made in a country where slave-purchasing was legal, ought or ought not to be supported in this country. Slavery is one of those institutions as to the absolute immorality of which even yet the public mind of all civilized States cannot be said to be completely made up.

Thus, even on the admitted principle that contracts must not be supported if immorality is thereby directly encouraged, the determination of what kind and amount of immorality,—as well as of what sort of encouragement of it,—is contemplated when the usual support of law is refused to an otherwise valid contract, involves questions of the utmost complexity. The general result has been in modern Europe and in the States of America, that the only cases in which legal support is refused to a contract on the ground of its object being immoral is where that object belongs to a small and definite class of immoral acts distinctly repudiated by the principles and general practice of all civilized countries, or where the object is directly in the face of some specific rule of law forbidding its pursuit.

There is better and more obvious reason for the interference of law in the matter of the persons who make contracts than for its interference in that of the subject matter. A contract is in all cases an *act* whereby a person binds his future acts, though it is also more than this, involving as it does the consent of another person, who by another *act* (unless the two acts happen to be simultaneous, and therefore to bear the appearance of a single act alone) signifies his knowledge of, and reliance upon, the exact degree in which the first person has restricted his future freedom. It is the two parties together who are said to make the contract. The rights, indeed, may be all on one side and the duties all on the other, or both persons may bind their future acts, each knowing and relying upon the other doing so, and so there may be both rights and duties on either side.

It thus appears that, in order to make a legal contract or, in fact, any fair contract, the persons must not only have all the capacity essential to do a voluntary act, but they must also have a sufficient knowledge of the world and of themselves both to know the exact meaning and character of the acts to which the contract has reference, and the ability which one, or other, or both of them has to do or to abstain from the acts contemplated. Now, considering the enormous range of subjects over which the possibility of making contracts extends, from the simplest purchase with a few hours' credit, to the carrying out of the most gigantic commercial enterprises, it is manifest that the doctrine of personal capacity, in respect of contract, must be an elastic doctrine, admitting of adaptation to the particular varieties of contracts which happen to be concerned.

From the mere statement of the nature of a contract it appears that the making of even the simplest contract involves higher mental qualities than are necessarily concerned in dealing effectually with property, or in committing a crime without exculpatory circumstances. The vitiating or disabling incidents to be guarded against in estimating the validity of a contract are (1) Incapacity to do a voluntary act, (2) Inexperience, (3) Fraud, and (4) Disease affecting the reality or clearness of intention, or otherwise perverting the patient's view of things, so as to present them in distorted relations with each other. The general causes which give rise to such facts or conditions as these are known to be extreme youth (or infancy), youth further advanced and at different stages, insanity, and such a combination of circumstances as, from a person's peculiar situation, render him especially exposed to the solicitations of fraud. Sometimes the situation of a person is permanently so unfavourable to the exercise either of freedom of the will in action or of balanced judgment in forming an intention, that the law treats a person in such a situation as permanently incapacitated; and a similar doctrine is sometimes extended to the contracts of two persons with one another, where their mutual relations render the good faith of one of them so open to temptations as to call for, at the least, excessive judicial vigilance.

The peculiar protection granted at one period of Roman Law to heirs against the extortion of money-lenders, and also to women against their own assumed weakness of will in monetary matters, are instances of the former kind of legal precaution. The contractual incapacity of married women by English common law is not such an instance, because this doctrine arises solely out of the peculiar relations in respect of property which exist between man and wife in England. It is not an imputation on the wife's experience or strength of mind, but is solely grounded on her not being assumed at common law to have sufficient command of her purse or of her future actions wherewith to procure the materials for making a contract. The legal presumption, then, is that she did not intend to make one, and, therefore, the allegation that she did make a contract would imply, on the face of it, a fraud. The English doctrine of "constructive fraud" by which certain kinds of contracts between persons standing in fiduciary relations to one another are disallowed, affords an illustration of the other mode above alluded to of combating fraud in the making of contracts.

The law, then, having determined what shall be the objects of the only contracts it will recognize, and what classes of persons alone shall make legal contracts, is next concerned with the character of the act which shall definitely signify to the contractors themselves and to all other persons that the contract is made. The purpose of law as to this matter is twofold. One object is to secure a complete mutual understanding between the parties; in other words, that the one knows exactly to what he is binding himself, that the other knows it also and relies upon it, and that the first knows that the other is relying upon his doing that which he knows he has engaged to do. Another object is to secure such a record or memorandum of the transaction as may both prevent the parties themselves or their representatives, at some future day, from being fraudulently tempted to put a different colour on the transaction from the true one, and as may facilitate to the utmost the ready investigation of the whole matter, should a controversy upon it ever take place in a court of justice.

All these considerations, taken by themselves, point to the expediency of enforcing the use of definite methods for the purpose both of clearly ascertaining the extent of a contract, and preserving evidence of it. But the argument applies with much less force to some kinds of contracts, and those the commonest, than to others. The large majority of the contracts that people make are of what may be called an every-day nature. They concern buying and selling, letting and hiring, borrowing, pledging, carriage, and service generally. The ordinary nature of each of these classes of contracts is clearly understood by every one who takes part in them. There are, indeed, individual circumstances which characterize each single contract, but they are usually simple enough, and scarcely admit of being misrepresented or forgotten. On the other hand, speed and economy of time are often essential in order that these constantly recurring contracts may be of the highest use of which they are capable in the conduct of the social and industrial intercourse of mankind.

On these grounds it is customary to dispense with any other formalities for the purpose either of fixing the moment of completing, or for the purpose of preserving a record of, the contract than those which the convenience of the parties spontaneously suggests to them. Sir H. S. Maine has noted how in primitive Roman times, even with respect to the commonest contracts, a cumbrous ceremonial or, at the least, an elaborately formal diction were indispensable both to the creating the obligation and to providing evidence of it. But public convenience gradually shook off all the hampering appendages till the fact of making a contract, however witnessed, became its own evidence.

The great development of modern commerce has had two distinct effects on the character of the legal evidence demanded to establish the fact of a contract. It has tended, on the one hand, to favour the use of a simple mode of evidence, owing to the great similarity and constant recurrence of some of the most important species of mercantile contracts, such as negotiable instruments of all sorts. These documents are worded in the shortest and simplest form; and by merely signing his name and passing on the document to another, a person not only becomes a contractor, but engages to do a great variety of acts which, though thoroughly understood by all persons concerned, are by no means expressed on the face of the document. Thus the uniformity of commercial methods tends to the condensation and abbreviation of the evidence of vast classes of commercial contracts.

But this same development of commerce, on the other hand, gives birth to contracts in which so many persons take part, and which have reference to such a variety of acts, depending on so complex a set of conditions, that it becomes the highest effort of law to secure satisfactory evidence in respect of them. In the case of contracts of this nature it is not sufficient for law to adopt the rigorous principle of insisting that the contract must be in writing, or even that the writing must be couched in certain definite terms and accompanied by the performance of certain solemnities. The English Statute of Frauds, and the later statutory supplements to it, have exhausted every possible contrivance in this direction. The old Roman contract "Literis," according to which the formal entry in the common household ledgers was sufficient or essential evidence of certain contracts, is a more primitive instance of the same effort, though the scope of this sort of contract was very limited. In some respects similar to this last is the modern evidence of a most important class of contracts supplied by registration in the books of a public company or on the records of a public office.

All attempts of this nature to secure definite and unimpeachable evidence of contracts no doubt possess considerable value and, in some measure, obtain their end. The infirmity of them, one and all, is that they are not, and never can be, elastic and plastic enough to adapt themselves to the actual transactions of mankind.

It is true that the general subject-matter of a contract can easily enough be expressed on the face of a writing or a deed, or be still more compendiously described by entering names in a public register. But it frequently, or most generally, happens that, side by side with every contract, there are also a number of subsidiary contracts which tend largely to explain or qualify the main contract.

Thus in the case of engaging to let a piece of land on lease there usually are a series of subsidiary contracts, such as to secure the incoming tenant against disturbance from persons claiming through the landlord; to rebuild premises destroyed by fire; to release the tenant from paying rent for a certain time in lieu of the landlord's making necessary improvements; and, possibly, to sell the land for a fixed price at the tenant's option. So again in conveying shares in a public company; besides the main contract which is evidenced by the transfer of names in a public register, it may be that the seller makes a subsidiary contract with the buyer that, in certain contingencies, a re-conveyance is to take place, or that, in consideration of the seller's having remitted part of the purchase money, the buyer is to devote what he has purchased to some definite end. Or the subsidiary contract may take the form of a guarantee relating either to past or to future transactions, and the main contract may be made to rest on the validity of the guarantee in such a way that if the guarantee prove to be worthless, the main contract fails with it.

Or, lastly, the main contract, however simple the form it finally assumes,—as of a mere promise to pay money at a definite date,—may depend for its validity upon the correctness of a long series of mutual accounts between the parties. The *bonâ fides* of the transaction may then wholly repose on this assumed correctness. If there has been any miscalculation, and, still more, if there has been anything of the nature of fraud, the law must regard the expectation, which is the very essence of the contract, as not grounded at all, or as improperly grounded, and therefore must treat the alleged contract as non-existent.

This is the meaning of what is called, in English law, the "consideration" for a contract. This "consideration" is no part of the contract itself. It is only one of the facts, or classes of facts, from which law judges that an actual contract has been made. It is, in truth, a general formula deduced from the ordinary experience of mankind. Men do not generally base expectations on the bare promise of others in the absence of all intelligible reason for the promise being made and kept. The reason may be of various kinds, such as a recollection of previous services done by the promisee to the promisor; the expectation of future services yet to be done by the same; the existence of moral obligations between the parties; or even nothing more than the solemnity and precision of the terms in which the promise is made.

Whatever the reason or ground of the expectation be, in judging of the fact as to whether the expectation is really formed, the law may well demand information as to this reason or ground. Should law, as does the law of England in the case of all contracts (not made in a very few definite ways), demand this information, it becomes itself part of the evidence of the contract. But, as has just been intimated, information as to the ground of a promise may extend over an infinity of complex transactions, tedious negociations, and even protracted controversies, the general result being that a certain definite expectation was aroused in the mind of one person, at the least, as to the future acts of another. At every stage in the progress of these preliminary circumstances an opening is afforded for the admixture of error, misrepresentation, forgetfulness, and fraud.

Thus it appears that, for large classes of the most important contracts, so many subsidiary contracts accompany the main one, that to provide evidence of a kind to explain and limit the main contract adequately, no sort of evidence which bears upon any one of the subsidiary contracts can properly be excluded. And even with respect to a contract, apparently one of the commonest and least artificial, it may be that the judicial investigation of the presence of a reason or "consideration" for it will open up all those very sources of hallucination which, by insisting on definite evidence of contracts, it is the policy of the law to prevent.

The general result of the inquiry seems to be that, though law may endeavour with some advantage to reduce the difficulty of obviating fraud and simplifying procedure in the course of supporting contracts, yet, nevertheless, the business of mankind is always likely to keep a long way ahead, in point of prolixity and complexity, of the capacity of law to deal with it in such a way as to obviate the necessity of most circuitous investigations and the possibility of occasional mishaps.

So soon as more or less satisfactory evidence is obtained of a contract having been really made and of its general character, the next points to be settled are the exact rights and duties of the parties and the nature of the remedy, if there be any.

The rights and duties of the parties may be either determined (expressly or implicitly) by the terms of the contract, or may be imputed by law as following from the ordinary nature of the contract, or may be partly determined in one way and partly imputed in the other. The extreme brevity and indefiniteness that attend the making of the most familiar contracts call for the application of presumptions founded on the general practice and expectations of mankind. These presumptions will, however, vary with the particular class of mankind immediately contemplated, and with the actual situation of the parties.

Thus it may be said, broadly, that there are three sources of information to which reference may be made on its appearing that the terms of a contract are insufficiently explicit or definite as to the detailed rights and duties of the parties.

The first source is that presented by the actual situation and antecedents of the parties. Previous transactions of a like kind, but more precise and intelligible, may explain the present one. A long series of negotiations between the parties, varying from the general course of like negotiations as pursued by others, may throw a light on what seems rare and peculiar in the present negotiation.

The second source of information to which reference may be made for the purpose of expounding a contract is the class, trade, profession, or place of abode of the contractors. Such a reference is not only important as serving to explain language, but also as importing into the contract customary usages to which, in the particular case, the expectation of the parties may be supposed to have been directed. Or the reverse process may take place of thereby excluding from the contract usages habitual elsewhere, but to which, among the class of persons in question, expectation could not have been directed. It is on these principles that the customs of the Stock-Exchange are admitted in English courts of justice to explain contracts for the buying and selling of stock; the customs of shipowners are admitted to explain navigation contracts; and even in narrower trades (as happened in one case in reference to the tobacco trade) the usage prevailing in them is similarly incorporated with the actual terms of the contract.

But if the special situation or generic habits of the parties do not serve to clear up the terms of the contract, the third source of information to which reference must be made is that supplied by the ordinary habits of mankind. It is natural that long experience should have formulated the conclusions drawn from the observation of these habits into general presumptions or maxims. These presumptions are partly general as applying to all contracts whatever; and partly special, as applying to the several kinds of the commonest contracts. The special presumptions, for instance, describe whether in the case of sale a warranty is to be held to accompany the sale, and if so, to what extent; whether a certain kind of debt does or does not carry interest, and to what amount; whether a contract of pledge leaves the pledgor at liberty to use the thing pledged, and to what extent; whether a contract of service extends to all the matters alleged to be included in it or only to some of them.

The more general presumptions affect the interpretation of every contract whatever, except in so far as they are rebutted by express agreement of the parties, or by one of the two classes of considerations already described. They relate to the general mode, measure, and time in which the contract must be performed. It is from presumptions of this nature that the artificial classifications of Diligence and Negligence have been concocted in Roman and in English law. These presumptions have a greater show of logical exhaustiveness than practical utility, inasmuch as, in any given case, the possible loss sustained by the breach of the contract must admit of far more numerous and fine gradations than could be commensurate with the formal classes into which diligence or negligence are distributable. Nevertheless the main principle upon which this last distribution rests is a true one, namely, that it may generally be anticipated that the less the payment made in return for diligence, the less the diligence that is expected; and if no payment at all is made, as little diligence as possible is usually expected, though it may be that some is.

In devising a remedy for breaches or apprehended breaches of contract, law may address itself either to restoring the parties to the original position they would have occupied if the contract had never been entered upon, or to giving the injured party as many as possible of those advantages which would have accrued from the contract, had it been performed. The former method is chiefly applicable when the breach has not yet taken place but is only apprehended, and the latter when a contract is already broken.

When there is good reason to suspect that a contract

will not be kept, whether that reason be based on a contractor doing an act inconsistent with the performance of his contract, or upon his means of performing his contract obviously failing him, the immediate object must be to take such steps without delay as may reduce to the utmost the other contractor's possible loss. One device of this sort is that called "lien," of which "stoppage *in transitu*" may be treated as an important species. The essence of "lien" is that a contractor is able to retain possession of things owned by the other contractor by way of security for his fulfilling his contract. In the event of proper fulfilment becoming no longer possible, the creditor with a lien is thus able to get an advantage over other creditors less favourably situated, and to re-imburse himself out of the value of the lien without even having recourse to legal proceedings. The process of "stoppage *in transitu*" is applicable in cases where a seller, after having technically parted with the possession of things sold, before their actually getting into the possession of the buyer, hears of the buyer's apprehended insolvency, and is thereupon legally entitled to recover possession of things sold while yet on their route.

There is an important class of contracts both in Roman and in modern law,—that of *intercessio* or suretyship,—the sole object of which is the providing security for a contractor in case of his co-contractor failing to fulfil his engagement. The rights and duties of the *sponsores*, or sureties, both in respect of the chief contractors and of one another; the various modes in which such a contract can be created; and the tests by which a surety may be distinguished from a principal, fill an important place in all legal systems.

But the most noticeable of the modes for reducing the possible loss of a contractor, owing to the failure of ability on the part of his co-contractor to fulfil his engagement, is that of Bankruptcy, a device as familiar to Roman law, under the title of *cessio bonorum*, as to every system of modern law.

The essential notion of bankruptcy is that, owing to a contractor doing some act, which, in the sight of the law, affords unmistakable evidence that he cannot fulfil all his contracts, he is at once compelled to take immediate steps to satisfy all his creditors as far as, at the present moment, he can, and he is further compelled to forbear entering upon any fresh enterprises, which might, by engendering still greater losses, disable him from giving even the amount of satisfaction which he can give now, or which might result in some creditor being favoured at the expense of others. The peril attaching to this stringent process is that, in a lengthy course of strictly honourable commercial transactions, the moment of apparent penuriousness may be a most unfortunate one at which to check the enterprise. It may ruin the debtor and seriously diminish the amount ultimately divisible among the creditors.

Thus one main object in a bankruptcy law must be that of selecting such acts to be conclusive signs of insolvency, present or future, as, in the experience of the ways of mankind, really are such. Another object is, the provision of a competent administrative body to gather in and estimate the bankrupt's assets and to distribute them proportionably among the several creditors according to their legal claims. Other objects, again, are the protection of the person of the bankrupt himself against ordinary legal process, and possibly the making such a provision for him as may best enable him hereafter to pay his debts in full, whether they be only morally due, or be treated, for some purposes, as still legally due. Voluntary composition with creditors, of a kind to exclude the necessity of a reference to courts of justice, are popular and valuable substitutes for the remedy employed in bankruptcy.

The remedies for the actual breach of contracts are twofold; one that of compelling actual performance in kind, the other that of exacting compensation for non-performance.

There are some classes of contracts to which the former species of remedy is obviously unsuitable. Such are those in which a moral, confidential, or friendly relationship is presupposed in the course of fulfilling the contract. Instances of these sorts of contracts are contracts to marry, to serve as an apprentice or domestic servant, to employ as an agent, or to enter into a partnership. In the case of these sorts of contracts, a compulsory fulfilment of them would be either impossible or only possible in outward appearance. But there are other contracts for which a compulsory fulfilment is the only adequate remedy. Such, eminently, are contracts for a sale, and for all that partakes of the nature of a sale, such as a lease, a mortgage, or the creation of a servitude. In these cases the object of the contract is in the highest degree definite and limited; while it may also be so precious and singularly desirable that no monetary substitute can be satisfactory. It is considerations such as these which have led to the evolution of the doctrine of "specific performance," as recognized and guardedly applied in English courts of equity. It is obviously only applicable where the acts of the plaintiff himself have not already rendered a return to the original situation impossible.

But the most obvious and generally convenient mode of applying a legal remedy in the case of a breach of contract is that of estimating the value of the loss by a monetary standard, that is, in the terms of a common medium of exchange. In the course of estimating the amount of the loss sustained, so as to translate it into a new language, a variety of considerations may have to be borne in mind which might at first escape attention; and these will differ with the different objects of contract.

Thus, in the case of a breach of contract to marry, the loss, though possibly of a pecuniary character in one of its aspects, cannot be only such. The possible injury to reputation, the risk to other matrimonial prospects, and the pain sustained by the feelings, are in themselves of a nature which defies calculation in the terms of a monetary scale. In such a case, if monetary compensation is the only possible one, the assessment of the amount of it can have only an arbitrary or accidental relation to the actual loss or suffering entailed by the breach of contract. In fact, other considerations than the actual measure of that loss are, perforce, admitted. Such considerations are the pecuniary position of both parties, and the sort of expectations to which that may naturally have given rise; the possibility of the defendant's making reparation out of his or her existing means; and the presence of aggravating circumstances of hardship and cruelty. When damages are thus increased on grounds other than the estimate of the actual pecuniary loss sustained, they are sometimes called "vindictive" or "exemplary" damages, and the estimation of damages in this way is carefully watched and restricted.

Another case, somewhat similar, may occur in which a pecuniary estimate is impossible. That is the case of service or labour, when, on the one hand, the loss sustained by the employer through a breach of contract at a particular moment may reach to such a variety of matters and may stretch so far and deep, that any attempt at a pecuniary estimate must be delusive. On the other hand, it is likely enough to happen that the servant or labourer is wholly unable to make any pecuniary compensation whatever. This question is one which presents great perplexities; and attempted solutions of it, both in the past time and the present, have led to the most tyrannical abuses.

It has seemed impossible to approach the question without regard to its political and social, as well as to its purely legal, bearings. The difficulty is that, if an employer has no means of enforcing a contract with a labourer or servant, he will not employ him. But if the labourer or servant is wholly destitute of property, it is thought that the only pressure he can be made to sustain at the hands of the law is a punishment similar to those inflicted for breaches of the criminal law. Thus, if an employer breaks his contract, a payment which will be trifling to him may be adequate compensation to his labourer, while for a similar breach of contract on the part of the labourer, the consequence may be that the labourer is treated as a criminal.

The question is further complicated by the modern, and constantly growing, habits of combination among labourers for a large number of purposes, and among others, for that of bringing pressure to bear upon employers by threatening what is regarded by some as wholesale breaches of contract in the event of non-compliance with their terms, in reference to such matters as raising wages, shortening hours of labour, allowing holidays, and the like. The capitalists or employers retaliate by the use of the offensive and defensive weapon which the law puts into their hands, that of imprisonment. When the combination is a fair and open one, and no tyrannical or fraudulent efforts are made to procure adherents to it, or to intimidate dissentients, or to take the employers at a gross disadvantage, it is scandalous that the law should throw so heavy a weight as the power of imprisonment implies into one scale of what ought to be treated as a purely economic contention.

It is different when the combination passes the limits here marked out and assumes the form of organized physical force. The latter case may properly be dealt with by the criminal legislation, somewhat of the form of the English "combination" statutes ; but such legislation has to be carefully restricted, because,—proceeding, as all legislation must,—directly from the more leisurely and opulent classes of society, the line (difficult at all times to draw) between what is natural and proper self-defence and what is tyrannical aggression, is most likely to swerve aside in favour of those classes of society to which members of the legislature usually belong.

With respect to the more ordinary contracts of labour and service, it is probable that the absence of any possible recourse to punishments such as belong to the criminal law would not be found seriously to prejudice the interests of employers. Regular employment is so necessary for the great mass of the population, and more especially for the poorest part of that mass, that the sentiment which stimulates to faithfulness to clearly understood engagements is not likely to be long weakened on any large scale. In those exceptional cases where contracts are broken on the side of servants or labourers without legal remedy or compensation being attainable, it is probable that public opinion will prove itself vigorous enough to award reprobation or consolation to one party or the other with sufficient justice to prevent a frequent recurrence of similar disasters.

Even in those contracts, however, for the breach of which a monetary compensation is a perfectly sufficient and natural remedy, the assessment of the compensation may involve peculiar difficulties. Thus, in case of a breach of contract to effect a purchase, to sell a cargo of goods, or to conduct a profitable mercantile negociation, the question may be presented as to whether the contractor who has suffered from the breach ought to be merely restored to the position he would have occupied if the contract had never been entered upon,—which may involve reparation for loss of time, loss of a market, loss of special opportunity as of a season for sailing and the like; or whether the probable benefit of the contract when fully performed ought to be estimated and the amount so calculated made the measure of the damages.

It is obvious that, for a vast number of the most important mercantile contracts, the very essence of them depends on a certain speculative uncertainty as to the profits to be expected from them. Thus any accurate measurement of the loss sustained by the breach of one of these classes of contracts must be impossible.

Assuming, nevertheless, that the second of the above two principles of compensation is the only just one, the following contrivances have been resorted to for the purpose of providing a distinct (though imperfect) measure of the problematical value of a broken contract. One contrivance is an estimation of its value by the parties themselves at the time of making the contract. This may take the form of a subsidiary engagement or bond to pay so much in case of non-fulfilment of the contract, and as an adequate measure of the damage sustained. Another contrivance is to make general presumptions, founded on the ordinary course of business or of the special business concerned, and to base the estimate of the loss on the truth of those presumptions if they are not rebutted by special facts. Such presumptions are those made habitually with respect to allowance of interest on bills of exchange, with respect to the calculation of the probable length of a voyage in navigation contracts, or with respect to the current value of money at a given time in different parts of the world. A third contrivance is to strike an average between the highest and the lowest possible gains to accrue from the contract if it had been kept. In the case of some very complicated contracts it may be that all these contrivances will have to be resorted to at once in order to estimate the loss incurred in different parts of the transaction.

The word "contract" has habitually been applied in all countries to a number of legal transactions which, on one ground or another, in no way satisfy the description of a true legal contract as given above. Such for instance are "quasi-contracts," which only resemble contracts in respect of the legal situation of the parties when once the situation they depict has been attained.
There are cases in which a person, through a series of accidental circumstances, may be in possession of what belongs to another, or may have parted with what belongs to himself on grounds which he afterwards discovers to be insufficient. He has committed no injury to a right of ownership, or has so far sustained none. But it is clearly inequitable that he should retain what does not belong to him or be unable to recover what does. He clearly is liable to a special *duty* as towards the owner of what he possesses, or has a special legal right against the person who possesses what belongs to himself. He has a duty to restore, or a right to enforce restoration. Or he may be in both positions at once, and then he is situated exactly in the same way as if he had made a pair of contracts, or a single two-sided or so-called "bilateral" contract. The rights and duties really belong to the law of ownership, and should be treated under that head; but their similarity to the obligatory relations arising out of a contract have, in many systems of law, led to their being affiliated to contract law, and being

treated under that head. The English expression "implied contracts" seems to cover assumed or fictitious engagements of this nature; and also to cover unmistakable contracts when the evidence for them has to be gathered from a number of surrounding circumstances rather than from the express language of the parties.

There are some important transactions to which the term *contract* is frequently applied, although they can in no way be said to satisfy the description of a legal contract as above given. Such, for instance, are *marriage* and *sale*. It is customary to speak not only of a contract to marry, which is an unmistakable legal contract, but of the act of marriage, or assemblage of acts which constitute a marriage, as being a contract. There is undoubtedly an analogy between the situation of two persons who marry one another and that of two persons who make a contract with each other; and this analogy may be closer in some countries and periods than in others. Indeed, the analogy may be so close in the case of some marriage laws that the difference between a marriage and a contract vanishes altogether.

The analogy consists in (1) the necessary reciprocity of sentiment and intention which accompanies the joint act; (2) the result of the joint act, which is that each of the parties has legal rights and duties in respect of the other; (3) the character and extent of some of these rights, which (frequently) may be qualified by the joint will of the parties as ascertained on the occasion of entering upon the marriage.

But this analogy is only an analogy, and no more, because the rights and duties of the parties are primarily fixed by the State; and such qualifications of those rights and duties by the parties themselves as the State allows

—as, with respect to property, management of business, education of children and the like—are treated as wholly subsidiary to the general policy of the State in respect to the rights themselves.

Again, in all States in which unrestricted liberty of divorce is not allowed, no mere agreement by the parties themselves can cancel the marriage; whereas it is of the very essence of a contract that either contractor can release the other from his duties to perform the contract. Thus though it is true that law often, in respect to certain matters, limits the region of free contract, and, to that extent, modifies the conception of contract altogether; yet in these cases persons are only restrained as to the matters to which the contract shall not extend. Whether or not it shall extend to all matters legally permissible is left to the free will of the parties.

But in marriage, as also in service in some states of society,—and not so long ago in England,—all the main rights and duties resulting from the relationship (and which are the expression of it) are sharply marked out both by positive and negative limits. The practical reliance (so far as the relationship is regarded from its legal and not its moral side) of each of the parties is placed, not on the good faith of the other leading him or her to do what has been promised, but on the presumed willingness of the other to conform to the course arbitrarily marked out for him or her by law.

It is obvious from this investigation, as has been already indicated, that marriage has a tendency to glide into a mere contract; and that the prevailing distinction between marriage and a contract must be tested by the amount of voluntariness permitted in constituting the terms of the relationship and the conditions of its duration. The formation and preservation of the family group is, however, in any healthy State, of far too great moment to be relegated to the capricious choice of individual persons in the community. On this ground marriage is an act by which a *status*, or special legal relationship sanctioned by the State, is entered upon, and not a mere contract made.

It is even a more inveterate habit to speak of a *contract of sale* than of a *contract of marriage;* and yet the transaction termed a *sale* is still less analogous to a true contract than marriage is. A sale is in itself nothing more than an exchange or mutual conveyance of property between two persons, the property (or a part of it) conveyed on one side being the common circulating medium of the country, that is, money.

All that is essential to a sale is that the parties should intend to effect it, and should in form effect it. When two parties make a mutual interchange of money for goods and intend that one shall represent the price or the reason for thus surrendering the other, all the necessary elements of a sale are completely present. In very primitive times, before the notion of contract, or even of good faith, has acquired any steadiness, no other sort of sale than this exists. The exact character of it is typified in the Roman solemnity of *mancipatio*, in which the notion of mutual conveyances was the only one present. In modern purchases in what is called "market overt," the same notion is alone to be found, and, there being no engagement reaching to the future, there is no room for the operation of contract.

But by a series of steps, some of the earlier of which have been skilfully tracked out by Sir H. S. Maine, the notion of contract becomes naturally imported into the more primitive and elementary notion of sale. First, the custom becomes habitual of one party conveying what belongs to him, while the other party abstains for a time from performing his reciprocal function; and, next, the custom becomes habitual of neither party making any conveyance at the time, but only of agreeing to make conveyances in the future. In this last case a contract for a future sale has taken the place, for the moment, of an actual sale; but the contract for a sale is not a substitute for a sale which must take place afterwards unless, as happens under some legal systems, courts of justice impart to certain contracts for a sale all the legal character and incidents of an actual sale.

The relation of a contract to a conveyance, and, more especially, of a contract for a sale to an actual sale, is perplexed by certain peculiarities in the transaction styled a sale, to which the habits and convenience of mankind have given birth.

Thus the case may be supposed that a sale has been made of the general kind recognized and supported by law, and yet that neither party has complied with the formalities (whatever they happen to be) which in every case are indispensable to the legal conveyance of the property or money.

Here the law occupies a somewhat ambiguous position. On the one hand, it asserts that the parties have conveyed that which, by the appropriate act, they signified their purpose to convey; on the other hand, the law asserts they have neither of them conveyed that which, without the forms appropriate in each case, could not be conveyed. It is from a sort of instinctive resistance to this ambiguity of attitude that the notion of sale itself slowly undergoes a metamorphosis. It acquires a double meaning; first, the simple and original one of mutual and reciprocal conveyance; secondly, the derivative meaning of a contract, the terms of which are that each party shall, *in default of immediate conveyance*, take such steps as may be needed to make an effectual conveyance at a future time.

In this way, by an extensive use of the term *sale*, the legal ambiguity above described is cured. The law no longer asserts that a sale means only simultaneous acts of mutual conveyance. It means this, but it also means contracts to convey in default of immediate conveyance.

Another source of complication in the relationship of contract to sale is that, in the case of most sales, a number of subsidiary contracts are usually either expressly made by the parties or implied by law, such legal implication being based on the ordinary habits of mankind, on general convenience, or on particular customs prevalent in respect of certain classes of transactions. Such are contracts with respect to rescission of the sale, or to compensation, in case of hidden defects, known or not known to the seller, coming afterwards to light; with respect to the possession of the thing sold, either before or after the actual conveyance has taken place; with respect to the responsibilities of the possessor for injuries to it sustained during the possession; with respect to giving compensation in case of eviction; and possibly, as in the case of an English common-law mortgage, with respect to re-sale hereafter on certain conditions being complied with by the seller.

The number of surrounding contracts which thus hang round all the most important sales naturally lead to the suppression of the notion of the sale itself as independent of these contracts. This is the more likely to be the case where, as in England, the same deed of conveyance commonly operates at once as transferring the property, and as furnishing evidence of, or, rather, as constituting, a series of subsidiary contracts.

There is one common notion with respect to contract which yet remains to be examined: that is, the notion of contracts being transferred in life; or, on death, descending by intestate succession or testamentary deposition. As above explained, a legal contract was seen to be eminently a personal agreement; that is to say, an agreement in which the promisor relied upon his own ability and disposition to keep his promise, and the promisee relied upon the same likewise. In pursuance of this essential conception, it must seem wholly anomalous to admit of any substitution of persons in the course of carrying out the contract; and yet the rapid play of commerce depends more upon what may be called the "marketable value" of contracts, than, perhaps, upon any other single legal institution. What is needed, then, is to understand what is meant by a contract being bought or sold, or descending to heirs and executors.

At this point the inconvenience is experienced in English law of having no word at hand like *obligatio*—signifying the legal relations created by a contract—to oppose to the *contract* itself, out of which the legal relation arises. In Roman and in Continental law, through the use of the term *obligatio*, there is no danger of confusing the rights and duties which it denotes with the formal act which is the cause and sign of their having accrued. But it is quite customary in England to hear of contracts descending to a man's heirs or executors, and of their being assigned and bought or sold. What is really meant is, that the rights and duties which have attached through the making of a contract are the subjects of the several legal operations indicated.

There are, indeed, cases in which it may be difficult to distinguish whether a person doing a certain act with the help of another person's name, and possibly by the use of documents signed by him, is simply (1) succeeding to the rights and duties of the other, arising out of his contract with a third person, or (2) making a fresh contract for himself, or (3) merely personating the original contractor, and, by such temporary intervention, assisting the actual contractor to avail himself of rights under the contract.

The first (1) of these cases is that of those contracts the benefit or burden of which descend to a man's heirs or successors, or of those which, in the words of English law, "run with the land," that is, which attach to every one into whose hands a certain piece of land comes, whether it be as landlord or as tenant. Whether the rights and duties under a contract shall descend and pass from one person to another in these or in any other ways must depend, as do all other qualifications of these rights and duties, upon the will of the contractor, subject, of course, to the recognition of such consequences on the part of the State. The convenience is so great of a man's being able to bind not only himself but also all those who inherit his estate, and of a man's being able to rely on the performance of an engagement, not only by the individual person who binds himself, but (if its object be yet unaccomplished at the time of that person's death) by those who succeed him and inherit his means of completing the performance, that the notion of succession to obligations—or to the rights and duties arising out of contracts—becomes a most familiar one in all systems of law; and the process of such succession is usually facilitated as much as possible by legislation.

In the second (2) case above alluded to a person might seem to be only availing himself of the contract of another when really he is also or solely making a new contract for himself. This is the case of the contracts made by what are called "negotiable instruments;" to which class of contracts belong those arising out of bills of exchange and promissory notes. These instruments are simple written forms conveying a promise to pay money to any possessor of the instrument at a certain date, the money either to be paid directly by the promisor, or indirectly through a third person, in whose hands the promisor has deposited money for the purpose of satisfying the demand. The essence of these instruments is that, by the mere transfer of the document, accompanied—it may be—with the affixing to it the transferor's name, a new set of rights and duties are called into being exactly reproducing the original ones created between the original promisor and promisee; and yet all the while the original promisor and each intermediate one continue bound to the actual possessor of the document. This process may be repeated any number of times. The peculiarity, however, is that, since each transfer of the document creates a fresh contract, all the successive contracts co-exist at the same time.

The real explanation of this is that each promisor in turn lays himself under a contingent duty to pay a certain sum of money to the person who holds the document and presents it at the proper time and place. He makes no contract with any one but the person to whom he immediately transfers the document; but the nature of the contract so made is such that any future holder of the document has all the rights arising under the contract which any previous contractor had. Thus each promisor is liable to pay the debt once to some person or other.

This contingent duty of paying to some one or other is one chief feature in this class of contracts. Another feature is that at each transfer of the document a fresh independent contract is made. The general result is extremely beneficial to the holder of the document, as he has a double kind of security for payment. In the first place, he looks to the person who immediately contracted with him; and, in the second place, he may avail himself of the right of action against an indefinite number of persons to whom he has succeeded through his possession of the document. In every system of law in which these contracts are recognized the most precious rules are laid down for marking the order in which these different classes of rights may be made available, and in which, after due notice, all the promisors may be successively sued. Sometimes it is said that a contract of this sort, by which each promisor so engages to pay only if an earlier promisor does not pay, is really one of suretyship.

The third (3) case in which the position of one who is presumably a contractor may be an ambiguous one is where it is doubtful how far one who is availing himself of rights under a contract is a successor to those rights, or is only doing, on behalf of the original contractor, the formal acts necessary to render them available. This must be a question of fact and of evidence, and belongs to the general subject of Agency.

The whole question of agency is one of evidence. Important as it practically is in a commercial country, the decision of questions arising upon it—that is, questions as to how to distinguish a principal from an agent, and how to protect principals against the acts of unauthorized agents and the public against both—must depend, partly, upon the use of that general wisdom which can be taught only by intercourse with the world, and partly upon the special adroitness with which legal presumptions and maxims founded upon that experience are gradually constructed.

There are, indeed, two distinct aspects in which the relation of principal and agent figures in the law of contract. There is first the contract of agency, which is nearly the same as the Roman *mandatum*, the object of which is to enable one person to repose confidence in the management of his affairs by another. In the ordinary business of life, and still more in the conduct of complicated commercial concerns, especially such as have offshoots in other countries, the convenience and necessity of such personal representation are sufficiently obvious. Like other contracts, this one may either be created by express language, written or spoken, or may have to be presumed from the acts of the parties (such as ratification of acts previously done) and from surrounding circumstances. In some cases the importance of guarding against abuses or frauds in this sort of substitution of persons is so great that law demands compliance with special forms in nominating an agent for certain purposes, as for appointing a *procurator* or *cognitor* at Rome and granting a "power of attorney" in England.

The other aspect in which Agency appears in contract-law arises out of the previous one, and relates to the capacity and power of an agent, when duly appointed, to make contracts on behalf of his principal. This belongs to the more general question as to the number and kind of legal purposes for which representation (*per nuntium* in Roman law) is admissible and what are the legal consequences to all the parties, conceivably interested, of such representation. The making of contracts is always held to be one of the purposes to which representation can extend. In this way the fact of agency first gives rise to a contract of agency between the principal and the agent; and, secondly, if the purpose of the agency is that of making contracts on behalf of the principal, that fact may qualify the liabilities arising under the contract presumedly made between the principal and third persons.

Perhaps the most remarkable of all applications of contract to diminish the uncertainty due to the precariousness of human life and to the prevalent liability to accidents of all sorts, by which calculation is baffled and the order of general existence disturbed, is the invention of contracts of Assurance. These, in modern society, take a large number of forms, according as the chances of death, fire, shipwreck, storms or other disasters,

CHAPTER X.

CRIMINAL LAW AND PROCEDURE.

THE topic of criminal law, while it is one of the oldest and the most universal, certainly yields in importance to none in a complete exposition of the science of law. The difficulty of treating the subject in what, from a scientific point of view, would be the most satisfactory manner, is due to the peculiar way in which legal, moral, and political considerations are here so intimately blended with one another. Even the purely legal view of the topic ought strictly to be broken up into two parts, that relating to the substance of criminal law and that relating to criminal procedure. But these two parts, again, are so implicated with one another that it is practically more convenient, and more conducive to a thoroughly clear statement of the whole phenomena, to anticipate, while treating of criminal law, so much of the general subject of procedure as concerns criminal procedure. The plan here adopted will be to handle the subject of criminal law as a whole, not scrupling to introduce moral and political considerations when they obviously present themselves, but guarding none the less sedulously against any confusion of those considerations with such as are only legal in the most strict and technical sense.

So far as recent historical research has contributed to throw light on the legal development of primitive communities, it would seem that what, at a later stage, grows into a system of criminal law appears, at the earliest stage, under two different phases. One phase has relation to private life; and, according to it, a *crime* is nothing more than the infringement of one of those general rights in which all members of the community equally share. Such rights are those to life, to free locomotion, to good fame, and to the general conditions of a healthy physical existence.

These rights, at first, are only very dimly and inadequately appreciated. They are discovered rather by the conscious shock attending the first early violations of them than by any antecedent reflexion upon their intrinsic importance. They are looked upon as belonging to individual persons, and not as having reference to the whole State—an abstraction which it is wholly alien to primitive ideas to declaim about, though it makes itself felt in a signal way which will shortly be described.

Thus a large part of early criminal law covers exactly the same ground as much of that covered in modern societies by the law of delicts or civil injuries or, as the mass of them are called in England, *torts*. From this conception flows the primitive practice of "composition" for certain kinds of crimes, and the identity of procedure in criminal law (such as it is) with that observed in matters of disputed ownership or contract. With some offences of this sort a strange superstitious element is frequently mixed up, especially in matters touching human life, or general religious duties. In the Twelve Tables it is impossible to distinguish the spirit in which mourning for the dead was restricted, burglary, libels, and sorcery were prohibited, and provision was made for a creditor getting satisfaction for his debt by hewing to pieces, with proper formalities, the body of his debtor.

The other phase in which early criminal law is presented is closely connected with the development of the abstract notion of the *State*. It is not long before, in the course of the early struggles of a community, a blow is inflicted on the community by some one of its members which causes widespread consternation and horror. It may take the form of an act of disloyalty and treachery; or of the assassination of a favourite leader or benefactor; or of the slaying of some private person with circumstances of peculiar cruelty or, as in parricide, in gross violation of the dictates of nature.

On the occurrence of one and another of such acts as these the national consciousness starts into existence: the people feel themselves injured and menaced as a corporate whole. A common compassion for an immediate sufferer mingles with a common apprehension of undefinable dangers to the nascent commonwealth. The result is that the people determine to judge the offender themselves, partly, in order to give dignity and solemnity to the proceedings; partly, because they alone are competent to assign an adequate punishment, or to avenge an unprecedented offence; and partly, because, as the injury is felt to be directed against themselves, their presence is as necessary as, in an ordinary case, is that of the private person despoiled of his rights.

Sir H. S. Maine describes the origin of this view of crime in his "Ancient Law" (p. 372), though he does not seem to recognize the private and public aspects of early criminal law as necessary co-existent. His words are as follows:—" Yet it is not to be supposed that a conception "so simple and elementary as that of wrong done to the "State was wanting in any primitive society. It seems "rather that the very distinctness with which this concep- "tion is realized is the true cause which at first prevents "the growth cf a criminal law. At all events when the "Roman community conceived itself to be injured, the "analogy of a personal wrong received was carried out "to its consequences with absolute literalness, and the "State avenged itself by a single act on the individual "wrong-doer. The result was that, in the infancy of "the commonwealth, every offence vitally touching its "security or its interest was punished by a separate enact- "ment of the legislature. And this is the earliest conception "of a *crimen* or crime, an act involving such high issues "that the State, instead of leaving its cognizance to the "civil tribunal or the religious court, directed a special "law or *privilegium* against the perpetrator. Every "indictment, therefore, took the form of a bill of pains "and penalties, and the trial of a *criminal* was a proceed- "ing wholly extraordinary, wholly irregular, wholly inde- "pendent of settled rules and fixed conditions. Conse- "quently, both for the reason that the tribunal dispensing "justice was the sovereign *State* itself, and also for the "reason that no classification of the acts prescribed or for- "bidden was possible, there was not at this epoch any *law* "of crimes, any criminal jurisprudence."

It is not necessary, for the purpose now in view, to follow Sir H. S. Maine's interesting sketch of the history of criminal law in Rome and in England, intermediate between that of its first development and that of its culminating point, so far as this, in England at least, has as yet been attained. The first two phases have here been dwelt upon in some detail because of the vivid illustration they present of the double aspect in which criminal law always presents itself; and which aspect imports so much perplexity into all theories on the subject and even into the procedure of criminal courts.

The twofold notion that by a crime, in most cases, some person has his rights violated, and at the same time that by a crime the State is more directly injured and menaced than by other violations of rights not classed as crimes, seems to be permanent and universal. In the case of an ordinary civil injury—which properly includes every violation of rights, even breaches of contracts—the State is only injured so far as the general security of rights given and guaranteed by the State may seem to be invaded. On this ground the State leaves the injured person to take the initiative in protecting his right or in obtaining amends for its violation.

The State may go so far as to expect a person interested in maintaining a right to be vigilant and diligent in giving notice of its infringement to the proper court of justice, and even to give securities for the *bona fides* of the complaint and of a resolution to proceed with it throughout. Thereupon the State provides all the judicial machinery needed to protect the right, or to ascertain whether it needs to be vindicated. It is the interest of all persons in the community that every right, of whatever sort it may be, should be guarded against infringement. But, as respects any particular right, it is still more eminently the interest of the person in whom it vests that it should be respected. On these grounds it is sufficient for the State to rely on the activity of individual persons to take the initiative in upholding their own rights. If a right is violated with impunity, owing to the remissness or indulgence of the person most concerned, the injury to the State is about as minute as can well be.

The gist of a *crime* is that, quite apart from the effect on the general security of rights and apart from the loss or suffering to individual persons, there are extrinsic reasons why the act constituting the crime should either be wholly prevented or be made of the rarest possible occurrence. A single act of treason, if successful, may overturn the Government; and, if political circumstances do not justify it, may threaten the stability, or permanently arrest the growth, of the State. Every murder, punished or unpunished (though more so in the latter case than in the former), destroys the sense of personal security, and, to that extent, defeats one great object for which the State exists. A successful forgery carries dismay into all mercantile circles; and a solitary case of perjury scatters uncertainty over the proceedings of every court of justice in the country. So with all the other leading crimes.

The object of the State is to devise special contrivances, adapted to the existing condition of society, and more particularly to the circumstances of those classes of persons by whom the several sorts of crimes are found to be commonly committed, so that the occurrence of crimes may, if possible, be absolutely prevented. Some of these contrivances take the form of a vigilant police, by which the probability of offences being committed may be made as little, and that of the detection of offenders may be made as great, as possible. Other contrivances appertain to the constitution and procedure of criminal tribunals; others again to the application of penalties, the choice and magnitude of which must be determined by a mass of considerations, the nature of which will be described lower down. Other contrivances, again, relate to modes of reforming habitual criminals and of removing, as far as possible, the more obvious incitements to crime.

The whole of these agencies have as their main and immediate end the diminution, or, if possible, the abolition, of crime, though some of these agencies may serve other useful purposes as well.

It has already been noticed that some acts, which the State designates as crimes, are nothing more than violations, in certain assigned ways, of general or particular rights of private persons. Sometimes the same act may be treated either as a civil injury or a crime, because it is in fact both. It will rest with the law of each particular State to determine how far in that State a person may be, at the same time and by the same process, proceeded against by a private person for a *civil injury* and by the State for a *crime*. This is allowable in France, but is not allowable in England. It may happen, again, that the circumstance that distinguishes a *crime* from a *civil injury* is one purely affecting the mental state of the offender, and not in any way qualifying the results of the offence.

Thus, in the case of a person being seriously injured by a railway accident, it may depend on the condition of the engine-driver's mind, as to attention to signals and the like, whether a mere civil action can be brought against the company for an injury to the person, or a criminal indictment can be framed against the servant of the company for manslaughter. A like case is presented when a person is injured through being improperly treated by a doctor. The violation of the person's right to be skilfully treated, and his personal loss in this respect, may be exactly the same whether the doctor was simply careless or was maliciously designing his patient's death.

These considerations might of themselves serve to indicate that the class of "crimes" is constructed on wholly different principles from that of civil injuries, though in certain places the two classes overlap. This will be all the plainer when it is borne in mind what a number of the most important crimes there are in all countries as to which it is not easy to say that the rights of any person whatever are infringed by their perpetration. Such are all crimes immediately directed against the State itself or some department of it, or against the administration of public justice.

Treason,—in some of its manifestations, and when the

stability of the Government alone and not the personal security of any human being is directly menaced by it,— coining, offences against the revenue, nuisances on public highways, and the neglect to repair bridges, all belong to a class of crimes in which the rights of persons invaded by them are either so vague, so remote, or so indefinitely and equally diffused, that no account can be taken of them in describing the offence. The gist of the crime in each case is, not that the rights of some person or persons are invaded, but that, in pursuance of a policy of its own, arbitrary or even capricious it may be, the State absolutely forbids such acts, and every measure is resorted to which seems likely to render them as infrequent as possible.

The distribution of acts which violate rights into *crimes* and *civil injuries* is further perplexed by the accidental and illogical way in which, in some countries, as in England, the line has historically been drawn between the two. There are some parts of criminal procedure in England which presuppose in theory that the object of the proceedings is the vindication of a private right and the punishment of its violation. There are other facts which presuppose, in theory, that the State, as represented technically by the Sovereign, occupies the place of a civil plaintiff in the prosecution of certain classes of crimes. But in either case the phenomenon is merely based on an eccentricity of historical development.

It took a long time in England for the two notions of the interest of the private person injured and the interest of the Sovereign to find their proper and philosophical place in relation to each other. The result has been that, in reference to the forms of initiating prosecutions, the conception of the interest of the person injured has adhered to all classes of crime, though the practical result is only so far significant as it seems to interpose a barrier to the substitution of a public prosecutor. The notion of the Sovereign's interest, connected though it is with the celebrated distinction between misdemeanours and felonies, has scarcely a single consequence of any practical importance at the present day.

Apart, however, from the particular circumstances under which criminal law comes into being, and the special modes in which wrong-doing is distributed into the two departments of civil injuries and crimes, there are certain internal characteristics of crimes which are wholly peculiar to them, and which render the investigation of the true nature of criminal law equally difficult and important.

It cannot be denied that criminal law is very closely connected with, and dependent upon, the existing condition of the moral sentiments of the community. The earlier parts of this treatise will have sufficiently established that every part of the law rests on an antecedent moral condition which alone renders its creation and general acceptance possible; though, on the other hand, law repays the debt by contributing largely to the substantiation and support of moral ideas. Criminal law is ultimately based on the moral conception of a *crime* which is anterior to, though also co-existent with, the legal conception. *Crime*, in the moral use of the term, and in the mixed moral and legal use (which is the popular use), signifies an abominable and atrocious act which is not only injurious to some members of the community and dangerous to all, but which proceeds from some exceptional wickedness in the person who perpetrates it.

It is in this idea of "wickedness" as contrasted with that of, what may be called, "dangerousness" that the moral conception of a crime differs from the legal conception. The common judgment of mankind estimates an act not only by its actual, or possible, consequences, but by the general character, in respect of moral excellence, of the agent, and also by the thoughts and feelings of the agent at the moment of action. Thus the acts most abominated are those which are most noxious in their actual or possible results; which are done by the most notoriously vicious men, or by men hitherto reputed to be the best men; and which, in any particular case under consideration, are done with the most malevolent or culpable motives. All these elements—some of them touching the act itself, and some of them touching the agent, either looked at generally or under special conditions—properly enter into the estimate of an act from a moral standing-point.

The process of evaluating acts is performed roughly and hastily enough by the bulk of the community, who have neither leisure, knowledge, nor disposition to look very far or very deep. It is performed with more precision and skill by the moral philosopher. But whether performed superficially, or with intelligent and conscientious thoroughness, the process of evaluating acts is always essentially the same, and the elements concerned in it are identical and invariable.

It is natural, then, that some classes of acts which usually are found to combine all the conditions by which atrocity is measured should obtain a generic name; and it is also what might have been expected,—considering that these acts are among those which it must ever be the policy of a State absolutely to prevent from so much as occurring at all,—that this generic name should in some countries be also the generic name for the acts which the State strains its uttermost to discourage by that part of the law which is called criminal law. Thus the term *crime* is one of the most notable meeting-points of law and morality.

It has thus been seen that "wickedness" in the agent is, from a moral point of view, one of the indices to the atrocity of an act which causes suffering or loss to others. The conception of "wickedness" must itself depend upon the moral criteria and the moral standard which happen to prevail in the community at the time. The word is, no doubt, vague and indeterminate, though by no means without intelligible meaning. It implies not only the absence of such concern for the welfare of others, and especially of the person injured, as, in the opinion of the community, *ought* to be there; but possibly, also the presence of sentiments which, in their opinion, ought not to be there. It imples, furthermore, that the agent was free, and, either at the moment of action, or at some other moment, could, if he had wished, have prevented the formation of the state of mind which ultimately dictated the act.

Thus in every moral judgment on an act, besides the estimate of the nature and consequences, actual or possible, of the act itself, there are present the several notions of, first, a standard of right sentiments; secondly, a dictation, or moral imperativeness, which directs conformity with that standard; and, thirdly, a moral responsibility or accountability in every one, except in circumstances of special exculpation, to conform to that standard.

The treatment of the self-same acts by the criminal law is illustrative of the differences between law and morality, and of their relations to each other. Law, like morality, directs attention, in the first place, to the act itself, as measured and circumscribed by its consequences, actual or possible, immediate or remote. It enumerates, with such precision as it can avail itself of, the acts to be abstained from, and usually classifies them under some scheme of arrangement suggested by the gradations, or the kind, of suffering or of danger they occasion, by the character and situation of the sufferers, or by reference to mere antiquarian and long familiar divisions.

In the second place law, like morality, addresses itself also to the perpetrators of the acts it forbids. The law, however, is here considerably at fault, and is, as it were, conscious of its own comparative impotence. The notion of "wickedness" involves far too numerous and subtle considerations to render it a possible basis of a judicial sentence. Law can venture so far in psychological inquiry as to determine whether an alleged *act* was really such, and was preceded by an exertion of the will, or whether it was merely an event. It can go further and test the *intention* of the agent's mind at the moment of acting. In other words, it can profess to ascertain the attitude of his mind towards the immediate consequences of his act. Law can even go further than this, and endeavour to discover an agent's *motive*, or the remote and ulterior consequence of which he was in pursuit, and to which the immediate consequence of the act was only a transitional, though an essential step.

This analysis of the presence or absence of will, intention, and motive, must serve to throw great light on the condition of the agent. If will is proved to have been present, the act was a true act for which the agent is accountable to law. If intention is proved to have been present, the agent knew what he was about, what was the character of his act, and what might be expected to follow from it; or, at least, a greater or less amount of such knowledge may be fairly imputed to him. If a motive is discovered, it is made plain whether the agent desired the consequences of this act, that is, either the immediate or remote consequences, or both; or whether he was indifferent to some of the consequences but desired others, or only desired some as a means or stepping-stone to others.

Now, the question is presented as to how far law has thus gone in competing with the moral investigation previously alluded to, and what is the purport and relevancy of the competition.

Throughout the enquiry law presupposes, just as morality does, a canon of right sentiment, a command that every one shall conform to that canon, and a corresponding legal and moral responsibility attaching to everybody who does not conform to it. Not, of course, that law ever judges, as does morality, thoughts and feelings by themselves, and apart from the outward acts which are the sole appropriate matters of its cognizance; but, in the course of estimating criminal liability for an act, of which, by the hypothesis, the chief characteristic is that it occasions suffering to others, or complex dangers to the State, law is bound to examine with scrupulous care the mental and even (so far as it can) the moral situation of the person accused.

There are, indeed, two distinct grounds why law, in that department of it which deals with crimes, is compelled to conduct, with such rude instruments as are at its disposal, a quasi-moral investigation so often as the legal responsibility of an alleged offender is called in question. One of these grounds is that a large number of legal crimes can scarcely be described in any other language than that supplied by the popular dialect of the day, and their very existence is largely based upon the moral notions and beliefs current at the day.

It has been seen that for the construction of many classes of crimes (in the legal and moral sense equally) moral sentiments and State policy have been invariably at one. Murder, robbery, theft, fraud, housebreaking, burglary, rape, and piracy are instances of crimes as to which almost as correct and exact a notion would be obtained by catechizing the first passer-by in the street, as by studying the most carefully considered judgments or the most elaborate codes. And it is probable that, however completely law written and codified absorbs unwritten law, increasing civilization will generate new forms of audacity and atrocity which will continue to be designated by some such generic term as *crimes*. It may also be expected that these new crimes, in the popular sense, will be successively made crimes in the legal sense; and that, too, by the spontaneous action of courts of justice in default of speedy legislation or amendment of the code.

It thus appears that, in respect to large and important classes of crimes, law is dependent, in some measure, on the popular sentiments of the day for a general description of them. It has also been shown that in such a description, for popular uses, the element of wickedness or mischievousness occupies a conspicuous place. It was further indicated that this last element could not be strictly or satisfactorily inquired into by the administrators of law, and that the only inquiry of the sort which they could conduct was as to the presence or absence of motive.

The question, then, now arises as to how far the legal investigation into motives coincides with the moral investigation into wickedness or mischievousness. The one will only coincide with the other if it is determined that the presence of certain definite sorts of motives are conclusive signs of that iniquitous state of mind which common morality condemns. Morality, indeed, could accept no such test, because it will not allow the region of considerations appropriate to itself in forming a judgment to be narrowed in any way. But law has no choice. It must either abandon the task of keeping large classes of crimes synonymous for law and for morality—an issue which would so much offend the sensibilities of the community as to be practically out of the question—or it must submit to convert, at every point of the judicial process, lax moral impressions into definite legal axioms.

There is another ground why a quasi-moral investigation is implied in the administration of a large part of criminal law. It is because legislators and judges have generally endeavoured to improve morality directly by the engine of criminal law.

It has been seen that the true use and purpose of the criminal law is to prevent absolutely (if possible) the occurrence of those acts, which, if frequent or more than very rare indeed, must result in the dissolution of the whole State. A subordinate purpose is the support in the most effective way of important classes of private rights. Yet a third purpose has generally flitted before the fancy of legislators and judges, and has largely influenced the history of criminal law,—that of directly promoting general morality. It is no doubt an object worthy enough in itself, though, if the search for it be not strictly watched and restrained, other and more appropriate objects may be unconsciously sacrificed to it.

The way in which this end has been pursued has been to turn much of the strength of the judicial investigation upon the moral situation of the accused person. In fact, a purely moral investigation (though delusive from its insufficiency) has been substituted for a legal one. A prisoner's family history has been ransacked to estimate his predisposition to crime, the story of his education has been told, all the influences of later years have been enumerated, not in order to prove him guiltless on the ground of insanity, but to ascertain and to fix the exact degree of his guilt. The fact of punishment as an adjunct to criminal law, and of its possible graduation, has done much to give credit to this inquisitorial process. But the tendency of such modes of judicial investigation is to substitute the idea of a school for that of a criminal tribunal. The confusion of these two ideas leads to many errors, especially in relation to the assignment and choice of punishments. This subject will come under consideration later on.

The peculiar relations of legal to moral ideas in the region of criminal law is especially marked in the use of such terms and expressions as *dolus, dolus malus, malice,* and *malice aforethought.* Such language occurring in formal criminal indictments, enhanced as it is in some countries by direct reference to the deplorable religious condition of the culprit, certainly would seem to point to "wickedness," in the purely moral sense above described, being the final test of criminal liability.

It has been seen, however, how it has come about that criminal law has thus, as it were, strained itself to become co-extensive with the canon of moral duty. But the attempt has, of course, been vain, and it needed a very short course of development in legal procedure to expose the impotency of the effort.

The wickedness—whether called *dolus* or *malice,* or by any other term—of which the rough mechanism of courts of justice could alone take account, must be susceptible of exact description and general recognition. Indeed, through the insufficiency of the analytical methods in its hands, law must often avail itself of presumptions, throwing the burden of their disproof upon the person accused; and sometimes, under the guidance of a discreet policy, it must raise presumptions of "wickedness" without any probable foundation in fact, and without any opportunity being allowed to the accused of removing them.

In English law, the expressions habitually used in indictments, "maliciously" and "with malice aforethought," as well as some of those current in legal judgments and literature as "malice in fact," "malice in law," "express malice" and "implied malice" are only capable of being explained and brought into harmony with each other by the help of such considerations as the above. What constitutes "malice," that is, the sort and degree of wickedness of which alone the law is cognizant, is again matter for exact legal circumscription; and such circumscription, as applicable to particular crimes, such as murder, libel, and injuries to property, is gradually wrought out by the concurrent decisions of successive generations of judges or else is formulated in statutes and codes.

In the course of creating a distinct legal measure of wickedness it is found that, owing to the impossibility of always exploring satisfactorily even those coarser states of mind, which are not generally beyond the reach of the instrumentality in the hands of law, a vast number of offences or pernicious acts of serious detriment to the commonwealth are likely to go unpunished. On this ground, in the case of any one being found in a situation which, as a matter of experience, is found to indicate (though not conclusively to establish) criminality, he is called upon to assist the administration of justice so far as to disprove positively his own guilt. In other words, malice is "implied" or presumed, and the accused must repel the presumption, at his own peril if he fails.

There are cases, indeed, in English and in Roman law in which apparently harsher steps are taken than this, and the presumption of malice is raised and is not allowed to be rebutted even in cases where wickedness, in the common sense of the term, is proved not to have been present. Such are cases in which excessive negligence is said to amount to malice; as happens in English law when a person has thoughtlessly killed another with a weapon which is of a very dangerous character and might have been known to be likely to kill. Mr. Austin has criticized the Latin phrase expressing this mode of imputation (*culpa dolo comparatur*), and objects that *culpa* eminently signifies the absence of a thought which ought to have been in the mind, and *dolus* the presence of one which ought not to have been there. The true meaning, however, and justification of the maxim, is the above, that the legal consequences of *neglect* are judicially made to be the same as those of actual *wickedness*.

The above account of the legal systematization of the moral notion of "wickedness" may be further illustrated by Mr. Austin's valuable analysis of the elements of legal responsibility in his "Notes on Criminal Law" appended to the different editions of his lectures. He says, "Every "crime supposes, on the part of the criminal, *criminal* "*knowledge* [criminal consciousness] or *negligence* [crimi- "nal inattention, criminal inadvertence], *vel scienter vel* "*negligenter*." "Criminal knowledge" he further divides into "criminal, unlawful, or evil design [intent or purpose]," and "criminal knowledge short of criminal design." The former, he says, is present "where the "production of the mischievous consequence which the "law seeks to prevent is an *end* (or object), ultimate or "mediate, of the criminal; and where, therefore, the "criminal *wishes* (or *wills*) the production of it; *e.g.*, "murder, or arson, out of malevolence; murdering to rob; "theft." In each of these cases the production of the mischievous consequence is the "very end of the criminal, or, at least, is a means to its attainment." Criminal knowledge, short of design, Mr. Austin says, is present "where the production of the mischievous consequence "which the law seeks to prevent is not an end, ultimate "or mediate, of the criminal; but where he *knows* that "such mischievous consequence (though he does not *wish* "the production of it) will follow, necessarily or probably, "his act or omission; *e.g.*, arson of a house adjoining his "own, through his setting fire to his own, with intent "to defraud his insurers. The destruction of his neigh-"bour's house will not subserve his end; but he knows "that the destruction of his neighbour's house will follow, "necessarily or probably, the firing of his own."

The very possibility of this exact analysis and classification of the states of mind of which a mature system of criminal law alone takes notice marks, of itself, the distance which law has travelled from the time at which the notion of legal and moral criminality were scarcely distinguishable. A similar opposition, and yet likeness, in legal and moral tests is supplied by a consideration of grounds of *exculpation*, a subject which forms as it were the negative or back view of criminal liability.

It is obvious that, inasmuch as all crimes are acts or omissions, all the reasons which affect the legal character or validity of any other alleged act or omission must apply to them, though (as will be seen) some further reasons of that nature there are which specially apply to them alone. Thus if a person cannot perform a voluntary act, or at any rate the voluntary act which the law commands him to perform; or if a person's mind and muscles are, through disease or external violence, so far out of natural accord with each other that an act commanded was impossible under the circumstances; or that which seems to have been the forbidden act was not an act at all, but only an event over which the agent had no control; in such cases exculpation follows as of course. An event, indeed, has happened or has not happened; but there is no person who has any mental relation to it, however much he may have physically intervened in causing or preventing it.

But, further, acts are qualified, in the eyes of the law, according to their immediate consequences; and the doers of them (if they are acts forbidden by law) are responsible according to this mental attitude towards those consequences, at the moment of acting; in other words, according to their *intention*. This intention, being a hidden mental state, can only be judged of by reference to a multitude of circumstances, including among others the attitude of the agent's mind towards the ulterior consequences of his act; that is, his susceptibility to the influences of a *motive*.

Now, this capacity to apprehend the immediate consequences of an act and to be allured or deterred by its remoter consequences must depend upon two conditions being satisfied; one that of sufficient mental foresight to look steadily beyond the muscular motion in which the act itself consists; the other, that of sufficient experience and knowledge of the general consequences of the class of acts to which that under consideration belongs in order to predict both the immediate and the remoter consequences of this particular act. The general incapacitating circumstances which, in certain cases, prevent these conditions being satisfied are well known to be such as infancy, idiocy, insanity, special inexperience (as that sometimes, and for some purposes, imputed to women, sailors, young men, and foreigners), and fraud or violence. It must depend upon the nature of the act or classes of acts in question, how far these several causes of incapacity exempt from ordinary liability.

Most of these causes of incapacity are, further, capable of graduation, and it may form one of the most perplexing parts of a judicial investigation to determine how far any one of them is present in any particular case. In the present place it is important to notice that the test of special incapacity is, usually, applied differently in the execution of the criminal law and in that of all other parts of the law.

It has been seen that a large part of the criminal law of every country is co-extensive with a large part of the moral system prevalent at the time in that country. The same acts and classes of acts are forbidden by both, though morality forbids a great deal more than the outward act forbidden by law, and applies much keener instruments than any which law possesses, in the process of ascertaining whether or not its dictates have been conformed to. Nevertheless law, depending, as it needs must, for its execution upon the co-operation of a number of persons, all speaking the language and replete with the sentiments of the current morality, cannot prevent a quasi-moral interpretation being constantly put upon the terms it is trying to rescue from a lax and uncertain use.

The general result is that, for a large and important part of the criminal law, legal and moral crimes are always tending to actual convergence, but never attaining it. This being so, it is not to be wondered at that courts of criminal justice should presume a more diffused acquaintance with the chief rules of the criminal law than with those of any other part of the law, and should even substitute the test of liability supplied by the current moral sentiments of the day for the more artificial one which the application of less well-known parts of the law necessitates.

For instance, it may be well to say that no person under the age of fourteen, twenty-one, or twenty-five (as the case may be), has sufficient experience of the world to make a Will or an important contract. Looking

CIVIL AND CRIMINAL INCAPACITY. 249

at the actual circumstances of society, at the age at which juvenile instruction usually ceases, and at the effects of climate in developing precocity,—and bearing in mind that certainty and universality in the rule are of the greatest moment,—some presumption founded on experience must be raised and an immovable rule based upon it. Or, to take another case, it may be well to estimate differently, and yet precisely, the legal consequences of the same stage of insanity, according as the purpose is to test the validity of a marriage, a bill of exchange, a Will, or a trespass, having reference to that stage; and it is probable that general rules based upon experience gathered within the walls of courts of justice themselves, and therefore of rather an incompressible and technical kind, will be framed for the regulation of those consequences.

But, in criminal law, the test of age, sanity, or moral and physical freedom will be applied in far closer connection with that pursued in the common judgments of mankind. In England, for instance, however demonstrable may be a case of insanity on all other grounds and for all other purposes, the mere capacity of knowing that the act was morally wrong is held to be a sufficient ground of criminal imputability. So, after the age of seven, evidence is admissible to prove the presence of such exceptional precocity as may rebut the general presumption of innocence.

If the criminal law was not supposed to stand upon quite a different footing in respect of a diffusion of a knowledge of it and of its close correspondence with the leading principles of morality current in the State at the time, these practices would be glaringly cruel and unjust. But so far from being so (although they admit of many improvements), they are obvious expedients for combining the policy of executing the criminal law in a rigorously universal manner with that of exculpating persons proved to be irresponsible.

It may be doubted, indeed, whether the extension of the principle to the protection of a wife who commits a crime in the presence of her husband is altogether favourable to public morality, or to the encouragement of wholesome relations between husbands and wives. And it is certain that, from a medical point of view, the test of a prisoner knowing that an act was morally wrong, is a most insufficient test. It is an instance of the inevitable tendency of the best and of the originally most elastic legal processes to harden into stringent rules.

Thus it is in accordance with what is best in the principle above expounded that when insanity is alleged as a ground of criminal exculpation, not only the fact of it, but the nature and extent of it, should be searchingly investigated. But it is against that principle to apply the test of mere knowledge on the patient's part of either moral or legal facts.

That attention is directed in the execution of criminal law to the mental situation and antecedents of the accused, in a much higher degree than in the execution of other parts of the law, is obvious from various indications supplied by the legal systems of all countries. Participation in a crime, even to the limited extent of what is meant in the language of English statutes by "aiding, abetting, comforting," must necessarily come under the control of the criminal law, as much as doing the main act in which the crime characteristically consists. But participation admits of an indefinite number of degrees; and though it may, at one end of the scale, be scarcely, if at all, distinguishable from the actual committal of the offence, yet, at the other end, it may be shaded off indefinitely till it becomes nothing more than a latent personal sympathy of some sort, possibly after the act, with the true offender. To describe in terms or to test by a judicial scrutiny the exact kind and degree of participation which is properly criminal is an extremely arduous task, and can only be achieved by fixing attention upon a number of purely mental or moral circumstances connected with the offence and the offenders. The process is furthermore a very precarious one for public liberty, and affords openings for the most flagitious abuses, especially in the case of offences against the Government. The only securities against such abuses are to be found (1) in a precisely written rule of law, explained and limited by interpretation clauses or illustrative cases; and (2) in a mode of appointing and maintaining in office judges whose ability shall be of the highest quality, and whose political motives shall be above suspicion.

The whole history of the English criminal law is a remarkable monument of the perilous tendency in this part of the law to overstep its natural bounds, and to become transformed into an instrument of moral inquisition, and thereby of political tyranny. This is especially illustrated in the cases of treason and of certain (so called) "misdemeanours," particularly that of conspiracy. The law of criminal libels might also, in some of its aspects, be cited to the same purpose.

It is said to have been the uncertainty of the law of treason and the abuses to which that uncertainty gave rise which occasioned the enactment of the leading, and still subsisting, statute on the subject, that of the twenty-fifth year of Edward III. It is curious, however, that even the legislature, which enacted that statute, expressly for the purpose of finally removing doubts and of arresting the arbitrary definitions of the crime of treason which were constantly springing up, seem to have distrusted their own work, and by express words left it open to the judges to consult the legislature as often as they chose, as to whether any new crime already committed did fall within the statute or not. The history of the "constructive" treasons which have been built upon this celebrated Act is well known. The terms of the Act themselves are remarkable in the present relation as showing how feebly an immature society grasps after the true functions of criminal law and yet how imperiously the necessity of the case obliges them to do homage to those functions.

The Statute of Treasons, and those later ones which are based upon it, are the only important laws in England which are expressly directed, not against outward acts, but against mental states. The main offence is "compassing or imagining" the death of the king. The test of the offence, however, is the being "provably attainted of open deed." Thus the open deed was not the offence, but the evidence of the offence. In the progress of time and of public liberty the nature of the crime became more and more precisely described by a long series of judicial decisions, and the sort of evidence essential to conviction more and more accurately defined by statutes.

Though the statute of Edward III. is still in force, it is not probable that the constructive extensions of it would be revived at the present day, should an indictment be framed upon it. Recent statutes, however, of the present reign have, by converting into ordinary felonies a vast number of offences previously comprehended, by constructive interpretation, under the statute of Edward III., gone far to supersede the necessity for recourse to that statute.

The history of the English distinction between felonies and misdemeanours, and of the gradual construction of the latter class of crimes, is a further instance of the divergence from its true course to which criminal law is peculiarly prone. The earliest crimes known to English law seem to have been all classed either as treasons or felonies. Both these classes of crimes had relation to the feudal obligations which every one, except the king, owed to a superior lord. "Treason" was a positive offence against the lord's person or authority, and implies (as Blackstone says) in its very name, "a betraying, treachery or breach of faith." "Felony" is a far more general term, though of very doubtful etymology. It imports all those offences of which the feudal consequence was the forfeiture of all the offender's lands and goods. Thus the original definition of the only term what covered the most signal crimes was entirely based on the technicalities of the feudal system, and no space was left for offences, however injurious to others or detrimental to the commonwealth, which did not fall within the definition.

Gradually, however, the courts of justice elaborated a new class of offences, in accordance with the demands of a rapidly developing society. The technical mode in which this new class of so-called "misdemeanours" first came to the surface was by treating them (as they are technically treated at this day) as civil injuries, delicts or "torts," in which the Crown represents the person injured, or plaintiff. From the nature of the case, however, there was no limiting definition of misdemeanours to start with; and the only description of them that could be given would be that of such infractions of the public peace or of private rights as were not contained in the class of felonies, and yet, from a joint moral and political standpoint, demanded punishment and repression. It has been said that the very laxity of such a description as this was of great service, because it enabled courts of justice to keep pace with the unceasing aggressions of influential persons who were exempt from all other control and would readily have evaded any precisely written rules of law. This may be historically true, but it is only saying in other words that, in a barbarous condition of society, law has a very feeble hold on even the weightiest persons in the country; and therefore that a subtitute, however rough and perilous, must be found for law in the despotic powers conceded to courts of justice. It is a defence of tyranny as the only refuge from anarchy.

Of the actual misdemeanours gradually created in the way above described, the creation of some has really conformed to the true aims of the criminal law, while that of others has signally conflicted with those aims. Among those misdemeanours the recognition of which is attended with the greatest public advantage are *attempts* to commit grave crimes.

There is often a moral, and always a political, distinction between an inchoate and a consummate crime. It may often be that a person pauses on commencing to commit an offence and is brought to a better mind by the very imminence of his own further action. He has willed the first step in the offence and has taken it; but as yet has not willed, or at least has not taken, a further step. There is every reason for encouraging an offender to pause at this stage; and this may be effected by varying the penalty at each stage of the offence, assuming the offence to be a divisible one.

The difficulty is that, though the consummate crime may be in the highest degree definite, what is an attempt may be, in an equal degree, indefinite. In the one case the completed act throws a backward light upon the intention; in the other case the absence of a completed act renders the intention, at the best, ambiguous, and therefore one the true character of which must be collected from surrounding circumstances. Thus, when a homicide has been actually committed, it may indeed call for a very long and anxious inquiry to determine whether it is a murder, a manslaughter, or accidental and justifiable killing. But if no man has been killed, and the only evidence there is points to some one having injured another in a way which might possibly have resulted in death, the question whether the injury was an ineffectual attempt to murder or was a completed act of its kind must depend upon a far larger and more complex class of considerations.

So in the English offence of "misprision" of treason, which is, in fact, a sort of misdemeanour, though generally called by its own specific name, the offence is one that in some aspects might seem purely mental and therefore open to the most dangerously uncertain constructions. "Misprision of treason," says Blackstone, "consists of the bare knowledge and concealment of treason, without any degree of assent thereto." This concealment becomes criminal if the party apprised of the treason does not, as soon as conveniently may be, reveal it to some judge of assize or justice of the peace. Thus, in truth, the actual offence is the not revealing the treason in the way prescribed.

But the most remarkable illustration of the dangerous licence into which judicial legislation on criminal law is apt to run is supplied by the English law of conspiracy, a law which has been defended in some quarters on the very ground of the arbitrary power it places in the hands of judges, and of the limitations of public liberty which it renders possible under the cloak of legal prosecutions.

"The modern law of conspiracy," says Mr. R. S. Wright, in his erudite and exhaustive treatise on the subject, " has grown out of the application to cases of con-
" spiracy, properly so called, and as defined by the statute
" of the 33 Edw. I., of the early doctrine that since
" the gist of a crime was in the intent, a criminal intent
" manifested by any act done in furtherance of it might
" be punishable, although the act done did not amount in
" law to an actual attempt." Mr. Wright goes on to point

out how the doctrine gradually took form that the criminality of a conspiracy is not to be measured by the criminality of the object of the conspiracy, and that "it has long been established law that a combination to defraud may be criminal, although the proposed deceit is not such as would be criminal apart from the combination." It will be seen at once how inimical this principle is to public liberty, when it is recollected upon what uncertain and multifarious sorts of evidence the fact of conspiracy, that is, of an agreement between two or more persons to do acts of certain specific kinds, must generally be established. How vague and how far related to merely moral considerations might be the object of an indictable conspiracy will be understood from the following language of Lord Mansfield in 1773:—"Whatever is *contra bonos mores et decorum* the principles of our law prohibit, and the king's court, as the general censor and guardian of the public manners, is bound to restrain and punish." This passage, indeed, may be called the *reductio ad absurdum* of that theory of the criminal law which treats it as a direct instrument, more than anything else, of improving national morality. The mere description of the general principle which has underlain the English law of conspiracy is in itself a sufficient refutation of the theory because of the moral and political dangers it conceals under a most plausible outside.

Sometimes a crime is said to be aggravated, and even its name changed, if it be committed concurrently with other crimes, or by a person previously convicted of crimes of a like nature. In these cases, the moral condition of the prisoner as a subject of punishment is the only reason for altering the conception of the crime. The matter more properly belongs to the general consideration of punishment.

It has been intimated above that criminal law vacillates between two dispositions drawing it in opposite directions—one, that of bestowing excessive attention on the ethical condition of the possible offender; the other, that of exhibiting comparative indifference to this condition, the main attention being concentrated on the nature and consequences of the act. It is in its latter aspect that criminal law most widely diverges, both positively and negatively, from the requirements of current moral sentiment. Criminal law erects into public offences a number of acts to which the moralist is wholly indifferent, and forbears to take cognizance of a vast number of not dissimilar acts which the moralist regards with the gravest concern.

This arbitrary creation of offences is most conspicuous in the long and ever increasing list of what are sometimes called "police offences" in English law, and which nearly correspond with the *contraventions* of the French criminal code. They are an eminently modern invention, and indeed flow, partly, from complexities of social existence which have no parallel in former times; and, partly, from theories of the relation of the individual citizen to the whole organism of which he is a member which are likewise, in their popular predominance at least, entirely novel. The general subject of the province of Government, in its wider aspects, will be discussed in a later chapter. The necessity and consequences of multiplying the classes of petty offences having no relation, or having only an inverted relation, to public morality, may appropriately be examined here by way of introduction to the topic of the administration of criminal law.

It is of great importance in estimating the value of a system of criminal law, especially in reference to the smaller and more artificial offences, not to allow the judgment to be blinded by the modern apology which is so commonly made for bad legislation, to the effect that when a nation has the advantage of representative institutions and self-government, all jealousy of undue encroachment on public liberty by the law-making authority is out of the question. No one is henceforth held to be entitled to utter a protest against any whole class of laws, though he may suitably enough advocate the repeal of some laws and the enactment of others on the ground of the superior utility of the one over the other. Representative institutions (it is said), if adequate to their purpose, are a sufficient guarantee against widespread abuses of the legislative power, and the ultimate hold which every citizen has upon his own representative is such as to relieve him from any continuing anxiety as to wholesale aggressions being made, in the name of law, upon public liberty.

The value, however, of representative institutions as a security against despotism depends, first, upon the amount of public attention which is directed to legislation; secondly, upon the kind of machinery employed in executing the criminal law, and the facility of redress provided in case of excess or abuse by officers of the executive; thirdly, upon the legislation, at all its stages, being direct and not delegated to subordinate authorities. It is needless to add that the truly representative composition of the legislative body,—as being an exact mirror of the interests, claims, and sentiments of all classes and persons in the community,—and the absence of all laws which on the face of them sacrifice the liberty of many or all to the advantage, or luxurious pursuits, or voluptuous habits, of a few, are essential conditions precedent to the existence of any security at all against despotism introduced under the covert of an interminable series of police offences.

In modern States, and notably in England, which enjoys more credit than any other for the success of its parliamentary and representative institutions, amidst the mass of incessant legislation, the topics which attract public attention are necessarily extremely few, and are generally least of all such as most nearly touch the ultimate nerve of public liberty. These last topics are devoid of any party interest, and are either handed over to a knot of specialists inflamed with the glowing report of a one-sided committee of either House, or are hastily dispatched, at the bidding of a minister of the Crown, in a thin and jaded assembly, and at an hour of the night or a time of the year when even the show of an animated controversy can safely be eluded.

The danger is the greater from the enormous multitude of projects which are constantly being pressed upon Parliament by small professional or fanatical coteries with no object at heart but that of securing a fair field for the temporary trial of their own nostrum. Resistance is all the more difficult from the prevalent fashion in political argument of making the decision of every question turn solely upon the calculable consequences of adopting a certain course. In this way the advocate for a new repressive measure has an enormous advantage over any opponent who might venture to withstand him, for the former can usually calculate some good or specious consequences to arise from the measure; while the latter, shut out from availing himself of the best and most exhaustive catalogue of consequences implied in a *principle*, may be unable to exhibit in a tabulated form all the possible evils of the proposed law.

The second test of the value of representative institutions, as a security for public liberty, so far as this is affected by the criminal law, was said to be the nature of the machinery employed in executing the law and the facility for redress provided in cases of abuse. The execution of the criminal law demands the co-operation of a vast number of subordinate officials, necessarily not very far removed in point of education, culture, or moral sentiment from the members of that section of society amongst which breaches of law may be commonly looked for. At the same time, these officials are, from the nature of their duties, in the closest *rapport* with one another, and are likely to be over stimulated by all the solicitations of professional zeal. The result must be that while circumstances are such that the temptations to intimidation, brutality, and corruption are likely to abound, those exposed to the temptations are most unfavourably situated for resistance.

It, no doubt, is true that by a careful selection of the officials and by efficient management the possible mischiefs may be largely reduced. But it is to be noticed that under a representative, just as much as, or even more than, under any other system of government, those who govern the police will protect those persons best who are capable of making most noise. And yet these persons, being generally rich and influential by comparison, are the very persons who can the best protect themselves.

It is to be noted again that a single rash or unscrupulous police official can every day inflict an amount of damage on innocent persons which all the discretion of the rest of the force cannot be said to atone for. In the case of some offences the mere preferring of a groundless charge, even if it be instantly disproved, may inflict an irreparable injury; and there are some charges closely connected with the general moral character which are easily made, and yet which it may require a mass of not easily procurable evidence to disprove.

What has been hitherto said applies to the police under all possible systems of criminal law, and, therefore, much of the evil and danger is inevitable. All that can be done is to endeavour to limit the mischief, and to resort to real securities, and not to the fondly fancied immunity supposed to be provided by representative institutions.

The real securities that may be resorted to are (1) the creation of no crimes in which the criminal act is not capable of being described with the highest amount of definiteness; (2) the refusal to any class of police officials, however presumably respectable, of any general control, having relation to moral character, of any order of persons, other than (perhaps) convicted criminals still undergoing a reformatory discipline; (3) insistance on the necessity of procuring a warrant from a magistrate for the committal of a prisoner in all cases either before or immediately after his apprehension; (4) maintenance of the principle that no prisoner should be detained longer than a week in custody, whatever the ground of detention, without a public or (only if he prefers it, a private) magisterial examination, in which the burden of proof is entirely cast on the accuser, who must give his evidence on oath or in such other form as makes him judicially responsible, and who must submit himself to cross-examination by the accused or those who represent him; (5) ample provision for rendering the police legally responsible for malicious, corrupt, or grossly careless prosecutions.

The above are cardinal·principles of public liberty which have gradually, after long struggles, welded themselves into the very fabric of the English constitution, and which, in all the best-known crimes, are invariably recognized. There are, however, offences recently created, in an evil hour, by act of parliament, as to which not one of these principles is recognized.

The sufferers are poor, helpless, and obscure. The end sought carries with it a plausible show of sanitary precautions. Selfish and indolent men and women call it "freedom when themselves are free;" and there are even honest persons, especially some of the most loyal and professedly religious, who are haunted by a confused and indolent notion that whatever a "representative" assembly wills is right.

It was said, thirdly, that any great use of subordinate legislation, even in a representative government, is likely to lead to a dangerous abuse of the criminal law. Such subordinate legislation is a necessary consequence of what has already been spoken of as the excessive amount of work which befalls a representative assembly in the present day. For instance, the English parliament is constantly deputing to persons or bodies of persons, in greater or less dependence on itself, the task of creating a vast number of the rules of law which practically become portion of the criminal law of the country.

Such persons or bodies are the different departments of the Privy Council, Municipal Corporations, the Home Secretary, and the head of the Metropolitan Police. The rules thus made are, to all intents, criminal laws, inasmuch as the persons who infringe them are punished in a definite way, and the State does its utmost to find out who they are, and to bring them to justice. But the public control over these laws is extremely infirm and irregularly exercised, owing to the indirectness and secrecy with which they are made; and, unless they accidentally attach themselves to some question of current interest, or unless newspapers, in the dearth of more entertaining matter, bring them into notice, the fact of their coming into existence is likely to escape attention altogether.

There is one other danger to public liberty, in the

earlier stages of the execution of the criminal law, which must here be alluded to; that is, the danger encountered by foreigners or even others of being delivered up to another Government on the ground of crimes alleged to have been committed by them in the territory of that Government. The danger is twofold; first, that a foreign Government may demand the delivery either of one of its own citizens or of some else on the ground of the commission of an offence which, if committed, is no offence at all by the laws of the country in which the fugitive is now residing, or is identical only in name with some offence recognized as such in that country. The direct object in this case may be a purely political one, and the allegation of crime may be only a subterfuge. Secondly, the evidence upon which an accused would be put upon his trial may be very different in the two countries.

The safest precautions to take are those now universally taken by England in all her Extradition Treaties. By a recent statute the offences in view of which extradition treaties may be made, though very numerous, are carefully tabulated. The same evidence which is needed for committal in cases of offences alleged to have been committed here is needed in the case of offences alleged to have been committed elsewhere. And at every stage of the proceedings opportunity is provided for the magistrate, a judge, or a secretary of State, to release the accused on the ground that a political motive is at the root of the charge.

The three points to which attention must chiefly be directed both in estimating and guarding the securities for personal liberty, as respects encroachments by the executive in any particular country, are apprehension, detention, and trial.

No persons or class of persons must be under the cringing fear of having imputed to them offences of which they are innocent, and of being taken into custody in consequence of such imputation. They must not be liable to be detained in custody without so much as a *prima facie* case being made out, such as, in the opinion of a responsible judicial officer, raises a presumption of guilt. They must not be liable to be detained for an indefinite time without having the question of their guilt or innocence investigated by the best attainable methods. When the fact comes to be inquired into, the best attainable methods of eliciting the truth must be used. In default of any one of these securities public liberty must be said to be proportionately at a very low ebb.

Assuming, then, that, in favour of public liberty, all crimes have been accurately defined by law, and that the police have been carefully selected and properly instructed; that, furthermore, every precaution has been taken to secure, at the earliest possible moment, the co-operation of a judicial authority such as is implied in the need of procuring a *warrant* for the apprehension of an accused person; and that the accused is not finally committed for trial without a formal preliminary investigation before a competent authority, nor without full opportunity being offered to the accused of explaining away suspicious appearances; the next essential conditions of public liberty are that the accused be not needlessly kept in prison if his appearance at his final trial can be ensured in some other way, and that the time of his trial be neither too long distant, nor be capable of change at the arbitrary will of the executive.

These two last conditions are ensured in England, and in those countries (including all the American States) which have borrowed their criminal procedure from England, by the constitutional principle that excessive "bail" shall not be required, and by the Habeas Corpus Act and the later amendments of it.

The question of "bail," or security for appearance at the time of trial, is one presenting peculiar difficulties, inasmuch as the propriety of letting an accused person out on bail, and the quantity of bail to be demanded, must necessarily depend upon a variety of circumstances peculiar to each particular case. Such circumstances are the atrocity of the offence and the punishment attached to it; the pecuniary means of the prisoner and of the persons whom he is able to present as ready to become securities for him; and even the general character of the evidence as already, at such an early stage of the proceedings, disclosed. The estimate of the value of the various considerations thus involved must be a purely discretionary matter, and, in many cases, no two magistrates would come to exactly the same decision. Thus it is impossible to direct magistrates by law when to require bail, and how much to require, without running a great risk of thereby frequently defeating the ends of justice. The discreet selection of magistrates and the publicity of the proceedings, accompanied by insistence upon the maxim that "excessive bail" is not to be demanded, are the solitary (though by no means valueless) safeguards of public liberty when threatened in this respect.

The English Habeas Corpus Act, introduced and carried with the utmost difficulty in Charles II.'s time, and having for its object the providing an effectual machinery for obtaining the ancient writ of "Habeas Corpus," is far the most stringent remedy ever devised in any country against illegal detention in prison and capricious postponement of trial. It has been extended so as to apply to all persons kept in forcible restraint or captivity, even where the officers of the executive are not the responsible persons.

The effect of the statute and of its more recent amendments is to enable any one detained anywhere against his will to have, at the shortest possible notice, the legality of his detention publicly investigated and adjudicated upon; and, in the event of the detention proving illegal, to obtain his instant release. In some cases a warrant of commitment for treason or felony, or a legal conviction, may be in itself a sufficient return to the writ, and may obviate further proceedings. But where such exceptions do not apply, heavy penalties are threatened against the judge who refuses to issue the writ and against inferior officers who do not execute it. Special provisions are made in the act for speedy trial of prisoners at a definitely named time.

It is impossible to read of or call to mind the long and cruel imprisonments for purely political purposes which, within very recent times, were so common in Rome and Naples, without insisting that the only effectual security against the possible occurrence of such abuses in any State is the enactment and loyal support of such a statute as this. There have been times indeed in which the English legislature has taken the bold step of temporarily suspending the Habeas Corpus Act, both in England and (more recently) in Ireland. But to give such uncontrolled power to the executive as this suspension carries with it implies either that a condition of civil war (and therefore the abrogation for the time of all law) is very nearly reached, or else that there is entertained a perilous confidence in that very Executive authority, the folly or supineness of which may, probably enough, have occasioned the evils which invite the remedy.

Assuming, then, that the prisoner is brought to trial in due course of law, the next question that presents itself is as to the mode of trial which is conducive in the highest degree to the vindication of innocence and the exposure of guilt. At this point one great institution which has prevailed most extensively in England, though it is now being copied by many of the European States, that of trial by jury, as applied in criminal procedure, claims attention.

The institution of trial by jury and the reason of its universal popularity would seem to have a close connection with what has already been pointed out as the moral element which is so conspicuous in the analysis of the most common legal crimes. The estimation of this moral element is somehow felt to be more satisfactory entrusted to a body of ordinary persons without any predisposition to adopt artificial distinctions, and without any technical training, than to a judge whose professional habits of thought might induce him to leave out of account some of the rougher elements of moral judgment which are the basis of action in common life. Furthermore, there is no doubt a scarcely conscious sentiment that the solemn act of awarding punishment demands the acquiescence of a representative body of the people as a whole; and that the jury, however casually chosen, forms such a representative body.

These explanations of the popular attachment to jury-trial are wholly independent of the more obvious reasons for introducing and adhering to it as the best possible corrective to such influences as, even in the best organized systems of administration, the executive may still contrive to exert over the judicial bench. The questions as to the number of persons required to constitute a jury, and as to the number of the jurymen required to assent to a verdict, are questions rather of calculable convenience than of political principle. A larger number, however, may well be required to constitute a jury for trying the heavier crimes; and, instead of requiring unanimity, the consent of some large number, short of all, would seem rather expedient in order to provide against the occasional presence of excessive prejudice, ignorance, or irrationality.

The fact already noticed that trial by jury supplies a popular and not unsuitable mode of estimating the moral element that enters into criminality also discloses the source of a serious difficulty which attends that form of trial. In any case that presents itself, the complete judicial investigation resolves itself into two parts which are always quite distinct from one another, though they may be blended in procedure; or, from its comparatively insignificant importance in any given case, one part may occasionally seem lost in the other.

These two parts are the inquiry (1) what is the rule of law which is alleged to have been infringed, and the inquiry (2) whether any given person has really infringed it. The second inquiry may present itself in three different forms, according as the fact of the infringement is doubtful, the identity of the person accused with the person who has committed the crime is doubtful, or both the one and the other are doubtful. The simplest cases, for instance, are where there is abundant and wholly unchallenged evidence that (say) a murder has been committed by some one, and the only question is whether the prisoner at the bar is the person who has committed the murder; or where there is good reason for doubt whether a blow was struck with intention to kill, but there is no doubt that it was the prisoner who struck the blow.

It is not, however, all criminal cases in which the line can be sharply drawn between questions of fact such as these, according to their various degrees of complexity, and what are called questions of law. In many cases the rule of law and the state of the facts are so implicated one with the other that it is very hard, if not impossible, to relegate one part of the inquiry to one tribunal and the other part to another.

In countries where trial by jury prevails, and most

decisively so in England, it is customary to reserve all questions in which the existence or interpretation of a rule of law is involved to a skilled and professional judge, and to leave all other questions to the jury. But, in some cases, the previous decision as to what is matter of law and what matter of fact, though a purely logical rather than a legal question, is usually left to the judge; and, through this loophole, a dangerous opportunity has been afforded for the encroachment of judges upon the province of the more popularly constituted tribunal.

It is true the line between the two classes of questions must, in each case of difficulty, be drawn by some one, and the judge, in all cases where he is not deflected from the right path by what Bentham called a "sinister" interest, is more likely to be competent to give a correct logical decision than a casually chosen jury. The only precaution in favour of public liberty that can be taken is to guard by statute the province of the jury in all those cases in which at once questions of law and of fact are particularly apt to be intermingled, and in which the political impartiality of judges, as a class, could in critical times least be relied upon.

Mr. Fox's Libel Act, which practically entitled juries to determine the question of whether an alleged libel was a libel or not, and freed them from the restraint, imposed upon them by high judicial authority, of being compelled to confine themselves to the question of publication,—the libellous quality of the writing being left for investigation by the judge,—affords a specimen both of the mode in which matters of law and of fact do become blended in practice, and of the mode in which, for purposes of political security, an arbitrary separation between them can be effected by statute.

Not indeed that this or any other statute can exempt juries from the necessity of finding their verdicts in accordance with law, and, therefore, of deferring to the guidance of the judge as to what the state of the law is. Mr. Fox's Libel Act gives juries as much freedom of acquitting or convicting in cases of Libel as juries have in the case of other crimes, but no more. Juries, indeed, are not, by the law of England, punishable for finding a perverse verdict, if it be not a corrupt one, and in criminal cases there is no appeal from the verdict of a jury. But it is none the less a strongly recognized moral and political duty of jurymen which is enforced by every sort of sanction, short of a legal one, to measure the guilt (if any) of the prisoner by the legal description of the offence, and not to strain the legal description of the offence so as to adapt it to the moral situation or deserts of the prisoner.

There is always a perceptible tendency, in the case of some of the most important class of crimes, to introduce, even with the connivance of the judge, a principle of haphazard justice or Lynch law which is only a rough alternative for anarchy. In the case of seditious or malicious libels, in that of seditious conspiracies, and in that of murder, the reluctance of juries to be guided by any definite legal rule, and the tendency of judges to warp the existing rules so as to cover or exclude the case before them, is a patent and ominous fact.

In France this tendency has given rise to the introduction of the verdict of "extenuating circumstances;" and in England it is proposed in some quarters to leave it to the jury to determine whether an offence which is murder according to the legal description shall be classed as in the "first" or in the "second degree," the capital penalty being assigned to the former class alone. There are, no doubt, peculiar difficulties in distinguishing the province of the judge and the jury in the case of murder, both because of the varieties of psychological eccentricity which, through the insufficiency of legal expression, are necessarily comprehended in one legal category, and because the penalty usually assigned to murder is neither susceptible of reparation, graduation, or recall. The French practice and the suggested English one have this in common that they refer the question of the infliction of the highest punishment to the casual sympathies or antipathies of a particular jury. In such circumstances moral considerations (including all the false moral notions prevalent in a partially educated and, perhaps, highly inflamed section of the community) are likely to have an overwhelming weight. What is an offence in one court is not one in another; and what is punished with death to-day is held to be an act attributable to the most generous and worthy motives to-morrow.

It is not probable that any solution of the real difficulty will be discovered so long as capital punishment is retained. The prerogative of pardon reserved to the executive is one familiar and largely used mode of solution. But, to the extent to which it is used, it induces insecurity in the administration of law, and counteracts the exemplary effect of a public trial and sentence. Not indeed that, in view of the rough and imperfect instrumentality at hand for discovering the truth, this ultimate preventive of cruel injustice can be dispensed with. But the more publicity that can be given to the proceedings of those who advise the exercise of the prerogative, and the more intelligible the grounds of the exercise, the less will be the amount of anarchy which the prerogative itself tends to introduce into the administration of criminal law.

In the whole course of criminal proceedings, from the apprehension of an accused person to the moment of his conviction or acquittal, there are two celebrated methods of procedure to some extent opposed to one another, and which may be roughly characterized as the English and the Foreign method. The two theories upon which the methods severally rest are closely connected with opposed views of the functions of Government and of the relation of the individual citizen to the State.

The whole tendency of the events which make up English history has been to develop the smaller groups, such as those of the family, the parish, the county, and the borough, at the expense, in some measure, of the centralized force of the greatest group of all, the State. Now, it is through the dignified self-consciousness and through the constant exercise of his faculties which membership of a confined group at once necessitates and develops that the individual person acquires a consciousness of moral claim and right which is anterior and superior to that of subordination to any system of mere external force.

It is true that important institutions have been constantly developing the relation of the smaller groups to the great one, otherwise the State could never have survived. Such institutions were the relics (long abiding) of the feudal system, the growing system of parliamentary representation, the circuits of the judges finally organized by Henry II., the central courts at Westminster, and the personal connection of the Church hierarchy and the aristocracy with the court. Parallels to these two sets of opposed influences, dissolving and uniting, could no doubt be produced from the histories of France, Germany, Italy, Spain.

But the peculiarity of the phenomenon, as exhibited in England, is that (owing, among other causes, to its insular position, to the peculiar circumstances of the Norman conquest, and to the course taken by the Reformation in this country) the free reciprocal action of the two sets of rival influences, centripetal and centrifugal, has proceeded with unbroken regularity for more than eight hundred years. The inheritance of this advantageous position (for such it must be named) has been reaped by the United States.

The consequence of this course which the development of English life has taken is that it has become a rooted constitutional principle that the pursuit of the guilty must be conducted, from first to last, with the utmost caution not to accuse or to implicate the innocent. It has been felt in England that criminal law and its administration are everywhere the natural avenues through which the executive encroaches on personal liberty. At some stages in the progress of the nation, the State trials afforded scandalous instances of this fact. But the national institutions and the fixed sentiment of liberty in this country were too strong for the example to spread or to last. In better times, the notion of individual claims to immunity from unfounded charges recovered itself, and became more and more connected with the demand that accused persons should be treated with the utmost indulgence and even tenderness up to the time of their conviction.

It was not, indeed, till very recent times that prisoners were allowed the help of counsel, or that the rules of evidence were construed as strictly against them as for them; but the origin of this difference no doubt lay in a belief that it was for the prosecutor to make out every part of his case so conclusively as to admit of no sort of conceivable defence.

Nor did this defence of the innocent spring from any softness in the English character or disposition to be lenient to criminals; on the contrary, the English have been exceptionally harsh, and almost savage, in awarding punishment to convicted criminals. In speaking of a severe statute passed in Henry VIII.'s reign, by which death was awarded as a punishment for persistent vagabondage Mr. Froude (vol. i. p. 86) says—" In point of justice as well "as of prudence, it harmonized with the iron temper of "the age, and it answered well for the government of a "fierce and powerful people, in whose hearts lay an intense "hatred of rascality, and among whom no one need have "lapsed into evil courses except by deliberate preference "for them. The moral substance of the English must have "been strong indeed when it admitted of such stringent "treatment; but, on the whole, they were ruled as they "preferred to be ruled; and if wisdom may be tested by "success, the manner in which they passed the great crisis "of the Reformation is the best justification of their "prince."

It is not saying too much with respect to what is characteristically the foreign method of criminal procedure to allege that, in the administration of criminal law, considerations of public liberty are wholly neglected. It is of course essential to the well-being of a State that most criminals should be detected and punished; but this must be done so as to be as much as possible consistent with attaining other equally important ends, one of which is the maintenance of personal liberty.

It may be that the English method, especially in the actual conduct of a trial, by not admitting the evidence of a prisoner, errs too much in one direction—indeed, so much as often to defeat the object intended. For an innocent person may only be able to establish his innocence by giving a connected account of a series of transactions which, taken by themselves, and apart from such explanatory evidence, are wholly adverse to him. It might be better at the least to allow a prisoner to be examined by the judge, the English rules of evidence which confine the whole inquiry to matters immediately connected with the actual crime being quite sufficient protection to the innocent against inquisitorial and irrelevant questions.

But the Continental method, of allowing unlimited license to the judge to parley throughout the trial with the prisoner, must be considered in connection with the other and preliminary parts of the proceedings. After an infinity of hypotheses, in the course of provisionally supporting each of which any number of innocent persons may have been imprisoned and privately examined, the police, with the help of the public prosecutor, frame a document the general upshot of which is to identify the accused with the person who committed the crime. The proof of this identification may depend upon an indefinite number of minute circumstances connected with the biography of the prisoner, and with his moral, social, and political proclivities from his youth up. In itself, so long a chain of circumstantial evidence may be of the highest value; but the evil is that it is this document which furnishes the groundwork of the judge's examination of the accused.

Such a course is obviously putting an innocent person at the grossest disadvantage. The very completeness and nicety of the theory is already a presumption against the prisoner; while his memory and habits of observation and introspection may wholly fail him in the attempt to explain the acts, sentiments, and motives of the past. No doubt such a system generally convicts the guilty, but, even where it does not also convict the innocent, it is an outrageous cruelty to practise upon them.

The general topic of *evidence* will be more conveniently treated in the chapter on the law of civil procedure, though there is one species of evidence which, considering its bearing on public liberty, properly belongs to this place,—that is, the evidence procurable from the alleged admission or so-called "confessions" of the accused. It is obvious that the admissions of an accused person, whether obtained before his apprehension or after it, may supply the best possible evidence concerning the fact in dispute. In some cases, it may be the only evidence procurable; and, in other cases, it may be accompanied by such strong confirmatory evidence from other quarters as to form an important link in a chain of criminating or exculpating proofs. This sort of evidence, however, when obtained out of court and not under the eye of the judge and the public, is open to two serious objections.

In the first place,—owing to the idiosyncrasy of particular persons, to the strangely mixed motives which are known to induce persons to confess crimes they have never committed, and to the obstacles which naturally lie in the way of obtaining an accurate report of what the alleged confession really amounts to,—alleged confessions are not only unreliable in general, but it is extremely difficult, and often impossible, to test the degree of reliability in any particular case.

But, in the second place, it is in the highest degree impolitic and opposed to public liberty to encourage a habit of making confessions, and still more, one of extorting or even of inviting them. From the ignorance of the law which generally prevails among those who are most frequently tempted to break it, and from incapacity to apprehend the relevancy of questions put to them, or the verbal import of their own answers, persons wholly innocent are frequently in danger of confessing to crimes they have never committed, and they who have committed one sort of crime of confessing to another.

English law, indeed, has done its utmost in outward form to surround prisoners with safeguards against the consequences of confessions elicited under any sort of pressure direct or indirect. But the number of alleged voluntary confessions cited in courts of justice every day as made to policemen by prisoners after their apprehension proves the impotency of these safeguards. The position of an accused person is of itself, apart from all extrinsic influence, wholly unfavourable to freedom of thought and act. Stupor, surprise, sense of novelty in the situation, and, most frequently of all, hope of conciliating the police by forbearing to give further trouble, all operate in favour of producing involuntary, and therefore generally worthless, confessions.

But the evil of encouraging the police to procure confessions is greater even than that involved in the particular injustice which the admission of them as evidence generally works. It has been seen that the hardest task a State has to engage in is to control the activity of the subordinate officers of the executive without compromising public order. To permit these officers to invite confessions of offences is to accord an illimitable and wholly uncontrolled extension to their functions. Instead of being the trusted and respected guardians of the public peace, and the allies of all in their war against the unhappy propensities of a few, they easily become transformed into the common enemies of all, suspected, hated, and feared by all.

It is needless to say that this consequence is most inexorably certain where a system of detective police undistinguished by a uniform, is used. The immediate result is that, instead of actively seeking for extrinsic evidence, the whole energy of the police is diverted into adroitly bringing pressure to bear upon the minds of those they suspect. The next result is a silent and widespread terrorism, and the birth of a corrupt brood of spies and informers. The final result is the immolation of public liberty, while its names and forms may still be scrupulously cherished.

Such a fate overtook Rome in its most brilliant days; and in the modern multiplication of laws, and the reckless extension of the province of government, coupled with the crowd of competing sanitary, economic, and social theories, loudly crying out for legislative recognition, may be seen signs of a like calamity befalling the most outwardly civilized states of Europe. The only bulwarks against the danger are to be sought in a deep and widely diffused conviction of the meaning and value of personal liberty and in a firm grasp of the immutable principles of national and individual morality.

Next in importance to the measure of the security afforded by the criminal law for public liberty in the mode of apprehending and trying alleged offenders, are the sorts of *punishments* to which convicted persons are subject, and the principles upon which the degree of punishment to be assigned in particular cases is estimated. The consideration of punishment is a very perplexed one, as it is difficult to confine it within the limits of any one branch of enquiry, and, therefore, it is equally claimed or appropriated by very opposite classes of reasoners who, through their combined efforts, somehow rather hamper than forward one another's work. It is quite possible, indeed, to isolate the question of criminal punishment in a variety of ways, though, by so doing, very erroneous and mischievous conclusions would be come to. The difficulty rather is to look at all sides of the subject at once, and to attribute its true relative value, and no more, to each separate class of considerations.

The first question to be answered is, as to the superior value of fixing by legislation an immutable scale of punishments, no discretion whatever being left to the judge as to the degree of punishment to be applied in the case of a prisoner convicted of a given crime; or of leaving to the judge either some, or an indefinite amount of, discretion in applying the punishment. This question cannot be answered without reviewing the several ends of punishments under the criminal law, an enquiry which will serve also to answer the next question to be proposed, —that of the most expedient forms of punishment for the different classes of crimes.

The commonly alleged ends of criminal punishment are, first and foremost, the prevention of a recurrence of the crime, either through the act of the convicted person himself, or through that of others; secondly, the moral advantage, generally, of the convicted person. This second end hardly comes within the purport of law, and much confusion of thought has flowed from fixing undue attention upon it and forgetting its relation to the former.

The true position of this alleged end is that of marking a limit to the modes of pursuing the former and only essential end. In marking such a limit it need not be said that the moral claims of the convicted person to being put in the best possible condition for retrieving his character are about as strong as can well be imagined. It is the great moral discovery of the present age that very much can be done in this direction without any sacrifice of objects more important than itself. Economical considerations, calling attention to the loss entailed on the community through the perversely conducted and wasted life of a single citizen, tend in the same direction. Sympathy and humanity, again, as they become richly developed in the community at large, cannot tolerate the infliction of any further amount of punishment than the public good or safety imperatively demands, while the same sentiments resent the infliction of certain kinds of punishment as an indignity to human nature, not to be submitted to as the price of any public good whatsoever.

In the invention and measurement of criminal punishments there is, undoubtedly, the widest possible field for the operation of instincts of benevolence and moral justice. The inducement to indulge these instincts freely is all the more potent when it is remembered to what extent society in general, by its selfish arrangements, its laxity in moral judgments, its encouragement of needless inequalities, and its permission of ignorance, is largely responsible for every crime that is committed. It is bound to make what reparation it can to the offender whose crime its own sins have nursed into life. Thus it is impossible to intensify the argument too strongly to the effect that the main end of criminal punishment must be carried out as far as possible in harmony with the secondary end of achieving the moral reformation of the particular offender.

But in some quarters there is a tendency to seek for no other end in devising and applying criminal punishments than that of reformation; or else, through pre-occupation in pursuit of this last end, to neglect to take the steps necessary for securing the higher end of enforcing universal obedience to the criminal law.

If a criminal law is wisely constructed, and based upon the needs of the whole community, and not upon the arbitrary and tyrannical prejudices of a class, general obedience to that law is the first and highest requisite of political existence. Want of general obedience implies approaching social dissolution. Universal disobedience implies that the State no longer exists. Thus the question of the reformation of any number of individual offenders is out of all proportion insignificant as compared with that of securing general obedience to law. The two cannot even be put in scales over against one another. They are incommensurable quantities.

Assuming, then, that the first object to be kept in

view is that of securing general obedience to law, it remains to be seen how punishments can best be chosen and measured in order to achieve this end, it not being forgotten that, in selecting between two kinds or degrees of punishment, equally efficacious otherwise, that is to be preferred which is least incompatible with the moral reformation of the culprit.

Criminal punishments may operate in the prevention of crimes in three distinct ways. Some punishments, as those of death, transportation, and imprisonment, by removing the offender temporarily or permanently from the midst of the society, to that extent forcibly prevent him from repeating his crime. The mutilation of those members which have been the instrument of committing crimes had a like effect, when such punishments were in use.

All punishments, again, quite apart from their actual quality or degree of severity, serve to mark in a distinct and public way the triumph of society over the devices or mischievous violence of a recalcitrant citizen. The actual infliction of the punishment re-establishes, as it were, the violated order. It reasserts in emphatic terms outraged authority. It proves decisively the weakness and puerility of guilt when brought into conflict with the mighty force, moral and physical, of the whole State. It is to be noticed that the success of this sort of operation must wholly depend upon the certainty of convictions and the rarity of misadventures in the administration of justice.

It happens, however, fortunately for mankind, that the lighter the punishment the more infallible is the process of convicting the guilty and of liberating the innocent. When the punishments are severe, or any attempt is made to assimilate, by a spurious and most misleading form of calculation, the suffering they cause with the hypothetical suffering resulting from the crime, convictions become proportionately irregular and uncertain. The attention of the tribunal (especially when it is a popular one) is unconsciously diverted from the consideration of evidence—a subject quite enough to occupy the whole mind—and is directed to the penal consequences of an adverse decision. Thus, in cases where the punishment is either very severe, or, under the circumstances of the particular case, wholly disproportioned to the moral guilt, and yet is inflexibly fixed, every shred of favourable testimony is laid hold of with the utmost possible zeal, and the prisoner is acquitted, not because it is believed he is innocent, but because it is too painful to encounter in thought the possibility of his punishment. Such an extreme crisis is not of course of very frequent occurrence; but so far as punishments are vindictive in their aspect, harsh in their quality, and admitting of no discretionary graduation by the judge, to that extent verdicts are likely to be determined at least as much by the promptings of sympathy as by the weight of evidence.

It may be looked for, at no distant day, that the whole vindictive theory of punishments, and the use of harsh and cruel punishments, shall have wholly vanished from the criminal code of every civilized State. It is a change which, no doubt, cannot be introduced all at once, but must be gradually approximated to. The increasingly numerous and humane advocates of reformatory movements will contribute much in this direction, though too often with an imperfect apprehension of all the ends in view.

The third mode in which criminal punishments operate is the coarsest and least worthy one, as appealing to the lowest and most cowardly feelings of man's nature. It is that mode, however, which seems to many superficial legislators the only one worthy to be taken into account. The mode is that of inflicting the exact amount of physical suffering which it is believed is sufficient to counterpoise the pleasure sought by the commission of the crime. Any such affected balance of a good and an evil must be extremely delusive; first, because any one contemplating the commission of a crime unconsciously takes into account, not only the actual punishment, but also the certainty of the punishment following the crime, and the date at which, if at all, it will follow; secondly, the moment of temptation to commit a crime is seldom, and least of all in the case of the worst educated people, the moment of the most discreet calculation.

It is true that fixed associations may gradually be formed in the minds of a whole population, founded on the connection of punishments and crimes; but this will be only a general association, and in very few cases will it be the association of a given crime with its corresponding punishment. Unless a person has himself actually committed the crime and then undergone the punishment, there is no force sufficiently strong to drive home such a purely arbitrary association. No doubt, in countries in which the crime of murder is punished with death, a popular association between the crime and the punishment is common enough. But there is some good reason to believe that this association is rarely of service in saving a person contemplating murder from the crime, inasmuch as ordinary persons (especially when in great turmoil of mind) seldom generalize sufficiently to present clearly before their own imaginations the exact legal name and description of the wrongful act they are about to perpetrate.

All these arguments tend in the same direction, that is, to establish the principles (1) that the most expedient quality and scale of punishments must be discovered by experience and not anticipated by deference to ancient customs, to prejudice, to vindictiveness, or to fallacious resemblances between the crime and the punishment; (2) that the least severe punishments are likely to be the most certain, and the most certain punishments the most effectual; (3) that the greater the latitude of discretion left to the judge the less pernicious are severe punishments; but that under a system of very light punishments, the reasons for admitting such latitude are proportionately less cogent.

The two propositions that the quality and degree of punishment which ought to be inflicted can only be determined by experience; and that, if punishments be not very light, the purpose of punishment can only be carried into effect by leaving to the judge a considerable amount of discretionary power in meting it out, involve certain logical consequences which are of the highest degree of importance, and yet the force of which is often very imperfectly apprehended.

If the nature of punishment is to be fixed, not in accordance with the dictates of inveterate custom, or with some antecedent conception of the appositeness of the punishment to the internal characteristics of the crime, but in view of its probable efficaciousness as tested by actual experience, then must punishments be constantly varying with the varying circumstances of advancing civilization. No punishment but one involving superfluous cruelty can be regarded as permanently excluded from the category of possible punishments; nor is it possible to affirm of any kind of punishment, however long disused, that it may not, in certain conditions of society, have to be recurred to again.

Punishment must have a relation not only to the physical apprehensions and moral susceptibilities of the nation taken as a whole, but of the small section of a nation in the midst of which certain classes of crimes happen to become prevalent. It may occur that, owing to general social causes, a small and definite stratum of the population has, in one or more particular respects, become shut out from the general influences of civilization which have permeated all the rest. Some particular crimes of the most odious sort may linger or revive here long after their very names and possibility have been all but forgotten everywhere else. Such an occasional experience is familiar in all highly developed States, and, in addition to other more hopeful agencies, those implied in the proportionately invigorated activity of the criminal law must not be neglected.

The sort of crimes which most frequently present themselves in this spasmodic form are setting fire to buildings or other property, violent assaults on the person, and brutal offences of all sorts against women and children. So soon as, in any festering corner of the community, the habit of committing such offences as these becomes anything like frequent, the first object of the criminal legislator is to break the habit at once, and absolutely. For this purpose he may have temporarily to resort to the use of punishments which have been long wisely discarded, and which, if further extended or even prolonged beyond the immediate necessity, would tend to national demoralization or would go far to counteract the best efforts that are being made in favour of the reformation of offenders.

The danger of adopting such punishments even provisionally is that, owing to the indolence of legislators in removing bad laws compared with their alacrity in providing the first remedy that comes to hand to meet a pressing emergency, such punishments readily become familiar and immovable portions of the legal system. The result is that, so often as a real necessity arises for exceptional penal legislation, the supporters and opponents of stringent modes of punishment become at once distributed into sharply divided and hostile camps. The one party call for a permanent increase in severity of punishment. The others deprecate any change whatever.

The only solution of such a difficulty is to be sought for in so wise and calm an appreciation, on both sides, of the true ends of punishment as may lead the one party patiently to acquiesce in the adoption of the only immediately efficacious remedy which, in accordance with the best attested evidence, the circumstances seem to admit of; and the other party to join with those they have been wont to regard as their adversaries, in securing an instant repeal of the anomalous laws so soon as ever the emergency which called for them can fairly be said to be over.

The value of leaving to the presiding judge a large amount of discretion in the assignment of punishment depends upon the importance of two distinct considerations. One is that of putting special obstacles in the way of those who, by repeated convictions, show themselves to be peculiarly exposed to temptations in certain definite directions. In some cases the legislature itself assigns an aggravation of punishment in the case of repeated crimes. In other cases (as is usual in England) the legislature simply allows to the judges a wider latitude in the assignment of punishment when the prisoner has, by previous conviction, displayed either a special propensity to commit certain offences or a character so depraved as to be beyond hope of being impressed by the ordinary penal sanctions. Similar principles apply to conjoint crimes whether of the same or of a different nature.

The other consideration which enforces the general value of leaving to the presiding judge a large amount of discretionary power in the matter of punishment is the importance of graduating the punishment in proportion to the varied shades of moral guilt.

It is true that this can only be a subordinate object, though the transparent conformity of legal to moral judgments cannot but conduce largely to carrying out the primary object of criminal law, that of, by some means or other, however coarse and mechanical, preventing the commission of crime. Nevertheless it is of great importance to render the administration of criminal justice as popular, and the grounds of sentences as intelligible, as possible; and this can only be effected by reproducing to some extent within the walls of a court of justice the opinion and judgment of the better part of the community outside. It is also true, as has just been shown above, that the worse men are, the more dangerous they are, and therefore a rough moral analysis of the general character of a culprit, over and above reference to previous crimes, can hardly be declined by the judge in determining the punishment. But when a judge enters upon such an analysis, however meagre the materials to his hand, he instantly passes beyond the limits of a merely legal inquiry.

Evidence of character may be produced either in an earlier stage of the proceedings to show that it is not probable a particular person committed the special crime charged; or to show after conviction, that, though it is true he did commit it, yet the act was so contrary to what might have been expected from his general disposition as to suggest that he must have been exposed to peculiar and rare temptations, and so to make it seem unlikely that either he or another man like him would do a similar act on another occasion.

Thus the judge is induced to pay regard, first, to

the fact of the legally defined crime having been committed by the person convicted; then to the surrounding circumstances which give the legal crime its peculiar moral complexion, whatever that is; and lastly, to the general or special antecedents of the prisoner. Out of all these elements he forms a rough moral judgment; and having regard first of all to the purely practical or political aims previously adverted to, he proceeds further to qualify the penalty in accordance with the degree of moral heinousness in the criminal act. The publicity of the moral teaching thus conveyed is of great value if only the moral criterion applied is a sound one, and so long as the main purpose of the criminal law, that of the prevention of crimes, is not sacrificed or imperilled.

The treatment of lunatics and of youthful criminals forms one of the most anxious parts of penal legislation, and the methods most in use in modern times are far from being satisfactory or even capable of scientific justification. The condition of insanity is not of that sharply defined character which English criminal law (for instance) supposes. Insanity is notoriously allowed to admit of an indefinite number of kinds and grades, and widely to differ in the case of different patients.

As has been already seen, the well-known tests supplied by the English criminal law by no means exhaust the possible conditions of lunacy, and it must be impossible to frame a definition which can quite keep pace with the researches of science or with the strange varieties of abnormal action,—ever afresh presenting themselves,—of mind and body. The only prudent course then, is, in each particular case in which the defence of insanity is set up, to investigate by the best attainable medical tests whether, at the time of committing the alleged crime, the muscles and the will were in the degree of health needed for voluntary action and whether the faculty of forming an intention existed in that degree of health necessary to form the particular sort of intention which is an essential constituent of the crime charged.

In estimating intention in such a case, it must be presumed or ascertained that the accused has his general faculties in such a healthful condition as to place him in the same situation as is occupied by any average person in the community with respect to the question whether the act is, or might be, forbidden by law. Thus there are general conditions of health to be inquired into, and also special conditions. It may indeed result that the prisoner was partially responsible, but not wholly so. He was quite sane enough to commit a crime, but not the actual or the whole crime charged.

This suggests the expediency of having a range of punishments specially set apart for the insane. It is certainly cruel and illogical to send a number of legally innocent persons *en masse* to a criminal lunatic asylum, wholly irrespective of the shades of their moral guilt, and solely on the ground of the accidental legal aspects of the unhappy calamity to which their disease has given rise.

The value of a reformatory or penitentiary system as a supplement to criminal law cannot be well overrated. It may, however, be doubted whether the application of such a violent penalty to boys (involving complete and permanent separation from all home ties) can safely be trusted to subordinate judges, or is at all appropriate to any except (after cogent proof) the most incorrigible offenders. There is distressing evidence the other way, and it is much to be feared that an over zeal in favour of a special mode of reclamation may operate as a serious invasion of public liberty, and, in not a few instances, occasion intolerable hardship.

CHAPTER XI.

THE LAW OF CIVIL PROCEDURE.

THERE is one large department of law which occupies a conspicuous place in both modern and ancient legal systems, and which it might seem proper to explore before passing to Laws of Procedure. This department is that which contains the law of what are called *delicts, civil injuries*, or, in English law, *torts*.

The Law of Delicts, however, has two distinct aspects, and it is only in one of these that it can be scientifically considered apart from other portions of the law. In one of these aspects, the Law of Delicts brings into distinct notice for the first time a number of rights, in themselves of the highest importance, yet which have not been previously considered under any other former head of law. Such are rights to personal liberty of locomotion, rights to personal security, rights to the essential conditions of health, rights to be fairly spoken about and written about.

In some codes these rights are superficially mentioned in an early portion of the code, but they are in themselves of too vague and indeterminate a nature to admit of being described with any precision, apart from the consideration of definite modes of infringement. These modes are capable of being accurately announced and limited; and, historically speaking, it is not till these modes have been discovered by experience that the reality, the value, and the extent of the rights is recognized. Thus, in one of its aspects, the law of civil injuries—which includes, among other matters, the mode of violating the general class of rights above described—affords the earliest introduction to this class of rights. These rights are obviously of the utmost importance to the welfare of the community, and they afford the most distinct proof of the function which law performs in defending the individual personality of the several members of all the constituent groups of which the State is composed.

It is different with the other leading classes of rights, such as the rights arising from special relationship, rights of ownership, and rights of contract. Most of these rights admit of being described and limited with the utmost precision; and therefore there is a certain convenience in treating all the rights together by themselves, and all the possible modes of infringing the rights also separately by themselves.

It might be supposed that these two portions of the law would exactly correspond, or, at least, be complementary, to each other. But, owing chiefly to historical causes, there are many rights—especially rights of ownership—which share in the indeterminateness already predicated of the essential rights of personal security. It has come about that violations to rights of ownership habitually take certain definite forms; and, though the law in no way professes to limit the rights by the negative standard supplied by such habitual modes of violation, yet an advantage (at least, for purposes of procedure) is gained by cataloguing together these habitual kinds of aggression, and imparting to them a distinctness which shall serve to ensure their immediate recognition.

The truth of this theory is illustrated by two circumstances. In the first place, it is not usual to include breaches of contract among civil injuries, and in English law they are, for some purposes, distinctly opposed to them. The reason of this is that, in contract, the breach of the right must presuppose an exact circumscription of the measure of the right. The artificial tie by which a contractor restricts his future action cannot be indefinite or vague; or, at least, if it be so, cannot for the first time be reduced to definiteness by the illegal act of the other contractor. The parties themselves (in dependence on the State) furnish the measure of the right, and therewith the measure of the injury. The one and the other exactly coincide, and can, for no useful purpose, be treated apart.

Where, on the contrary, it is the State which directly furnishes the measure of the right, as in the case of rights to personal security and rights of ownership, it may invite the co-operation of its own courts of justice, as guided by the experience of the most habitual modes of trespass or aggression, to give precision and definiteness to the general rights it accords. Another circumstance illustrating the theory, that it is chiefly for convenience of procedure that violations of the most important rights are often treated apart from the rights themselves, is the close juxtaposition of delicts and actions in Justinian's Institutes; and this, too, in spite of the formally closer connection of contracts and delicts, both giving rise to obligations.

There is no part of the law on which what may be called the success of the whole legal system more obviously depends than that part which is concerned with the administration of justice, or, in the largest sense of the expression, on "laws of procedure." The object of this part of the law is to secure that the most expeditious and convenient remedy is accorded in the case of the actual or threatened violation of rights. The essence of a right is that the State will lend its aid, in case of need, to maintain and enforce it. If the State is tardy in lending its aid, or if the conditions of accepting that aid are onerous or expensive, or if the machinery for supplying the aid is unreliable in its movements, to that extent the rights conceded by the State are worthless, and the law which affects to create and protect them is abrogated.

It must then be the care of the State to ensure that (1) the rights and duties which it originates are clearly ascertained; and, in case of controversy as to their existence or extent, that the persons immediately concerned may, with as little a loss as possible to themselves, further than is caused by their own acts or defaults, have a ready opportunity afforded them of clearing up doubts. The State must again ensure (2) that in case of a right being actually violated, or of its violation seeming imminent, the person invested with the right have a ready opportunity of making his complaint known; of having the exact measure of the actual or possible injury (which includes the measure of the particular right in question) correctly determined by responsible State officials; and of claiming the interference of these officials to award him redress or protection. The State must (3) further provide effective means of putting an injured person as far as possible in the same situation in which he would have been but for the injury; and this, partly, on the ground of good faith towards the person invested with the violated right, and, partly, in order, by way of general admonishment, to render more secure all rights not as yet violated.

The first duty of the State—that of anticipating controversy by making the nature and measure of rights and duties unmistakably clear—may be performed, and in an advanced condition of society is performed, in two ways;

one that of bestowing as much pains as possible upon the formal expression and publication of the law, and the other that of calling into existence and fostering a legal profession.

Both these tasks are for many ages spontaneously proceeded with long before they are made distinct objects of conscious State policy. Nevertheless, in a seemingly advanced state of society, such as that of England at this day, it is customary, in some quarters, to confuse the legal profession with other professions; and to resist schemes for the education of it at the hands of the State on the ground that it is not so much the concern of the State as of the individual suitor whether a legal profession is a well-educated or ill-educated body, and that the individual suitor may be trusted to discover for himself the standard of learning and skill which he thinks essential to his purpose.

It is obvious, however, that the analogy between the legal profession and a body of voluntary practitioners of any other art is wholly delusive, because the relation of the subject-matter concerned—that is, law—to the vitality of the State itself, wholly independently of its relation to the interests of particular persons, is left out of account. It is of the most vital moment to the State that the legal system be correctly expounded, so as to prevent needless litigation, and gradually to dispense with all litigation; that the slow and spontaneous growth of law—which, even under the best codified system of law, must ceaselessly proceed—should be as little irregular and capricious as possible; that the arguments of advocates in courts of justice should be as concise, as unsophistical, as helpful to the real enucleation of the points in dispute, and as conducive to the administration of certain and speedy justice as possible; and that a race of men should be in constant training of the highest sort, either to take their seats on the judicial bench, or to give efficient and reliable aid to the Legislature when engaged in contemplating amendments of the law.

In the previous chapter, on Criminal Law, it was found necessary to anticipate some of the proper subject-matter of the present chapter, inasmuch as the general process of a judicial investigation, as concerned with the hypothetical existence of a rule of law on the one hand, and with an alleged condition of facts on the other, is the same whatever the part of the legal system involved. In that chapter, however, the prominent topic kept in view was the mode of successfully prosecuting crimes without sacrificing the claims of public liberty. There are yet other considerations to be borne in mind in the administration of justice, which will more appropriately be entered upon here.

Assuming that litigation is really to take place, and that all means of peaceable settlement of disputed rights, whether by seeking professional and extra-judicial counsel, or by reference to arbitration, have been exhausted without effect, it must be the care of the State that the public judicial inquiry be conducted with the utmost despatch, economy, convenience to suitors, and certainty. It is only by long empirical experience and a tedious course of disastrous failures that the value of these ends becomes appreciated, or the possibility of attaining them by conscious effort so much as conjectured. Nevertheless, the experience of Rome and England, which is in a large measure an independent one in each case, goes to prove that there is an inevitable course through which judicial procedure travels, and a definite character to the attainment of which it unceasingly tends.

It seems universally confessed that the whole proceedings necessarily resolve themselves into two distinct parts—the one concerned with ascertaining the real point or points in dispute between the parties; and the other with determining the reality of essential facts alleged on either side, and the existence or applicability of cited rules of law. The first part of the process is a necessary interlude or transitional stage between the vague and indefinite controversy which a sense of injury produces, and which passion fans into a flame, and the cold and emotionless inquiry which is conducted within the walls of a court of justice.

The process of ascertaining what are the facts which one party alleges, and the other denies, and of separating them from facts either admitted by both parties or wholly irrelevant to the true issue, is one which needs, indeed, the general supervision of a judicial officer, but does not call for the active interposition of a court of justice. How many facts are relevant to the issue in any given case may be a difficult question to answer, and much injustice may follow from a rash or precipitate judgment in the matter. Much must depend upon the subject-matter of the suit, and the actual complication of the affairs which have led to it. Much must also depend upon the nature of the tribunal to which the ultimate decision on the law or on the facts, or on both of them, have to be referred.

If the tribunal be popularly constituted, and composed of persons possessed of no previous legal training, a greater care may have to be taken in the preliminary sifting of the facts than where the tribunal consists of a single Judge or body of Judges.

It is to be remembered that there are two opposite risks to which the process of separating the essential facts in dispute from the non-essential, and questions of law from questions of fact, is liable. One of these is that of forcing the statement of the case on either side into a purely artificial and conventional groove, which, in default of timely correction, is always liable to become technical in the extreme. The result is that, as often as not, through mere accidental nonconformity with the established system, the object of the parties is defeated, and the real issue never goes to trial. It may be, indeed, that a wholly false and side issue becomes substituted for it. It is true that, in the formulary system of pleading at Rome and the common-law system of pleading in England, ingenious devices were, and are, resorted to, to obviate or diminish this danger. Such are what are known as the "*præscriptum*," "amended pleadings," "new assignments," and "multiplicity of pleading." These remedies are undoubtedly of great value, though the necessity for their presence points to the characteristic evils of the whole system.

The other risk alluded to is the admission of such a loose preliminary statement of the facts on both sides as, while retaining many of the disadvantages inherent in the last-mentioned system of pleading, has none of its advantages in the way of saving the labour of the judicial tribunal. It was, no doubt, a consciousness of the existence of both these risks that led, in Rome, to the popularity and final establishment of the *cognitiones extraordinariæ*, and, in England, to the existing simplicity of pleading adopted in the Divorce Court and the modern County Court.

The process of the *cognitiones extraordinariæ* had for its purpose the formal merger of what had hitherto constituted two distinct parts of the procedure, without sacrificing what was really precious in either. The pleadings were no longer modes of determining, before the actual trial, what was the issue between the parties, but rather modes of conducting the actual litigation in the very heat of the struggle. The pleading (if such it could still be called) took place after the parties had come into court, and were under the eye of the judge. The judge was now no longer distinguished from the superior magistrate who, in earlier times, simply supervised the whole process, and, after finding the issues, referred them to the decision of such judge or judges as he chose to nominate. Still the formal modes of statement and counter-statement, of "confession and avoidance," and blank denial, were still preserved in their ancient dress; the difference being that, in point of time, the pleas succeeded the "*litis contestatio*," or commencement of the actual trial, instead of preceding it, and the language in which they were conveyed might be as informal as possible, the whole being taken down in writing at the time by public officers named *epistolares* or *officiales*.

The modern English innovation on the old formal system of pleading, though mostly confined as yet to such courts as have been recently created, is connected with the same causes that gave rise to the growth of the simpler system at Rome; that is, the reduction of the functions of the jury, and the aggregation of all judicial functions in the person of a single judge. In the English County Courts, and in the new Probate and Divorce court, the jury has been made only a possible and occasional, instead of being a necessary and universal, tribunal. In these courts, for the vast multitude of cases, the judge is the sole arbiter both as to the law and the facts. It thus becomes less necessary, in general, to distinguish, previously to the trial, between the questions of law and of fact; and it becomes more necessary to afford the judge the largest possible opportunity of making himself complete master of the real relative situation of the parties, without hampering him by technical rules. The usual kinds of cases in the courts into which the simpler modes of pleading have as yet been alone introduced, and the extreme similarity or identity in the character of the facts to which the general routine of business relates, have made the experiment of the new method a peculiarly safe one. It probably, however, marks a real stage in the general history of pleading at which the procedure pursued in all the other courts is likely sooner or later to arrive. The Supreme Court of Judicature Act of 1873 affords substantial encouragement to these expectations.

So soon as the real questions in dispute between the parties have been ascertained, and questions as to the existence or exact purport of the rules of law applicable have been separated from those relating to controverted facts, it becomes necessary to provide a convenient mechanism for testing, in the most speedy, economic, and infallible method, the comparative value of the evidence produced by the rival parties. Such a mechanism is found in what are called "rules of evidence," which are, in fact, series of propositions, partly theoretical and partly practical, founded upon experience, and having for their purpose the simplification and shortening of the process of proof. The character of these rules varies considerably from country to country, and from age to age. They have always afforded a curious reflection of the state of society in which they have grown up, and they have generally been largely infected with the superstitions, prejudices, antipathies, and false or inadequate scientific and logical notions of the day. Thus, the superior guiltiness of a thief caught in the act, the conclusiveness of the trial by ordeal, the value of torture, and the habitual mendaciousness of persons not believing in a future state of rewards and punishments, have at one time or another impressed themselves on the national consciousness of very different nations; while the last of them has a certain amount of weight in England even at the present day.

It is, however, one of the most signal marks of modern legal progress that the subject of evidence is now treated as one requiring for its due consideration all the light that can be thrown upon it by logical science, judicial experience, and regard for administrative speed and economy. It is still habitually recognized that it is the proper task of the judge to control and regulate the production of evidence; and, in order to prevent the operation of arbitrary caprice in discharging this task, it is necessary to mark by law the limits of the judge's functions in this respect. But the only recognized objects of a law of evidence in modern times are (1) to shorten and simplify legal proceedings by excluding evidence on the ground of its invariable unreliableness or its useless prolixity; (2) to determine the mode of taking evidence both in court and out of court, and to devise such securities as may seem most expedient for imparting to it the greatest possible value.

The first question to be settled is as to which of the two parties incurs the burden or responsibility of bringing positive proof of the assertions already made in the preparatory pleadings. This question is determined partly by regarding the actual situation of the argument at the time of coming into court, and partly by framing what are called legal *presumptions* in favour of one side or the other. These presumptions, which may or may not be held capable of being rebutted by extrinsic proof, are general propositions originally formed on a vast amount of forensic experience, found to be of great and practical value.

Such presumptions are that a prisoner is to be held innocent till he is positively proved to be guilty; that a will, deed, or other document, regular in form, and purporting, on the face of it, to have been duly witnessed and executed, has been duly witnessed and executed; that the holder of a bill of exchange has paid a price for it to the person who has transferred it to him; that a person in possession of housebreaking tools is intending to use them for an unlawful purpose. It is obvious that these presumptions travel through a very long range, some of them—as the one last quoted, and the similar one regarding the possession of stolen goods—being nothing more than the everyday generalizations of the most vulgar experience; and others,—such as that of the presumed compliance with forms, in the case of documents purporting on their face to be formal,—being in the highest degree artificial and arbitrary.

Some presumptions, indeed, which are not allowed to be rebutted, are in special cases directly opposed to facts, and yet they are supported solely on the ground of the greater inconvenience of constantly listening to evidence adduced to prove that they do not apply. The incapacity of persons under a certain age to make contracts, and, under a lower age, to commit crimes, are nothing more than presumptions of personal immaturity, which can never really be determined by reference to a sharply described age. But, whatever the origin or substance of these presumptions, their general purpose is invariably the same—that of either excluding the necessity of producing evidence altogether, or of determining the order in which it must be produced.

It was said that one main purpose of laws of evidence was the exclusion of some sorts of evidence on the ground of its invariable unreliableness. It has, however, now become an established principle that general assumptions of the unreliableness of certain sorts of evidence are extremely precarious, and must be admitted with the utmost parsimony. Because evidence is unreliable, it is not therefore of necessity valueless; and a great mass of evidence, mostly unreliable, may, by proper sifting, be made to disclose seeds of truth of the utmost value. The old English doctrine of the expediency of excluding witnesses on the ground of real or supposed interest in the case must, as often as not, have excluded all the people who were near enough at hand to know anything about the matter. This is especially true of the parties to the suit themselves. In the case of an oral contract between two parties, it must surely be better to hear what they have to say, and to compare the rival accounts together, than to shut one's ears for fear of hearing a good deal of falsehood.

There is no doubt some subtraction to be made from the general value of the evidence of certain particular classes of persons, and notably so of children, policemen, and scientific theorists of all sorts. Much good can be done by cataloguing the general infirmities to which the evidence of such persons is frequently liable. This liability, however, is no ground for excluding the evidence, but only for commenting upon it.

Assuming, then, that sound principle is in favour of excluding no witness whatever on the grounds of supposed interest in the suit, of connection with the parties, or even of known bad character (a ground of exclusion which at Rome was the most familiar of all), the next question presented is as to the expediency of limiting the topics on which evidence may be offered, or of otherwise restricting the matter which a witness may be allowed or invited to speak to. One obvious rule must here be made, that the purpose of the trial be kept in view throughout, and therefore that the evidence offered must have a bearing, direct or indirect, on the issue to be decided.

It is attended with great public inconvenience,

besides waste of labour and time, to allow witnesses to take advantage of the opportunity to obtrude on the court masses of irrelevant matter which can in no way affect the decision of the suit. It may be difficult for the judge, or even for the suitors and their legal advisers, always to predict what matters are likely to prove relevant to the issue and what not. But the difficulty of drawing the line with accuracy for all cases is no reason for drawing no line at all in any. The responsibility must be cast upon the judge of determining how far, upon these principles, evidence shall be limited.

It is sometimes even attempted to fix by law what shall be held relevant evidence. (See the Indian Evidence Act of 1872.) But the danger of occasionally excluding important evidence, not falling under the legal category of "relevant facts," is so great that it is doubtful whether such a description, by anticipation, can prove really satisfactory or safe in practice. The only secure plan is to leave a very large discretion to the judge, while providing that, in the case of an obvious miscarriage of justice ensuing through an unwise exercise of his discretion, the suffering party be at liberty to have the trial over again. This is the practice at present in England in civil cases, and the "new trials" which it occasions are not frequent enough to give rise to reasonable complaint.

Even with respect to really relevant facts, however, a distinction must be made between what has come under the witness's personal observation, and matters which he is led to believe only through his reliance upon the credibility of some one else, or, at least, through his personal estimate of the value of some evidence or other. This evidence covers not only the speech of the persons on whom the witness is accustomed to rely, but writings and documents which he has seen, and upon which, believing in their genuineness, he has based certain opinions. The manifest distinction here indicated has given rise in England to the familiar description of all evidence not directly based on the personal observations of a witness as "hearsay." There is, beyond doubt, much practical use in giving a distinct name and place to all that class of evidence, the probative value of which rests on some other considerations than the mere trustworthiness of the senses of a present witness, tested by such logical processes as the tribunal may employ in order to ascertain the truth.

It is necessary here to interpose, parenthetically, the distinction between "direct" and "circumstantial" evidence; the former kind of evidence implying that what the witnesses saw, or heard, or felt, constitutes the fact or facts which are the essential topics of the investigation; and the latter kind, that the reported sensations of the witnesses—taken together, it may be, with other kinds of proof—need, in addition, a train of reasoning from which the existence or nonexistence of essential facts may be presumed. In either kind of evidence, the sensations of the witnesses are equally important; and in either kind it might, or might not, be allowable to admit "hearsay" evidence—that is, evidence deriving some of its value from the credibility of absent persons or documents, and not from the mere reported sensations of present witnesses.

The distinction of "hearsay" from other evidence has sometimes being complained of as unnecessary and impracticable. But it is a real and essential one, though fault may be found with the practice of absolutely excluding all evidence classed as "hearsay." It is obvious that it is the lowest and least valuable form of evidence, since the persons or documents to which credence is invited are absent, and were, most likely, never subjected to that severe scrutiny which alone could have sufficed to test their real meaning or character. English law has allowed a good many exceptions to the rule excluding "hearsay" evidence; but it has occasionally proceeded by the rather indirect path of saying that the evidence which it determined not to exclude was not "hearsay." Thus English law is generally consistent with itself in excluding "hearsay;" though the legal and the logical distinctions between evidence believed on the authority of present witnesses as to what they themselves heard or saw, and evidence believed on the reported authority of absent persons and documents, are not always strictly in accord.

The remarks that have above been made, on the principles which apply to the discussion of how far evidence should be excluded or restricted, chiefly relate to witnesses giving oral evidence in court. But there are kinds of evidence other than that capable of being supplied by the mouths of witnesses actually present at the trial; and there are occasions in the process of conducting certain classes of suits in which it may be desirable to have the evidence received in the first instance out of court, and only the result of it produced in court, if called for.

This last process is especially applicable in cases in which a certain number of facts are admitted on both sides, and, in fact, are presupposed in the statement of the case of each of the parties. The formal establishment of these facts may be none the less necessary in order to prevent ulterior or accidental disputes. Such facts are the dates of births, deaths, marriages, the due registration of documents, and other facts of a like kind. It may be convenient for the court before which the trial takes place to have all the facts which are either indisputable, or not disputed, clearly ascertained beforehand, so as to be able to address itself with undivided attention to the facts actually in dispute.

In some cases this evidence thus received out of court may consist of the reported proceedings of an inferior court, which has made a preliminary investigation. The report of these proceedings may be turned to account at the actual trial, especially in criminal cases, either because other evidence proves defective, or because it seems hopelessly contradictory, and needs all the help that can be obtained from any quarter. It is upon such a principle as this that, at the trial of a prisoner in England, the "depositions" of the witnesses taken before the magistrate at the previous investigation are occasionally, but not invariably, read, either at the wish of the prisoner or of the prosecuting counsel. Similarly, the depositions of witnesses at the point of death, and who have since died, and of persons in foreign countries who cannot be present at the trial, are admitted as supplementary, if not as essential, evidence. Such evidence, again, is sometimes allowed to be specially prepared in order to facilitate the process of pleading,—as by means of sworn "interrogatories" administered out of court, and to be answered on oath.

With respect to the admission of some of the last-mentioned kinds of evidence one useful rule obtains in English law, which operates in the way of beneficially restricting the whole amount of evidence received. The rule is that the best evidence must always be produced; or, rather, that no evidence will be received which expresses on the face of it that a more reliable form of evidence than itself could be produced. This rule is nearly allied to that excluding evidence consisting of the assertions of absent persons; but the two rules are by no means co-extensive with one another. The rule now mentioned, for instance, excludes oral evidence of a contract if it appears that it has been reduced to writing, as well as evidence of the contents of any document so long as there is no insuperable obstacle to the production of the document itself. The rule against "hearsay," strictly interpreted, would exclude such evidence in either case absolutely.

It was said that laws of evidence have for their purpose not only the regulation of the admissibility of evidence, but also that of the modes of taking evidence. These modes must be determined by considerations of convenience, despatch, economy of labour and expense, and security against fraud and impostures. The four main kinds of evidence are (1) personal witnesses, (2) documents, (3) public records, and (4) physical monuments.

With respect to the three last, the only security possible is to take ordinary precautions against forgery; to insist, as far as it is practicable, on the production of originals instead of copies; and, where this is impracticable, to regulate the mode in which the faithfulness of the copies shall be guaranteed.

With respect to the first species of evidence, the most obvious and commendable of all methods is the oral examination of witnesses in open court, attended with what is called "cross-examination,"—that is, a process of rigid questioning from the opposite side directed to searching the grounds of the witness's answers, and to testing his capacity and opportunities for observation, as well as his general credibility. In England, even this oral examination has been considerably restricted by definite rules which, in criminal cases at least, are of great importance to public liberty. Such a rule is that of abstaining from asking leading questions, or questions which in their structure suggest the form and matter of the answer. Such questions are, however, freely admitted in cross-examination. It was not so long ago that leading questions were only discouraged when put by prisoners examining adverse witnesses; while they were freely allowed to the prosecution. But this scandalous injustice is now entirely abolished, and the same rule is applied with strict impartiality to the prisoner and the prosecuting counsel. The abuse implied in leading questions would seem to be the darkest spot on the administration of justice in Continental countries.

The notion of an "oath," in its religious aspect, as the main security for the trustworthiness of a witness, is almost equally obsolete in modern times with a belief in the value of torture as a test of truth. It is generally accepted, at the present day, that the imposition of an oath adds no fresh guarantee for credibility in the case of a morally disposed witness, while it affords to an immoral witness a shelter and stimulus for his mendacity. To a witness not believing in the theological facts to the truth of which the form of the oath appeals, the application of the oath is either a puerility or an offence, or both. In this last case the feelings provoked are the least of all likely to make the witness highly susceptible to the obligations of truth.

The only justification for the preservation of the oath, in the administration of justice, is that some solemn form is needed to remind the witness of the importance of the occasion, of the serious issues at stake, and of the legal penalties which follow the offence of wilfully giving false evidence. No form is more solemn to persons who believe in a God than one which reminds them, on the face of it, of His character and government; and where the bulk of the witnesses examined in courts of justice have such a belief, such a form may be rather beneficial than otherwise, so far as they are concerned. But the greatest possible facility should be provided for having the form dispensed with in case of conscientious objections to it, though even the throwing the burden of making any objection to an almost universal practice may press very heavily in particular cases.

Some observations must be made upon one class of witnesses, the examination of whom is attended with peculiar difficulties. The class is that of specially skilled witnesses, or so-called *experts*. They are summoned in cases in which facts have to be examined wholly removed from ordinary experience, and with which only certain limited classes of persons are conversant. Such facts are those relating to exceptional sorts of manufactures; to the identity of handwriting; and especially to morbid conditions of mind and body and bodily accidents.

On all such matters there are a few persons who, from a rare taste, or lifelong occupation, or professional training, stand in a wholly different position towards the facts forming the subject-matter of the inquiry from that occupied by the general public, and therefore (most probably) by the members of a popular tribunal. The members of the tribunal are thus unfavourably situated both for estimating the value and meaning of the evidence of any one such witness, and still more for comparing the relative authority of each one of a number of such witnesses. The tribunal can therefore generally be guided by nothing else than by the demeanour of the witnesses in court, or by general impressions received from a number of indefinite sources outside the court. These tests are less and less appropriate in proportion to the recondite character of the scientific facts involved and the real ability of the witness, which last is little likely to be appreciated by the vulgar who dispense the meed of public fame.

Another difficulty is added, however, by the fact

that, in some cases,—as in that of a murder, manslaughter, railway accident, or sudden seizure of illness,—the witnesses cannot (as in Patent cases and some others) be chosen at leisure, but must include those who actually chanced to be first called to the spot at the moment indicated. The evidence of such persons will not, and cannot, be confined to mere matters of descriptive fact, but must include those of scientific opinion. These accidental witnesses may thus be pitted against men of the highest degree of professional eminence; but a popular tribunal, and even a judge, may be wholly unable to compare the scientific value of the opinions on either side. In this way the decision becomes a mere matter of accident.

Many solutions of this difficulty have been proposed. They almost all point to the public organization of bodies of skilled witnesses in each of the important departments in which they are constantly demanded, and to a special preference being given to their evidence in the administration of justice. Such witnesses might have to make a preliminary report to the court on the scientific character of the other evidence to be offered, and on the professional authority of the witnesses; and this report might be simply read at the trial, or also made the basis for the cross-examination of those who have prepared it. Or the report might be merely tendered subsequently to the reception of the other evidence, and as a comment upon it, thus forming mere material for the summing-up of the judge. It is possible that, in Patent cases, even a special court, with scientific assessors to the judge, might be organized in some way after the model of foreign tribunals of commerce. At the same time, with respect to all these suggestions, it is not to be forgotten that there is an inherent political danger in organizing and multiplying special professional coteries appointed by, in constant communication with, and under the control of, the Government.

As a legal system approaches a high degree of development, there are a variety of facts which lead to the gradual introduction of the practice of professional Advocacy. As a good deal of misapprehension prevails with respect to the nature and objects of advocacy, and as in some quarters it is believed to have no moral justification whatever, it will be worth while to examine with care the real reasons upon which the use of advocacy is based.

A litigant needs the assistance of a properly qualified adviser and representative for a variety of purposes quite distinct from one another. Such purposes are (1) information as to the procedure of the court, and as to the formal mode of pressing his claim or of resisting the claim or charge of another; (2) aid in eliciting relevant evidence from witnesses in his favour, and in exposing the irrelevancy, inconsistency, or general incredibility of the evidence produced on the other side; (3) aid in arranging in the most concise and manageable form the facts of his own case, as well as those of his adversary's, so as to lay the foundation of a simply reasoned argument in his own favour; (4) aid in availing himself of the rules of law which are in his favour and in exposing the inapplicability of those which are or may be quoted against him.

It will be seen that part of this work is logical and psychological, and part of it connected with a professedly erudite knowledge of law and of practice. All of it, however, demands special skill and experience; and where the witnesses are numerous, the facts complicated, and the law uncertain, to be destitute of such professional help it must put a litigant,—brought, it may be, for the first time in his life, within the walls of a court of justice, —at a most serious disadvantage. Nevertheless, it could hardly be credited that it was only at the close of the last reign that prisoners in England were first allowed the assistance of counsel. It had been customary, indeed, to allow counsel to prisoners in cases of treason; but they had no constitutional right to the advantage, and the concession of it was often refused, or hampered with limitations, just as the whim of the judge happened to dictate.

It is, however, as much to the interest of the judge and the State that the practice of employing counsel should be encouraged and facilitated as to that of litigants themselves. There is no more miserable spectacle than that of a rude and uneducated clown, with the poorest command of language, the dullest apprehension of the meaning of evidence, or even of law, and with complete inexperience of the proceedings of a court of justice, setting to work to defend himself. It is useless to tell him he must ask questions at one time and make a statement at another, because the difference between a question and a statement is one wholly ignored by him in his ordinary speech. It is equally useless to tell him what are the facts which are against him and which he must address himself to controvert, and what are the facts in his favour and which he must not allow to be controverted. He is plunged in a sea of obscurity and mystery, and nothing but the casual benevolence and untiring patience of the presiding judge can help him out of it.

Similarly, in a civil case, any one who attends courts of justice knows how erratic, prolix, and perverse is the course taken by a suitor who insists on advocating his own cause, or who is not able to procure a professional advocate. The time of the court and the country is wasted, the minds and temper of every one concerned are tortured, and the ends of justice are always in special peril of being defeated. On all these grounds it is obvious that a highly-developed legal system and a complete state of civilization enforces the necessity of creating and maintaining a legal profession; and that in the conduct of all suits, civil and criminal, not of the simplest description, the co-operation of a professional advocate should be provided for, if necessary, at the expense of the State.

The stigma of immorality that has proverbially been held to attach to the profession of advocacy is founded partly upon an entire misconception of its purposes, and partly upon an exaggerated notion of the extent to which immoral advocacy really prevails. There is no doubt that the temptations to an unfair representation of facts, to a rhetorical abuse of language, and to an unconscientious allegation of false, or denial of true, convictions are constantly present to the advocate, and often assail him with overpowering force. But they are temptations to wrong, and not the measure of what is recognized as right. It is the same with the advocate as with other men. The more complex the duty, the nobler is the successful achievement of it, and the deeper the disgrace of an unworthy failure in it. It is for the public and for the legal profession itself to set before the advocate the highest possible standard of integrity and faithfulness to moral truth, and then to denounce all symptoms of an immoral use of his opportunities as gross and inexcusable deflections from that standard.

In the administration of any mature body of laws, there will be needed a large number of courts having very different jurisdictions. One principal division of courts is that into Courts of Original Jurisdiction and Courts of Appeal. The necessity for appeal courts is caused not merely by the uncertainty of the actual purport of large portions of the legal system, but by the way in which the uncertain parts of law are closely implicated with the certain parts, and, in procedure, questions of law with questions of fact. In a vast number of cases, the decision of a single judge on a point of law may be readily accepted as final by both parties, and the point itself is not sufficiently doubtful to encourage the unsuccessful party to incur the risk of having it reconsidered elsewhere. But there are confessedly doubtful points of law on which it may be in the highest degree expedient that the judge, at the moment of dealing with the facts, should express an unhesitating, though provisional, opinion. The mode in which the appeal should be conducted, and the amount of discretion which may be left to the judge as to allowing it or not, and the terms upon which he may allow it, are details upon which different legal systems will differ much from one another, and the same legal system will differ with respect to different sorts of cases.

Another important division of courts is that into Courts of Inferior and Courts of Superior Jurisdiction. In all countries there are a class of cases, both civil and criminal, which may be described as being of a routine character, and yet multitudinous in quantity. The facts are easily ascertainable, and the law scarcely admits of dispute except in very peculiar and rarely occurring circumstances. On these grounds there is much convenience in establishing a set of courts, distributed as far as possible throughout the country, in which the proceedings are exempt from many of the formalities which are essential to the fair solution of more difficult questions. The test of suitability of a case for the higher or lower order of courts may be founded on the amount of money-value at stake, or (in criminal cases) of the penalty liable to be incurred, or else on the mere option of one or both of the parties,—with or without the concurrence of the judge, and with or without security being given for future costs, that is, the expenses of proceeding in the higher courts. It may even be expedient, as in France (and in some few classes of causes in England), to have the earlier stages of every trial travelled over in inferior courts.

The next main division of courts is that founded on the nature of the subject-matter, a certain peculiarity of procedure being either inherently adapted to certain kinds of business, or (through historical causes) being traditionally associated with them. Such courts are Courts of Probate and Divorce, of Bankruptcy, of Admiralty, Church Courts, and Tribunals of Commerce. The object of the institution of these several courts is sufficiently indicated by their titles. They also differ from one another according to the extent of their jurisdiction; the procedure, for instance, of Courts of Bankruptcy and of Probate and Divorce—the jurisdiction of which extends to matters of a purely administrative character—differing from that of others in respect of the nature of the pleadings, of the forms of conducting the actual trial, and especially of the constitution of the tribunal.

The most remarkable variation from the normal type is that supplied by the Continental institution of *Tribunals of Commerce*. One essential characteristic of these tribunals, as at present existing, is that the judges are eminent merchants, elected by their fellow-merchants as being *recommendables par la probité, l'esprit d'ordre, et l'économie.*" (See French *Code de Commerce*, 618.) Another characteristic is the absence of the formalities, technicalities, and consequent delays, by which proceedings in other courts of justice are usually or necessarily attended. The reason for instituting courts of this nature is found, partly, in the peculiarity of the subject-matter, conversance with commercial habits and practices being held to be here of higher value as a judicial qualification than knowledge of law,—and partly in the importance of commercial disputes being settled with the utmost promptitude, an importance held almost to exceed that of obtaining a greater security for justice in awaiting a more patient process, and in a more rigorous observance of precautionary solemnities. The value to foreign merchants of having ready to their hands a tribunal in which the proceedings are exempt from the technicalities of the national system of law, is also dwelt upon as a special recommendation of these courts.

Should these courts be introduced into England, it may be expedient to combine a professional legal, with the lay, element in the constitution of the tribunals. It has indeed been said that the practice of summoning "special juries" of merchants in important commercial cases renders the institution of Tribunals of Commerce a superfluity. But this objection, however valid within its own limits, takes no account of what is said to be the great recommendation of the institution as existing abroad, that even where only small sums are at stake, justice is administered far more cheaply, rapidly, and satisfactorily to both parties than in the ordinary tribunals. (See Report of Select Committee of House of Commons, 1871.)

The subject of "costs," that is, of who is to pay the expenses of the trial, is one of far greater magnitude and moment than perhaps, at the first glance, it seems. The interests of three parties have to be considered—those of the plaintiff, of the defendant, and of the State. It has been said by some, with much force, that all the expenses of every trial should be borne by the State alone, because it may be imputed to the shortcomings of the State that the law is so uncertain as to admit of any doubt as to its meaning; and even where litigation is concerned with the settlement of disputed facts, the State, in conceding a right, is bound to supply freely the means of protecting the right, and is not entitled to throw its own burden upon either of the contending parties, whichever happens to be in the wrong.

On the other hand, it is urged that the only possible mode of prohibiting incessant litigation of the most needless and vexatious sort, is to make the party who is proved to be in the wrong bear some of the expenses which the State incurs in setting its judicial machinery in motion. It may also be said that the necessity of contributing to these expenses, in case of defeat, is at once a check upon wrong-doing and an encouragement to amicable arrangement of controverted claims.

The true objection, however, to this practice of throwing the expenses, or part of them, on one or other of the suitors, is that it makes it far easier and safer for a rich man to go to law than for a poor man. It thus operates directly as an encouragement to the rich to prey upon the poor. The institution of the English County Courts where the costs are small, and the constant extension of their jurisdiction, have been most important steps in the opposite direction in England. It is probable that a greater simplification of procedure in the Superior Courts, accompanied by a re-publication of the whole law on a readily comprehended basis of arrangement, and with the use of the utmost clearness of expression, would (even if costs were no longer payable by either party) go a long way towards bringing before those courts questions which are now improperly and tyrannically excluded, and towards largely reducing the number of those which are now needlessly admitted.

There is one great branch of law which has yet to be considered, though the place it must occupy in a scientific exposition is somewhat doubtful. It is sometimes described as "Private International Law," and sometimes as the "Conflict of Laws." Neither expression is exact enough to indicate the true nature and limits of the laws to which reference is made. The first expression suggests a closer relation than the facts justify to that International Law which deals with the legal relations of States; and the second expression hints merely at some of the occasions which have called the new body of law into being, but suggests no information as to its character or whereabouts. The true nature of the law or laws now alluded to will be best understood by a brief description of the circumstances through which it was originally created, and is still maintained and developed, in every civilized State.

The courts of justice of a State can only have jurisdiction over the persons of those who are either permanently or temporarily members of the State, and only with respect to things lying within the territory of the State, or over which, as in the case of things on the high seas, the executive power of the State can (if permitted by law) extend its control. Further than this, courts of justice can only (except by special arrangement between two States) control the acts of the citizens who are generally subject to their jurisdiction so long as they are within the national territory. With respect to acts done elsewhere, it must rest entirely in the discretion of a court of justice in what aspect it shall regard them, either as it affects the doer of them or other persons.

But the progress of society, and of international, social, and commercial intercourse, gives rise to circumstances which practically enforce on courts of justice what may be called a great usurpation of jurisdiction in all these respects, and it is the rules which mark out the province and extent of this enlarged jurisdiction which constitute the branch of law now under consideration.

It is to be distinctly observed that the existence of these rules owes its immediate origin to a discretionary, or rather tentative, exercise of jurisdiction by courts of justice; that the continuing validity of these rules, just as much as the validity of all other rules of law, depends on the acquiescence, implied or expressed, of the supreme political authority; and hence that these rules, so far as they have any validity, are part of the national law of the State, and not (as some seem to suppose) a bodiless phantom of law floating about in the presence of all States, but attached to none. It is true (though much to be regretted) that the rules appertaining to this part of the law are only partly identical for many States, and are partly different for each. This has induced writers to confound what is desirable with what really exists; and to believe that a real body of (so-called) Private International Law exists somewhere, though many States are exceedingly perverse in the interpretation they put upon its rules.

The facts which have given rise to the extension of jurisdiction in question are the sojourning of citizens of one State in the territory of another; marriages, divorces, and contracts between the citizens of the same State in the territory of some other State, or between citizens of different States; land and goods lying in the territory of one State and owned or conveyed by the citizens of another; judgments and bankruptcies decreed in the territory of one State against the citizens of another. It will be seen that on adjudicating in the territory of any particular State upon such facts as these, there may be as many as four different legal systems which the judge may, on a single occasion, be invited to apply.

One of these, and the most obvious one, is the law of his own country, that which he administers in all other cases (*lex fori*). According to this law, strictly interpreted, he might have simply to abstain from all interference in the case on the grounds already explained. Any way it is by this law that the form of the remedy must be determined. Another system, applicable where ownership is involved, is that of the place where the things are (*lex loci rei sitæ*). But this is generally only adaptable to immovable things, as the actual situation of movable things may be matter of interminable controversy. A third system of law is that of the place where an important act was done, or (if a contract) where performance of an act promised was to take place (*lex loci actus, lex loci contractus*). A fourth system is that of the State to which the person immediately concerned may be held to be permanently subject through the fact of an intentional residence in its territory without any distinct purpose of going elsewhere (*lex domicilii*).

It must be a matter for each State to determine for itself which of these several systems of law shall be followed in any case in which a selection between them is possible. In some cases all the different systems may have to be followed in adjudicating upon the different parts of one and the same continuous transaction. It is a misfortune that the civilized States of the world refuse to follow identical principles in the adoption or recognition of each other's laws. Sometimes a selfish commercial policy, and sometimes a narrow-minded national prejudice or moral susceptibility, stand in the way. Nevertheless, considerable progress has been made, especially in America, in establishing the true methods upon which the construction of this part of the law must proceed. It is obvious that what has been said above of the laws of different States is equally applicable to the different legal systems prevailing in different provinces of the same State. The relations of England and Scotland, and of the States of the American Union, sufficiently illustrate this.

CHAPTER XII.

INTERNATIONAL LAW.

The scientific study of law seems to attain its highest perfection and its noblest uses when it is directed to what is now generally known as "International Law," or the "Law of Nations." A preliminary difficulty is here encountered as to whether the rules of reciprocal action, to which the Governments of modern civilized States practically submit themselves with more or less steadiness, can properly be held to constitute a body of *law* in the same sense of this term as is involved when the rules for the internal government of any particular State are concerned. There are, no doubt, obvious resemblances between the two sorts of rules, and there are also obvious discrepancies. The question is, whether a new term should be invented to designate the rules practically guiding the mutual action of States in certain respects, or whether it is rather expedient that the meaning of the term *law* should be extended to admit of its covering both classes of rules. This inquiry opens out another, as to whether the definition of the term *law*, as given by the most recent and celebrated school of English legal writers, is not based on too restricted a conception of the phenomena to which it relates; and it is only at the moment of attempting to apply the former definition of *law* to international uses that the insufficiency of that definition is discovered.

Mr. Austin, indeed, endeavoured to escape the necessity of reconstructing his own definition by denying to the rules for regulating the mutual relations of States the name of *law*. He styled those rules, in their assemblage, *morality*. Two inconvenient consequences followed from this innovation. In the first place, the word *morality* was restricted to expressing the sort of outward and formal acts which alone belong to the well-recognized region of the "Law of Nations." In the second place, and following from the former consequence, the field for moral action and for moral rights and duties as between States—so far as that action and those rights and duties do not admit of the precise and logical circumscription demanded in courts of justice—was entirely ignored. In fact, morality, as between States, was made to exhibit itself in nothing else than in the limited number of precisely ascertained rules hitherto making up the so-called "Law of Nations," and the name *morality* was implicitly denied to every other standard of mutual responsibility between States.

Had this language prevailed, the indirect influence of it must have been to conflict with one of the most promising tendencies of the present age,—that is, to recognize moral rights and duties as existing between States wholly independently of the strictly legal rights and duties which properly belong to the great structure called the "Law of Nations" or "International Law." Those moral rights and duties, like the moral rights and duties of private life, reach far too deeply, and extend too widely, to be ever made the topic of forensic circumscription or legislative enactment. Legal rights and duties are their signs and buttresses, but not their substitutes. Law is ever the handmaid of morality, but where the notion of morality is limited by that of law, morality and law will soon perish together.

To return from this apparent, though not real, digression occasioned by Mr. Austin's attempt to make "International Law" and "International Morality" convertible expressions, it becomes necessary to consider the true lesson enforced by the seemingly impracticable phenomenon presented by the body of rules forming the bulk of what is called the "Law of Nations." This lesson is that the distinguishing characteristics of true law must be sought for somewhere else than in the nature of the authority from whence it proceeds, and in the certainty of the punishment by which its infraction is attended.

It is not necessary to warn a Continental student of the importance of this lesson. None of the words *recht*, *droit*, nor *jus* have ever been restricted to the narrow meaning that, in the hands of Bentham and Austin, the word *law* has acquired in England. And yet it is true that the excessive precision by which the use of the word *law* has of late been narrowed in this country has tended to save English students from many of the pitfalls of vagueness and indeterminateness, not to say sentimentality, to which some foreign writers are undoubtedly prone. But precision, valuable as it is, must not be sought at the expense of truth; and the question is now presented, as to whether recent English legal writers have not, in aspiring after clearness and brevity, entailed upon themselves a loss which is not appreciable at the full till the problem of the scientific nature of so called "International Law" comes under treatment.

Assuming then (what, in view of the mighty expansion which there is reason to believe International Law is likely to undergo, it is proper to assume) that the distinguishing characteristics of law must be those which are common to it when looked at as determining the

LAW IN THE INTERNATIONAL SENSE. 325

outward relations of persons to one another within a particular State, and as determining the relations of States to one another in the great commonwealth of States, the following may be taken as among those characteristics.

Both within the limits of a particular State, and in the commonwealth of States, law (if it is accepted and generally obeyed) is a "command of a supreme political authority." The main difficulty is as to what is meant by a "supreme political authority" in a society of, presumably, equal States, and with no greater or more effective organization for enforcing their general will on recalcitrant individual States than at present exists.

The exact analogy to this state of things is to be found in that described by Sir H. S. Maine as existing at one time, and even to some extent still, in the village communities of India. From time immemorial rules of ownership, of procedure, and of family succession existed in those communities in the absence of any recognized government from without, and of any permanent organization, of the nature of government, within. The rules were very generally, or almost universally, observed. They were felt, as it were unconsciously, to be part of the order of nature, against which resistance or objection could not so much as suggest itself. They were obeyed far better than are the laws of most highly organized States, and yet both a supreme political authority and a punishment for disobedience might be said to be entirely wanting.

This analogical case must be considered in connection with the known phenomenon of the actual existence and potency (up to a certain point) of a body of international law, and further, with the historical circumstance that in every known civilized country law and government have grown together, the existence of a definite political authority being generally later, in point of time, than the foundation of the nation's laws. The result proves that, though law, when fully developed, presupposes the presence of a supreme political authority, yet binding rules of action are recognized, and the habit of obedience to such rules is formed, long before that political authority, to which ultimately law will owe its main efficacy, is actually constituted.

It may be said, indeed, that the constitution of a central, definite, generally recognizable, and indisputable, political authority is the last and greatest triumph of law. The history of law is that of the evolution of customary rules out of the innate genius of the people, and of the conscious modification or extension of those rules by a series of tentative political authorities operating from without. A final reconciliation and balance between the rival influences is achieved so soon as a supreme political authority exists which is in perfect harmony with the tendencies and aspirations of the popular life.

At this stage the further development of customary law is arrested, because it is no longer serviceable. All the legislation proceeds henceforward directly from the supreme political authority which finally represents the political conscience of the nation. Not that even here, further changes—introduced by new influences working on the popular mind—may not still have to be undergone. A fresh stratum of customary law may gradually form itself, and the whole series of events included in the above political narrative may again repeat themselves.

Exactly the same course of events may be anticipated in the formation of a body of international law. It is no disparagement to the description of that sort of law, as being a " command of a supreme political authority," to say, that at present no such authority is anywhere to be found, and that if anywhere it were to be found, it would be as soon as possible repudiated.

Every improvement that is introduced into the rules

of international law; every attempt that is made to produce uniformity, certainty, and publicity; every effort that is made after harmony of spirit and of interpretative method on the part of the public lawyers of different States; all point to the gradual elaboration among States of what may be properly called a supreme political authority. What form this authority will take it may be impossible for us, in this generation, so much as to guess; just as the members of an early, spontaneously developing village community had no materials from which to construct a notion of civil government in its later sense.

It is not possible that the authority of the future will take the form of the governor of an universal empire, supported by military force. Nor is it easy to see the steps by which the States of Europe, physically and morally unequal, can ever be brought to confederate themselves on wise and permanent conditions. These are matters for the political speculator, and will serve rather to animate the hopes, than to engage the activity, of the practical statesman. The question is as yet too far ahead for it to be worth while to bestow much serious labour upon its discussion. What, however, is indisputable, and, in relation to the nature of international law, of the highest importance, is that the actual existence and continuous amelioration of international law involves in itself the sure and gradual formation of a supreme political authority among the States of the world.

The progressive steps towards the publication of a definite system of rights and duties by which the legal relations of States are, in fact, governed, imply a system of procedure for ascertaining how far rights have been maintained or violated, and duties performed or omitted. A system of procedure involving courts and judges will thus be introduced and supported by a competent authority.

This authority is the supreme political authority; and if, in the existing reign of war, no symptoms of the appearance of such an authority are as yet descried, still the actual prevalence of international law, amidst all obstacles, is a sufficient witness of the advent of that authority.

The above investigation has been conducted merely in order to establish that, in passing from the consideration of the sort of rules which publicly regulate the social relations of persons within the limits of a particular State, to the consideration of those rules which affect to regulate the relations of States to one another, no real change of conception is encountered; and that one and the same definition of the term *law* will serve to cover the applications of the term to both sorts of rules. The investigation is very far from being an unprofitable one. On the contrary, it is of the utmost moment to establish that, in the development of the moral life of humanity, an unbroken continuity is observable, though at certain points in the progress it may be peculiarly difficult to discover the junction.

It is obvious that the simple rules upon which the integrity of family life and the prosecution of agriculture in the earliest ages depend are, in their nature, scarcely distinguishable from the highly perfected customary code by which an extensive village community is enabled to develop all the conditions of a free and peaceful industrial life. It is, again, confessedly hard to draw a sharp line between this customary code and what is called true law, as existing in a fully-organized State and as proceeding from a determinate supreme political authority.

But even at this point the course of progress is not concluded. As the intimacy between the States of the world increases, a fresh career for law is opened out; and if unprecedented difficulties are encountered at this stage, it is only because the elements that have to be subdued are more hard and unmanageable, and, on that very account, the ultimate triumph of law will be more conspicuous and complete.

It is true there are certain great differences in the materials with which international and national law have severally to deal, and it may be well to examine these carefully, in order to estimate the exact value of the likeness and the unlikeness of the two sorts of law.

The main ground of unlikeness between the two sorts of law is to be found in the fact that the subjects of national law are individual human beings; and of international law, certain peculiar assemblages of human beings, denominated States. These States are looked upon as imperishable in their nature, and as preserving through all time a continuing identity. Not that it is true in fact that all States live for ever, or that States are not occasionally so much dislocated and divided as to lose all identity for any purpose whatever. But while, in national law, death, birth, succession, adoption and other like events are the familiar topics with which law deals and for which it has to make provision by a carefully calculated estimate of the advantages and disadvantages of different lines of policy; in international law, the event of the dissolution or disruption of an old State, or the appearance of a new one, is a strange anomaly for which, in view of its rarity and, as it were, its unnaturalness, little provision can usefully be made by anticipation.

Another peculiarity in the situation of States as representing the individual human beings alone contemplated by national law, is that every State is a composite body made up of such individual human beings, each more or less capable by himself of counteracting the policy of the State itself. The power of the State over all its living members is of course theoretically complete; and it might be supposed that it were not worth while to consider the occasional consequences of the rare conflict of action that may take place between the State and its members. But this power is never practically complete, and for some matters, and at some periods, is much less complete than at others.

It happens, however, that the action of even a very small proportion of the whole community, if out of harmony with the public action of the State, may succeed in largely countervailing the general course of that public action. Instances may be taken from the extreme difficulty experienced by modern States, in view of all the appliances of modern navigation, and the habits of free commercial intercourse, to discharge properly the duties of neutrality. A few recalcitrant citizens of a neutral State may render the most valuable aid to one or other of two belligerents, and the high prices paid for the service are likely to present the most inordinate temptations. So, in the case of extradition and of international copyright, a State may, in spite of all its corporate efforts to the contrary, fail to discharge its international duties through the delinquencies and disloyalty of a few of its own citizens, or even through those unavoidable failures of justice by which the best administered system of law is occasionally disfigured.

So again, a State may be compromised by the rash, imprudent, or injurious acts of its citizens resident in the territory of foreign States. These citizens may either be private citizens, or may be persons directly representing the State, whether in a civil or military capacity. That a State should be ready to protect every one of its members when travelling abroad under the assurance of that protection, and when conducting themselves with proper regard to the laws and customs of the people with whom they take up their abode, is a proposition which no one would contest. But the proposition has been too frequently extended in practice to signify that for whatever purpose citizens of one State sojourn in the territory of another, and however they demean themselves, the so-called "honour" of their State compels it to interfere on their behalf, even if the result should be war. This is, no doubt, an abuse, and would now generally be admitted to be such; but it serves to illustrate the peculiar character of international law, owing to the composite elements out of which a State is constructed.

This idea, however, of composite units is very far from strange to national law; and the whole historical progress of that law, as indicated in the gradual development of all the groups out of which a fully organized nation is constituted, may be treated as a preparation for the peculiar features of international law. The conception of a mercantile "corporation," which is one of the last, as that of the family is the first, of the products of national law, carries with it many of the very same incidents which have just been described as especially distinguishing international from national law. Thus, for some purposes, a corporation, as a whole, is responsible for the acts of every one of its members; and is liable, under some circumstances, for his contracts, defaults, and wrong doings. A mercantile corporation is generally made to be only temporary in its duration, but it does not come to an end by any such natural event as death,—universally contemplated by law in the case of other "persons,"—and it contains within itself the seeds of a perpetual existence.

Some corporations, indeed, as those for religious, educational, and charitable purposes, seem by their constitution to be as imperishable as the State itself. Thus the leading notions on which the validity of international law depends, especially those of the permanence of States and of the relations of the State to its members, cannot but be familiar to the citizen of every developed State, from the facts which lie on every side of him in his own system of national law. It is not necessary to insist further on the evenness of the progress from national to international law.

It is worth while, however, glancing at the actual circumstances to which the existence of the body of European international law is due. It will be found, that if it is true that the study of national law, in a scientific spirit, is a main aid to the comprehension of the true nature of international law, it is also true that a study of the history of international law serves to throw back no small light on the true mode of growth of national law.

It deserves notice that the very fact that international law was a later growth than national law is one of the greatest relevancy, and yet one which has scarcely, as yet, attracted any attention. It was an enormous advantage to all the founders of the international law of Europe—whether legislators who published ordinances for the guidance of the subjects of particular States, or diplomatists who based treaties on the confessed validity of special doctrines, or text-book writers who gave an organic shape to a multitude of casual usages—to be already familiar, each in his own State, with a body of national law which had already matured itself into a system at once copious, well-compacted, and generally just.

It was not only that Roman law was, as it were, the vernacular tongue of all the statesmen, diplomatists, and lawyers of Europe, but that every thinker and writer on the topic of a law of nations was familiarly conversant, in the daily life of his own particular country, with legal machinery, legal conceptions and methods of disputation, and legal solutions for the complicated claims presented by the ordinary intercourse and occupations of mankind. Thus, when once the idea began to prevail, that the governors of the several States of Europe were subject to some body of laws, bearing an analogy to the national law of each State, there was no need for a long incubating process, during which the substance of this new law should slowly acquire its true shape and size. The substance was fully developed at once in all its proportions.

Not of course that room for indefinite improvement was not still left: the more so as a new commercial, social, and military era was just about to commence, which must call for doctrines of mutual relationship between States wholly unknown or inapplicable before. But whereas national law had to grow in the dark, slowly making its way through the dreary and accidental course of self-developed custom, there being no guide, standard, nor example to direct the primitive lawgiver, international law had guides and types and examples in abundance, and best of all, had a legal language ready to its hand.

Thus different have been the circumstances, with respect to the presence or absence of a pre-existing legal ideal, which have attended the growth of the two sorts of law. It need scarcely be noticed that a difference quite as striking is perceptible in respect of the pre-existence of a high moral ideal at the epoch of the foundation of international law. The ideal may not have been the highest or even so high as exists at this day; but, at the epoch of the foundation of systems of national law, there was generally no consciously perceived moral ideal at all.

The function which the so-called "law of nature" has performed in the development of a law of nations, is a proof, were such needed, that, at the time at which the rules for regulating the mutual relations of States were beginning to be systematized, a prevalent conception existed of a great moral order in which States, like individual persons, must find their place. The exact requisitions which this moral order implied were indeed very obscurely perceived, and were drawn from quarters of the most opposite character. Thus the maxims of primitive Christianity were mingled with the conclusions of Middle-age casuists; and the prescriptions of knight-errantry, with the suggestions of a rudely-calculated expediency. Nevertheless, for the conduct of individual life within the limits of a single State, although actual moral excellence was diffused over a very narrow space, the moral standard was high and composed of the richest elements. These elements included justice, mercy, patience, fidelity, truthfulness, self-sacrifice, generosity, and humanity in the largest sense.

It could not fail to strike a thoughtful and good man in the seventeenth century, casting his eyes over the battle-fields of Europe, that, in practice, the rulers of States and the leaders of armies confessed a very different creed in their conduct toward each other from that which they confessed and loudly extolled when seated peacefully at home. The contrast was obvious and could not fail to suggest itself. The only obstacle in the way of drawing instructive lessons from the contrast was to be found in the fact that war was as old as morality and religion themselves, and that a belief seemed to be ineradicably fixed, that men might and ought to be cruel, unsparing, and treacherous in one department of action, and none the less gentle, forgiving, and loyal in another.

So long as this sharp opposition between the moral standard for peace and for war, as between the citizens of the same State and between the citizens of different States, or (what meant much the same) between friends and between enemies, held its ground, the actual emergence of International Law was impossible, though the possibility of its future appearance was involved in the very fact of a higher moral standard co-existing in the world side by side with the lower one.

The most important steps in the evolution of international law were those by which the notion of the entire separation of the moral provinces in peace and in war, as between friends and as between enemies, was gradually got rid of. Such a step, eminently, was the remarkable institution of Chivalry. The influence of chivalry in carrying over the loftiest virtues of peaceful life into a life of war, otherwise so strange to them, cannot be exhibited more forcibly than by the following quotation from the second volume of Mr. Ward's well-known "Enquiry into the Foundation and History of the Law of Nations," p. 161. "Whatever savageness of temper
" a man might naturally have possessed, the 'point of
" honour' and spirit of knighthood had the most palpable
" and beneficial influence in generating a continued
" antidote to its consequences. So early as the middle of
" the tenth century, when the Emperor Henry I. intro-
" duced tournaments into Germany (which it is well
" known were the fairest graces of chivalry), it was
" ordained that no one should be admitted to that most
" honourable of all amusements who did not profess
" Christianity, or who had been known to have been
" guilty of perjury, treason, slaughter in cold blood,
" sacrilege, or violation of women. Certain it is, that
" from about this and the next century (to which the
" full birth of chivalry is generally ascribed) we are able,
" notwithstanding the barbarities that have been related
" to discover, nearly all over Europe, a change of manners
" which was evidently forced, because other improvements
" did not keep pace with them, and which may fairly be
" attributed to a chivalrous origin." Mr. Ward, in the

course of a deeply interesting chapter on this subject, gives a series of historic examples of the mode in which, under the influence of chivalric notions, the amount of ransom for prisoners was reduced, good faith was observed with enemies, treachery was punished, and the current harshness of practice in war was in a variety of ways mitigated.

Another important step in breaking up the distinction between the moral qualities appropriate in peace and in war was Feudalism, by which the semi-private relations of the rulers of the different European States to one another were often so complicated, that either war became impossible between them, or the consequences of war were largely mitigated through the active interposition of a superior feudal lord. In the same way, the ecclesiastical institutions of Europe, centering as they did in the Pope at Rome, were in the highest degree conducive to the creation of a moral tribunal to which kings, emperors, and soldiers were as much amenable as the peasant and the priest.

It may here be noted that one favourable circumstance which facilitated the creation of a system of International Law was the monarchical form of government which, up to comparatively recent times, has universally prevailed in modern Europe. The states of Europe were thus saved from being looked upon as mere abstractions or lifeless corporations. Each State was bound up with, and to a certain extent lost in, the individuality and fortunes of its particular sovereign for the time being. The sovereign, on the other hand, by his acquisitions or losses, by his marriage, by his treaties, by his enmities, and by his wars, irreparably committed the State he represented, and his conduct in these respects was only to a small extent influenced by any constitutional forces within the State itself.

Now, bearing in mind that the sovereign was a member of a Christian commonwealth and, as such, stood in relations of the closest intimacy both with the Pope and with his brother sovereigns; that, in many cases, he was bound in the ties of a close feudal union with other sovereigns; that by family ties he was dynastically related to them; and that in all public action it was the personal king and not the people he governed who appeared on the scene,—it can scarcely be wondered at if some canon of wise, rightful, honest action for the guidance of these sovereigns in their mutual intercourse should gradually be conceived and come into force. Such a canon in fact was the international law of Europe in its inchoate form.

In the actual erection of the complete structure of international law, there have been two celebrated schools which severally have affected to extract from different, or even from opposite, sources the rules of which the body of law is composed. The one school has rested the authority for an European law of nations upon the actual usage, and the assent implied in the fact of that usage, of the States of Europe. The other school has not felt itself bound by the limitations implied in actual usage or assent, but has conceived itself entitled to make the European law of nations repose on the authority of an antecedent "law of nature." This law of nature is here intended to imply a body of prescriptions of universal and necessary validity, the exact terms of them being discoverable on the application of certain wide and general maxims of justice, truth, mercy, and humanity, to the particular circumstances of the case for which the rule is demanded.

It cannot be denied that if the latter method is the more superficially attractive, the former one is likely to lead to results of greater practical value. As a matter of fact, it is useless to construct a law of nations, even on the most admirable and unimpeachable principles if the States of the world will not obey it. The best, or only, guide as to what rules States are likely to obey in the future are the rules by which they have actually guided themselves in the past. Nor is the systematization of these rules a superfluous task. The intermittent and desultory observance, indeed, of a certain beneficial practice may be a sufficient indication that the practice is not unsuited to the times and to the disposition of the States observing it. Yet a great deal may further have to be done to ensure its permanent ascendancy, to emphasize its importance, and, by advising common action, to secure the States adopting it against the inconveniences sometimes attendant upon isolated action.

In this way the formation of a compendious and logically distributed scheme of the best rules widely observed among the States of Europe could not fail of going a great way towards introducing principles of order into the intercourse of nations. It was, in fact, just this task which Grotius succeeded in effecting, and the permanent influence and authority of his great Work is a sufficient proof of the value of the cautious and, as it were, tentative method he adopted. The shortcomings of that method were that, if nothing but actual usage was to be introduced into European law, the growth and development of that law must mainly be determined by the accidental fortunes and tendencies of the several States.

The fact is that international law, like national law, must necessarily grow in two directions at once. One part of it comes upwards from the spontaneous habits and customs of those who are subject to it. The other part comes downward from the legislator, whose province it is to take a large and a wide view of all the necessities and probabilities of the case; to stimulate tendencies scarcely as yet apparent; to arrest proclivities before they come fixed; and, generally, to provide that such habits and dispositions may gradually be formed as may render even spontaneous customs more equitable and wise.

In the case of international law the functions of the legislator have to be discharged by a number of different persons. One of these is the statesman, who, in making a treaty, does his utmost to bind two nations, if not more, to the observance of new rules dictated by a sense of general expediency and justice, and therefore deserving of being universally adopted. Another of the persons performing the functions of the legislator is the text-book writer on international law, who, in describing the rules actually obtaining among States, occasionally steps aside to point out how far those rules conflict with the general interests of humanity and how far they subserve those interests; and what supplementary rules might advantageously be adopted in order to make the moral gain the highest conceivable. Grotius himself was not neglectful of this part of his task, and perhaps the error of some modern writers on the subject has been that of amplifying their task as legislators to the neglect of their task as narrators or historians. There is a place for the exercise of both functions, and the success of attempted reforms in the substance of international law must largely depend on the skill and moderation with which they are blended together.

In order to estimate the existing condition of a body of law, there are three points to which attention must be directed. In the first place, in view of the demands of the persons for whose use the law is designed, its copiousness affords an important index to its general sufficiency. In the second place, such an index is afforded by the degree of symmetrical form in which the law is presented and arranged. In the third place, the law must be tested by reference to the justice and moral adequacy of its provisions. In view, then, of these several requirements—that is to say, of copiousness or richness of material, of symmetry of form, and of legislative wisdom—modern international law may advantageously be examined in order to ascertain what lesson it has to teach with respect to the progress and prospects of law universally.

First, with respect to richness of material, there is no doubt that the international law of the present day covers a vast number of subjects, and contains a mass of rules and principles, which were scarcely so much as hinted at in the encyclopædic work of Grotius. In the time of Grotius, and even of Vattel, the only prominent topics of international law were the rights and duties of ambassadors, the obligations arising from treaties, the just causes of war, the rights and duties of allies, the rights and duties of neutrals, and certain alleged qualifications of the exercise of the extreme right of war. Doctrines upon these and a limited number of other topics were announced in the broadest form; but, with respect to some matters, such as the limitations of severity in war, it was openly confessed that there was no law at all, though, according to Grotius, there were a number of *temperamenta*, or modifying principles, which inculcated the observance of a practice gentler than that which was strictly legal with respect to putting prisoners to death, destroying the enemy's property, and annexing the enemy's territory.

According to Vattel, there was a distinction between the "necessary" and the "voluntary" law of nations. "Let us leave," he says, Book III., chap. xii., "the strict-"ness of the necessary law of nature to the conscience "of sovereigns; undoubtedly they are never allowed to "deviate from it. But as to the external effects of the "law among men, we must necessarily have recourse to "rules that shall be more certain and easy in the appli- "cation, and this for the safety and advantage of the great "society of mankind. These are the rules of the voluntary "law of nations." This distinction was, in fact, based upon the double origin of international law from essential moral principles—that is, the so-called law of nature— and from the actual customs which, in fact, regulated the intercourse of States.

The effect of the distinction was the same as that introduced by Grotius between what was *summum jus*, and what was a *temperamentum*. It was to recognize one part of international law as stable and eternally the same, based as it was on general and broad doctrines of what seemed to be of transparent validity; and another part as shifting and changeable with the changing manners, fashions, creeds, and customs, of the European States.

It is this last part of international law, the voluntary law and the field of the *temperamenta*, which has undergone improvements during the past century, to such an extent, indeed, as practically to abrogate and supersede much of what originally was thought to be its main substance or stronghold.

Modern international law is mostly made up of rules indebted for their existence to physical and social conditions which did not exist two centuries ago. At the present day, owing to the facilities of locomotion, and to postal and telegraph communication, as well as to wider moral conceptions and more enlightened commercial principles, the intercourse of nations with each other and of the citizens of one nation with those of another is far more noticeable and important in time of peace than in time of war.

Thus, while international law has the functions to perform of facilitating the intercourse of States and their citizens in time of peace; of obviating and determining the occasions of war; and of moderating the severities and restricting the area of war; the two last of these functions have been for the last two centuries acquiring a less and less degree of importance in proportion to the development of the first. Not that the function of restricting the area of war and tempering its severity is to be held of small account in itself. On the contrary, some of the most beneficial innovations which international law is daily witnessing have no other purpose in view than this. But the tendency of these very innovations, as of every other part of international law, is to equalize States in point of military opportunity and thereby to render war a less and less satisfactory criterion of their real relative prowess and strength. Hence, while the improvements in the laws of war have been preparing the way for the abolition of that whole topic as one belonging to international law, the improvements in that part of the law which concerns the peaceful relations of States are such as to warrant the hope of definite expansion. The latter matters escape attention, to a great extent, even in textbooks on the subject, because the mode in which this part of the law is developed is usually by treaty, and therefore the legal handling of it is sufficiently performed by referring to the general head of treaties. But when the mass of subjects with which modern treaties deal is considered, and when the number of treaties to which every State is a party is calculated, some idea may be formed of the mass of rights and duties, almost wholly unrecognized in the times of Grotius and even of Vattel, which now form the subjects of international law.

In the second place, it was said that the symmetrical

form of the law afforded a test whereby to estimate the height of development it had obtained. International law has gained much in point of form from having been cast into the mould of Roman law by the first writers—such as Balthazar Ayala, Albericus Gentilis, Grotius, and Puffendorf,—who published its principles and rules in an organic shape. This form has never been lost by Continental writers on the subject; though, as might perhaps have been expected, American and English text-book writers have proceeded independently of any particular form other than the one which seemed at the moment most conducive to convenience of arrangement and reference.

There is, indeed, a peculiar difficulty in giving harmony of appearance to the doctrines of international law owing to the very diverse basis on which those doctrines rest, the varying amounts of authority and certainty they carry with them, and the indefinite qualification of the doctrines themselves by the operation of innumerable treaties. Some eminent writers of the present day have endeavoured to ride over these difficulties by publishing so-called "codes" of international law, which purport either to present the law as it is at this day,—with only such additions or modifications as are imperatively called for by the fact of glaring gaps or contradictions or ambiguities,—or else to present the law in the complete shape it ought finally to assume, however far it may seem to be away from attaining it at the present day. The code of Professor Bluntschli represents one belonging to the first of the two types, and that of Mr. Dudley Field of New York represents one belonging to the other. It is scarcely possible to speak too highly of both these tentative efforts, and they cannot fail both to prove most valuable guide-books to the student, as well as standing remembrancers to statesmen of ideals to which the public law of Europe ought increasingly to conform itself.

This leads to the consideration of the third test, that of the wisdom and justice of the existing rules of international law. It has been seen that two leading principles originally guided the development of international law; one, the claims of the law of nature, and the other the claims of actual custom. There have been apparent of late years conscious energetic efforts to direct the course of international law by reference to a fresh standard, that of the common and permanent interests of all the nations concerned. It was the misfortune of international law, for a long period of its history, to have its course directed, or rather perverted, by the influence of the special nations which, for the time, happened to be most potent by land or by sea.

The influence of England in manufacturing the prevalent doctrines relative to neutral commerce, and of France and of the United States in combating these doctrines, is sufficiently familiar to all, and is usually alluded to by French and German writers with considerable emphasis. Such an influence, however, was far more conspicuous and important while war was the main topic with which international law had to deal.

So soon as nations began, in times of profound peace, to make treaties with one another from a presumedly equal standing-point and comprehending such varied matters as the use of harbours, navigable rivers and fisheries, commercial privileges, patents, trade-mark, copyright, and extradition, it was natural that exactly similar considerations should guide the policy of each contracting State as habitually guided the policy of the State in matters of purely internal administration. In this way a vast accession has been made to international law, in respect of topics as to which no corrupt aims or indirect purposes are so much as conceivable. It may be hoped too that, owing to the increased publicity which now attends all international transactions, and to the growing tendency to introduce into public life the morality demanded in private life, the era of secret treaties, by which two States have been wont to bind themselves in a way designedly disadvantageous to a third, is passing away.

It may thus be expected that a habit of thought will be formed to the effect that—just as in national law the institutions of property and contract have the good of the State as much in view as that of individual persons, and just as no private rights can exist which are opposed to the well-being of the State—so in international law every rule shall and must be based on the prospective benefit of all, not on that of a few alone, and, least of all, on that of the most unscrupulous and the strongest.

It remains to consider what influence the modern improvements in international law are likely to have in attaining their greatest and noblest end, the abolition of war.

It may first be noted that it is not true that the main cause of war is the uncertainty or backward condition of international law. This uncertainty or absence of law is rather a consequence than a cause of the state of things which leads to war. The real cause of modern European wars must be sought in the fact that most or all of the States of Europe are, in respect of their mutual relations, still sunk in that primitive rudeness which in all societies of men necessarily precedes a truly legal condition. For the attainment of such a condition, equality in respect of all the essential elements of subsistence must exist, and must be generally admitted to exist.

Now, as to the States of Europe at the present day,

their equality is a pure fiction, or rather a sanguine anticipation, of international lawyers. The notion of leading and inferior, great and little, strong and weak, important and insignificant, States has become so fixed in the diplomatic and historical, and thereby in the public, mind, that the legal notion of all States being equal is one wholly removed from the experience of actual life, and therefore is practically discarded. The past struggles of these States, and the prevalence of such doctrines as the Balance of Power, which no doubt also performed some useful service in arresting these struggles, are largely accountable for this, and Europe cannot all at once get free from her own past.

Nor is it only that States are at the present time unequal, whether equality be tested by extent of territory, by amount of population, by wealth, by military strength, by advantages of climate, or by number and kind of treaty obligations. Owing to an incessant change which is at work in the value of each of these elements, the relative preponderance and significance of States is constantly undergoing alteration. It thus comes about that each State, as it emerges from a condition of weakness to one of strength, aspires to liberate itself from shackles imposed on it in the hour of depression or defeat. It demands the "revision" of ancient treaties, or fresh bulwarks and securities against possible invasion on the part of powerful neighbours, or a public confession, in the conduct of diplomatic negociations, of its own growing importance.

Such aspirations as these can never be noticed by the best constructed systems of international law. These are too indefinite, too peculiar to each particular case, too dependent upon unaccountable national impulses and traditional modes of thought, to fall within the province of even the most refined legal language. The aspirations themselves may, in a certain sense, be termed "natural," and even irreproachable, though the issue of war to which they frequently lead is terrible and barbarous in the extreme. It is probable, indeed, that the State which in the way above described is endeavouring to pass beyond its existing bounds will either try to clothe its claims with the semblance of legal right, or else will provoke a quarrel with the State which it desires to encounter, so as to defy international law itself to find any other solution but that of war.

Now there are two popular methods for the diminution of war: the one, that of improving the substance as well as the form of international law; the other, that of introducing a general system of arbitration, by way of "substitute" (as it is called) for war. It will be well to examine at some length the applicability of these several methods to the purpose in view, and to consider whether any, and what, qualifications must be made in the mode of stating and employing these methods in order to impart to them the utmost possible validity.

The weak side of these methods is that they, as generally explained, seem to ignore the most prevalent causes of war, and to overrate the actual disposition of the European States in favour of peace. It is not true that the uncertainties or imperfect promulgation of international law are the main causes of modern wars, and it is equally untrue that the governments of most of the leading European States are sincerely desirous of permanent peace. This constitutes the imperfection of the analogy between national law as existing in a civilized State, and international law as existing in an imperfectly civilized society of States. In the case of national law, the prevalence of disorder and crime is a pretty sure index of bad laws and bad government; and in every State it may be assumed that the bulk of the population are desirous to have their disputes decided by the peaceful processes of courts of justice rather than by the violence of physical conflict. The bulk of the community do not wish to get more than the law gives them, though, through the blindness of passion or selfishness, individual persons may often be tempted to persuade themselves that the law gives them more than it does.

It is true that one reason of the acquiescence of the bulk of a national community in the laws by which they are governed is a knowledge of the central force which is always behind the laws, and which is ready to support them. Such a force is at present absent from international law; and it might be said that one commonly suggested mode of improving that law is the creation of such a force. But here, again, the same fallacy lurks behind. The States of Europe do not at present wish to submit themselves to any central force, nor even to create such a force out of their own body by the most adequate representative system imaginable.

Again, with respect to Arbitration, this method, invaluable as it is, at least presupposes a certain measure of assent by both parties who resort to it. It implies a belief on the part of both that either a legal or quasi-legal question is involved, and that each is, in his own opinion, in the right; or, in other words, that, when the state of the facts is carefully examined, and the law or equitable principle accurately expounded, each hopes and thinks the result will be in his own favour. A *bona fide* belief in the justice of one's own cause is an essential element in a successful arbitration. If such a belief is absent, there can be no readiness to obey the award, and the same causes of acrimony exist after the award as before it.

In national law, indeed, an award may be converted into what is called a "rule of court," that is, may have impressed upon it all the validity of a judicial sentence. This finally ends litigation, and the whole process is only a special method of conducting it. But the existence of a judicial and executive machinery, as a prop to arbitration, is not presupposed in the notion of arbitration itself; and the demand for such machinery, in the mouths of those who most loudly call for an universal system of international arbitration, is quite distinguishable from the demand for this last. It is here fully recognized that the proposal for the extension of the practice of arbitration is, at present, a far more moderate and hopeful one than the suggested creation of a central authority prepared to carry out, in the name of all the States of Europe, the sentence of a court of arbitration against any one of them.

If it be true, then, as has been indicated above, that the most fruitful causes of war are not to be sought in the condition of international law, but in the condition, relations, and temperament of the European States, the field for the application of arbitration might seem to be a comparatively narrow one. The alleged limitations to the practice of arbitration may be expressed in the following words of Professor Mountague Bernard in a letter to the *Times* of October 18th, 1873:—"Arbitration "is an expedient of the highest value for terminating "international controversies; but it is not applicable to "all cases or under all circumstances, and the cases and "circumstances to which it is not applicable do not admit "of precise definition. Arbitration, therefore, must of "necessity be voluntary; and though it may sometimes "be a moral duty to resort to it, cannot be commanded in "any form by what is called the positive law of nations."

The explanation of this passage, no doubt, is that when a State is bent upon doing what, on the simplest reading of the most elementary principles of international law, is an act of injustice or aggression, neither the trespassing State will, nor the State trespassed upon ought to, refer the question to the decision of third parties. It may be maintained in defence of this position that, in the existing inequality of European States, no tribunal can be constituted which shall be possessed of the authority, wisdom, and moral character needed to decide upon points which, in the view of a State suffering from aggression, seem to touch its independence and national existence; and that, even could such a tribunal be found, no State would ever believe in the moral competency of the tribunal sufficiently to entrust to it a decision upon a question involving issues so great.

The difficulty may be expressed by saying that arbitration seems to be the only means of perfecting relations of order, equity, and mutual confidence, between States; the pre-existence, however, of which very relations must be treated as a condition precedent to the universal application of arbitration. Looking at the present state of things, it is not at once apparent how designing and ambitious States can be made contented, revengeful States made oblivious, timid States made confident, by the mere magic of an appeal to the duty of referring to arbitration legal or political complications which they are well aware do not exist. These complications are, as often as not, gossamer cobwebs spun in order to conceal the hideous spirit of avarice, or passion, or national pride which dominates within. The most competent tribunal imaginable, so far from being welcomed, would only be shunned in proportion to its competency and its purity; while an award which adjudged a sentence of extinction (or what might be treated as such) against the life of a State would be simply repudiated.

It would be well if all lovers and promoters of peace were seriously to lay to heart these considerations, and not to underrate, through ignorance or thoughtlessness, the hardness of the task to which they have devoted themselves. There is no doubt that both those who look upon the difficulties in the path as almost insuperable, and those who all but ignore them, have a common end in view; and, if they would only learn of one another, patiently and respectfully, would find themselves not so far removed from each other as they suppose. In the hope of contributing somewhat to bring about such a reconciliation, the following remarks are offered.

If it be true that wars mostly arise, as has above been explained, from what has been called the existing inequality of States, it is obvious that every political or social measure that tends to bring about permanent equality tends, to that extent, to reduce the probabilities of war. Hence, even where it may be impossible to equalize physical areas, or numerical estimates of population, or even climatic advantages and national opportunities, still it may be of great use to propagate doctrines which insist on that equality of contribution and on that equality of moral and spiritual value which, in instituting a comparison between States, the population of each may properly claim for itself.

Every influence which increases the economical dependence of States upon each other, every barrier which is removed from free commercial intercourse and free locomotion and communication, not only makes war more and more opposed to the obvious interest of all classes of persons in every State, but brings home more and more distinctly the fact that even States apparently the weakest and smallest have a function to perform in the great society of States, which, in dignity and importance, may vie with that performed by the most pretentious. Every measure that gives political enfranchisement and personal liberty to large classes of the population must tend to the disuse of the enormous European armaments which absorb so much of the wealth of all States, and which, by keeping up a fictitious and delusive inequality among States, as well as by nursing a childish passion for military "glory," tends to a like extent to promote war. Again, every movement that unites together the mass of the population of different countries, by teaching them what is their common interest, by removing traditional prejudices and antipathies, and by bringing them, through locomotion and mutual interchange of labour, face to face with each other, must tend to diminish the possibility of war.

While the attention, however, continues fixed upon all these more general methods of rendering the nations of Europe unused to war, there is no doubt that the improvement and codification of international law, and the assimilation of the national laws of the several States, must tend largely to prevent the chance of, or to diminish the excuses for, armed conflict.

Then, too, a resort to arbitration cannot be too earnestly recommended nor too perseveringly pressed. It is only through a change in the public opinion and feeling of the several States that a condition of legal relationship can succeed to the existing condition of rivalry and violence. But this public feeling itself must be largely influenced by familiarity with legal procedure in the place of the dread familiarity it already has with the struggles of war. The new familiarity will be largely promoted by supporting, in every possible way, the practice of arbitration, and by never admitting it to be an impossible solution of a difficulty till after it has proved to be such. The way in which this familiarity operates will be described lower down.

There are two important avenues to the improvement of international law. One is that of imparting increased certainty and publicity to the rules which compose it; the other is that of recommending for adoption by States new rules, by way of supplementing or modifying the old ones; such new rules to be ostensibly founded on principles of general expediency and abstract justice. There are great and obvious difficulties in the way of the success of each of these measures. As to the first one, any one acquainted with the character of existing international law, and with the dubious and contracted nature of the evidence on which the validity of even the best approved rules rests, will recognize at once that the attempt to secure general acquiescence in the mode of stating the whole mass of rules must involve obstacles all but, if not quite, insuperable. It must be remembered that the republication of even a national system of law, where a large part of it is comprised in tolerably explicit statutes and the rest in the reports of authoritatively decided cases or in the accredited comments of competent writers on a clearly written text, is a task from which, on the ground of the hazard attending the operation, some of the ablest minds have universally been known to shrink.

But international law, in spite of the scarcity and thinness of its materials, when contrasted with a fully developed system of national law, must, from the nature of the case, far excel in ambiguity and indefiniteness the most tortuously grown system of law in any civilized State. The absence of any legislative authority, and of courts of justice purporting to act in the name of such an authority, throws all the responsibility of ascertaining the rules (such as they are) of international law on the private students and investigators in each particular country. The materials which these private persons possess for their researches, instead of being explicit statutes or decisions by publicly authorized judges or commentators, are composed of nothing more certain than the frequently repeated language of treaties between particular States, the utterances of judges in the Prize Courts instituted during particular wars, the varying and conflicting ordinances and regulations of particular sovereigns, the forced logic of individual diplomatists and popular or parliamentary orators, and the wire-spun refinements of the scholastic closet student.

This statement of the difficulties which beset any one who attempts to republish in a systematized form the rules and principles of the international law of Europe is not made in a spirit of scepticism, as intimating that the existence of such law is a mere illusion. In spite of the indefiniteness and obscurity of the quarters from which a knowledge of the law has to be drawn, it cannot be denied that true legal relationships between the States of Europe have, for the last seven or eight centuries, been gradually forming themselves; and the rules which have sprung from and expressed those relationships have been more and more exactly adapted to the requirements of general convenience and justice.

The progress has undoubtedly been all the slower, and occasional retrogressions the more frequent, from the mistiness of the path through which the law has been compelled to march. Each State, as it has become overweeningly powerful and unscrupulous, has endeavoured to wrest the existing rules of international law, by interpretation or open amendment, into conformity with what its own interests immediately demanded. A strong State has imposed upon a weak one in the hour of defeat the necessity of confessing by treaty the existence of some one-sided and spurious rules; while the fact of the treaty itself has, in no long time, become a main evidence of the universal validity of the new rules. The misfortune has been, too, that States have generally been supported in their iniquity by the consentient voice of text-book writers among their own citizens. Even at the present day, in treating of the subject historically, this spurious patriotism is too apt to manifest itself, and the writers in each country seem often enough as though they were the paid apologists of the acts of their own State in every age.

The above described abuses of international law by ascendant States may be taken as, in some way, a tribute to the actuality and energy of that law. It is seldom that States, even in the flush of victory, have dared ostentatiously to offend against a generally admitted principle of international law. The methods of evading the operation of the principle have been either to deny the fact of the existence of such a principle; or to deny its applicability under the special circumstances of the case; or to wrest the language in which it is customarily expressed in such a way as to alter its meaning; or by a sort of play at legislation to abrogate it by a formal convention entered into with States which are momentarily dependent; or to obtain from professedly learned citizens of its own and under its own influence direct or indirect scientific opinion in derogation of the true compass and import of the principle.

If this view be historically correct, it both establishes the supreme value of immutable principles of international law, and indicates the sort of machinery which may be advantageously called into being for the foundation of such principles.

It has been seen that the main obstacle to the creation of a definite and settled system of international law has been the isolation and narrow patriotism of the 'earned men who have chiefly helped to develop it. This obstacle can only be overcome by promoting a closer sympathy between all the students and professors of international law in different States. Signs of the growth of such a sympathy are already apparent; and one and another institution has been founded for the purpose of giving organized completeness to the movement. If once all the scientific students of international law throughout Europe come to be of one mind as to the principles and leading rules of which that law is composed, there will no longer be any hope for an ambitious and reckless State in endeavouring to wrest the interpretation of the rules of international law in its own favour.

It is none the less to be feared, on the grounds above described, that for a long time to come States will now and again endeavour to burst their bounds and to assail the independence of their neighbours. But when once the principles and rules of international law shall have been reduced to definiteness and certainty, and the leading students of that law in all the several States shall have pledged themselves to support one interpretation and one only, every outrage committed by any State will stand out in plain colours to be condemned, and not countenanced, by the international law of the world. The influence of such a judgment will be all the greater, inasmuch as, by the same process by which international law is freed from the distortions introduced by particular States, it will gain infinitely in authority and moral reputation. It will stand forth, as gradually becoming, what in its own nature it essentially is, an embodiment of the purest reason and the loftiest morality, and as having for its sole end such an adjustment of the relations of the several States of the world as may best enable each to contribute its share to the welfare and moral advancement of all.

It will thus be seen what place the further work of suggesting amendments and additions must occupy in the general task of completing the development of international law. The first object to be attained (as will be seen) is to provide for the organization of a body of persons who shall form such a scientific opinion on the existing state of the law as shall command universal respect. There is no doubt that the mere process of presenting the scattered and much disputed rules of international law in a more compact and definite shape must of necessity compel a certain amount of alteration in those rules. The very filling in of gaps which have been left open through the accidental facts of European history must imply a certain measure of what is, practically, legislation. But the most that is here contemplated, as a sort of accident in the course of republishing a diffuse system of law in a condensed form, is very far removed from what some mean by the project of constructing an European code.

According to these, a code is to be at once devised of the utmost possible completeness, not only gathering up all the principles and rules of international law which possess a fair amount of authority, but also extending to all the rules of international intercourse which, in view of the social and commercial relations likely progressively to develop among the citizens of the several States, it may ever become desirable or indispensible to enact. Such matters are those which, at present, so far as they are made subject-matters of law at all, are provided for by special treaties between particular States. Of this kind are, for instance, all the topics of what is sometimes called "private international law," and all the rules appertaining to the navigation of the high seas, to copyright, to trade-marks, to patents, and to extradition.

With respect to some of these matters, there is no doubt that uniformity of practice among all States in the conduct of their mutual relations must be of inestimable value, and might well form the subject of a general code to which each State should be invited to signify its adherence. But, however numerous the topics comprehended in such a code, there must always be some outlying topics which, in view of the peculiar situation and circumstances of particular States, must continue to be more appropriately dealt with in private treaties. The general adoption, indeed, of so comprehensive a code as that here alluded to, cannot be hoped for till a greater amount of actual equality is brought about among the States of Europe, though the perfecting of such an equality would be largely accomplished by the use of such a code.

Whatever be the prospects of such a code, however, the value of sketching it out and of constantly holding it forth as an ideal to be attained sooner or later cannot but exercise an important influence on the formation of public opinion, and thereby on that of the members of representative assemblies to which statesmen are finally accountable. In the mean time the earlier, and more modest, as well as more purely scientific, work is of the most immediate promise, and cannot afford to be delayed.

This whole discussion of the means of improving international law is closely related to that of the advantages or possibility of introducing a general system of arbitration. The difficulties in the way of making such a system obligatory have been clearly indicated. But, however menacing these difficulties, it is to be remembered that the principal change to be introduced into the society of States is to substitute a notion of legal relationship, of legal right, legal duty, legal accountability, and of legal penalty, in the stead of that of spasmodic and self-determined violence. So long as statesmen, on the slightest provocation, talk of the "honour" of their State being wounded, and not of a legal right being infringed or threatened, so long the hope of permanent peace is vain. It ought, then, to be the aim of every lover of peace to secure that each apparent ground for quarrel is treated as having a relation to a legal right and duty. To improve and propagate a knowledge of international law is one great part of the work to be done; to lose no occasion to recommend arbitration, and to devise expedients for facilitating the practice of arbitration, is another and equally important one.

CHAPTER XIII.

CODIFICATION.

When it is remembered by what tedious and apparently accidental processes every system of national law comes into being, it can scarcely be wondered at that an epoch sooner or later arrives in the history of every State, at which a loud cry is heard for simplification and republication of the law. It has been seen that the mass of the laws in every country spring up, as it were, spontaneously, being necessary links and bonds for the purpose of holding together, with the cohesiveness which is indispensable, the several groups out of which the State is constituted, and for maintaining the unity and rigidity of the individual groups themselves. These essential laws cannot be accurately described as "customs," this term signifying either what is merely an occasional and irregular growth upon a pre-existing body of law, or else the eccentric variations of usage which, in a partially civilized society, precede the existence of the State, and of law in the true sense. Nevertheless, it is these primitive customs, in the latter sense of the term, which are the foundation of true law, and which contain in themselves the germs of all the most important classes of law. Thus, as was seen in a former chapter, the family, government, property, and contract, being at the first only obscurely hinted at in the desultory practices of a people, become gradually marked out as subject-matter for strict regulation by definite rules; and the relations of these several topics to one another, and to the State as a whole, become more and more clearly ascertained.

This work was accomplished by what cannot be designated in more intelligible language than that which speaks of it as a spontaneous moral impetus of the people themselves. No doubt this spontaneity itself is determined by a number of general causes which operate in some places and not in others, and at some times and not at others. It is also true, that in the course of the development of a State, it usually happens that certain more special causes concur to give energy and determinateness to the legislation of the State. Such causes are the wide prevalence of religious beliefs, together with the concentrated influence of a priestly hierarchy resulting therefrom; and the facts of military domination and military discipline, or of peculiar institutions, such as the feudal system and chivalry.

The result of the actual process by which a system of law is thus gradually built up is that, however much accustomed to it the people may have become, and, therefore, however little its disadvantages are actually experienced, yet the obscure and involved condition of the laws presents at once a dangerous opening for governmental abuses of all sorts, and a steady opposition to the invasion of reform. These evils are largely exaggerated in course of time by the inordinate growth of law; brought about partly through the mere process of administering it in courts of justice, and partly through the direct and spasmodic interposition of the legislature. The legislature, in enacting statutes, and the courts of justice in framing decisions on the state of the law, as occasion needs, having no formal standard or type to guide themselves by, severally proceed in their own independent paths, gradually creating notions and rules of interpretation solely for their own use, and having no relation to the whole system of law, which indeed cannot be said to exist in an organic shape.

This condition of things is not peculiar to any one country, but is an universal consequence of the mode in which civilization progresses. It is only less conspicuous in those countries in which the spontaneous development of law has, at an earlier stage, been interfered with through the effects either of internal revolutions, accompanied by violent changes of government, or of foreign conquest. It is in countries such as England, which has been exempt from or has resisted both these interfering influences, and which has progressed a long way in the path of civilization, that the anarchical condition of the legal system, as above described, is seen in its most characteristic phase. The following quotation from Mr. John Stuart Mill's well-known essay on Bentham, republished in his "Dissertations and Discussions," vol. i. p. 368, will exactly illustrate the general phenomena here alluded to:—

"The laws which were suitable to the first of these "states of society could have no manner of relation to "the circumstances of the second; which could not even "have come into existence unless something had been "done to adapt those laws to it. But the adaptation "was not the result of thought and design; it arose, not "from any comprehensive consideration of the new state "of society and its exigencies. What was done, was "done by a struggle of centuries between the old bar- "barism and the new civilization; between the feudal "aristocracy of conquerors, holding fast to the rude "system they had established, and the conquered effect- "ing their emancipation. The last was the growing "power, but was never strong enough to break its bonds,

"though, ever and anon, some weak point gave way.
"Hence, the law came to be like the costume of a full-
"grown man, who had never put off the clothes made for
"him when he first went school. Band after band had
"been burst, and, as the rent widened, then, without
"removing anything except what might drop off of itself,
"the hole was darned, or patches of fresh law were bought
"from the nearest shop and stuck on. Hence all ages of
"English history have given one another rendezvous in
"English law; their several products may be seen all
"together, not interfused, but heaped one upon another,
"as many different ages of the earth may be read in some
"perpendicular section of its surface,—the deposits of
"each successive period, not substituted, but super-
"imposed on those of the preceding. And in the world of
"law, no less than in the physical world, every com-
"motion and conflict of the elements has left its mark
"behind, in some breach or irregularity of the strata;
"every struggle which ever rent the bosom of society
"is apparent in the disjointed condition of the part of
"the field of law which covers the spot; nay, the very
"traps and pitfalls, which one contending party set for
"another, are still standing, and the teeth, not of hyenas
"only, but of foxes and all cunning animals, are im-
"printed on the curious remains found in these ante-
"diluvian caves."

This account is probably less true of all those countries in which the Roman law proper, the "codes of the barbarians," and the canon law, have had an enduring vitality; though, as to such countries, and pre-eminently France and Germany, other causes, such as the aggregation under one dominion of a number of provinces, each with its own system and customary law, have tended to produce a chaos different in kind from, but equal in degree to, that found in English law.

EVILS TO BE REMEDIED.

Admitting then that a time must arrive when a State becomes conscious of the inadequacy in form, as well as in substance, of its own laws, the question is presented as to what is the best remedy to provide. It is needless to premise that the remedy required may be different for different countries, and at different epochs; and, therefore, in laying down the most general propositions on the subject, openings must always be left for the qualifications which the circumstances of particular countries may call for. Be it remembered, at the outset, that the exact evils to be provided against are (1) the actual uncertainty in the law, owing to the obscurity, indefiniteness, and conflict of the authorities from which a knowledge of it is to be derived; (2) the amount of labour and time consumed both by judges and private legal practitioners in the process of ascertaining the state of the law, either for the purpose of giving final judgment, or of merely rendering professional assistance; (3) the want of publicity in the law, whereby the most serious obstacles are placed in the way of all persons in the community coming by a knowledge of their rights and duties; (4) the want of acquaintance with, or of opportunity of informing himself upon, the leading doctrines of the law, which must ceaselessly hamper the legislator in his effort to amend any special branch of the law.

These four classes of evils, which are entirely independent of one another, and yet all of the most serious importance, must all be kept in view in any attempted remedy for the unsystematic character of a body of law. No remedy, or mode of applying a remedy, which leaves one of these evils wholly out of account, however effectually it deals with the rest, can be deemed sufficient. It may be better even to wait longer for a more complete and adequate remedy than to close hastily with a more immediate remedy which only cures a part of the disease, and puts the attainment of perfect health at a greater distance than ever.

Now, the remedy which is in everybody's mouth for the evils above enumerated, and for all that disorderly condition of a nation's laws which results in those distinct evils, is "codification." But, inasmuch as this term is made to mean something very different by each person who uses it, the recommendation itself is not of very much service until the nature of the codification recommended is made plain. The following meanings (among others) are given to the term *codification* by different classes of reasoners. Some mean by it the mere conversion of the whole unwritten law of a country into written law, in such a way that no secret or inaccessible principles of law may hereafter exist, and that all persons in the country may have an equal opportunity with judges and lawyers of acquainting themselves with the state of the law. In this meaning of the term, publicity and explicitness are the essentials rather than unity and correct classification. This must have been the sense in the mind of those who procured the publication of those ancient codes of which Sir H. S. Maine writes in his "Ancient Law," p. 1 ':—" In " Greece, in Italy, on the Hellenized sea-board of " Western Asia, these codes all made their appearance " at periods much the same everywhere; not, I mean, " at periods identical in point of time, but similar in " point of the relative progress of the community. " Everywhere, in the countries I have named, laws " engraven on tablets and published to the people take " the place of usages deposited with the recollection " of a privileged oligarchy. It must not for a moment " be supposed that the refined considerations now urged " in favour of what is called codification had any part "or place in the change I have described. The ancient codes were doubtless originally suggested by the discovery and diffusion of the art of writing. It is true that the aristocracies seem to have abused their monopoly of legal knowledge; and at all events their exclusive possession of the law was a formidable impediment to the success of those popular movements which began to be universal in the western world. But, though democratic sentiment may have added to their popularity, the codes were certainly in the main a direct result of the invention of writing. Inscribed tablets were seen to be a better depository of law, and a better security for its accurate preservation, than the memory of a number of persons, however strengthened by political exercise." It would seem that even to Bentham's mind, organizer as he was, the main service of a code seemed to be that of arresting the progress of "judge-made law," and getting finally rid of the notion that there are any recondite principles of law traditionally handed down from one generation of judges to another, and not accessible to the general public.

Those who use the term *codification*, in the sense now being examined, may be distributed into three classes, two of which classes may be said to have generated, in England at least, influential schools of opinion on the subject. To the first class belong those who mean by a *code* nothing more nor less than a written republication of the whole mass of existing law, statute and common law, written and unwritten law, attention being mainly paid, in the way just described, to the certainty and publicity of the new body of law, and questions of arrangement and even of consistency in terminology being treated as of very subordinate importance.

To the second class belong those who, like the last-mentioned persons, consider publicity and certainty the main purpose of a code, but desire to adhere as closely as possible to the language, conceptions, and methods of arrangement familiar in the old law. They would codify the statute and the common law apart from one another, and would think it a hazardous experiment to attempt to frame a new scientific vocabulary and logical mould to which both departments of law might be forced to adapt themselves. In the eyes of these reasoners, who represent some of the most able and thoughtful practitioners at the English bar, the essence of so-called codification is not the attainment of the highest possible amount of unity and symmetry, but the liberation of old law from the antinomies and obscurities which impeded its free and natural growth.

Thus the main part of the codifier's work would be that of comparing the results of decided cases, for the purpose of throwing the weight of his influence into the scale of one set of authorities rather than of another; of announcing the existence of irreconcilable contradictions, for the purpose of inviting legislative interference; of declaring certain principles and rules to have become practically obsolete, and certain decisions, once regarded as authoritative, to be now finally overruled; and, lastly, of stating the general results of decided cases in the form of brief and compendious propositions, yet with the least possible encroachment on the old legal conceptions and language. This process is sometimes called *digesting*, or making a *digest*, and is contrasted with *codifying*, or making a *code*.

There is, undoubtedly, a cautiousness and moderation attaching to the suggested process which goes far to render it popular with many who, from daily experience, are well aware of the delay, inconvenience, and injustice occasioned by a chaotic condition of the law authorities, and yet, from constitutional timidity or acquired professional wariness, shrink from the bolder schemes advocated in other quarters. The objections to this method will be more clear when other current notions of what codification does and ought to imply have been evolved. In the mean time it is sufficient to notice that such a scheme as the above involves a large part of exactly the same labour as would be required in recasting the whole body of the law into a new and symmetrical shape better adapted to the demands of modern society. So far the work is a necessary one in any case, and, in the least sanguine view, may be treated as a preparatory step to the creation of a more systematic work. But, on the other hand, all that part of the work (and that not the least laborious) which is concerned with the re-expression, in brief rules of law, of the general result of decided cases would have to be done over again if ever a more systematic project were hereafter adopted.

If a great national waste is not to be incurred, the decision on the superior claims of some one of various rival methods must be made at once; and, before entering upon any of them, it must be borne in mind that the most serious objections to the preparation of this sort of "digest," as a substitute for a more organically complete work, are that the bulk of the work must be enormous; the facilities for reference and study must be of a very inferior sort; and, in the place of taking occasion to reconstruct the form of English law after a fashion better adapted to the exigences of the present day and in closer sympathy with the form of Continental systems of law, every antique fossil is carefully preserved (if only its existence is indubitably established), and the accidental divisions and language generated in semi-civilized times are embalmed and reverentially handed down to supply the necessities of endless generations to come.

The third class of adherents to the cause of *codification* generally, in the first sense of the term above noted, place a high value upon certainty and publicity, and yet, unlike the members of the last class, have no lingering fondness for the forms and language of the past. On the other hand, they consider complete logical unity and consistency, as applied to the complete reconstruction of a whole body of national law, as of very subordinate importance. These persons belong to what is sometimes characterized as an essentially "practical" type. They consider not only what is best, but what is possible; and the temptation that besets them is to take what is very inferior, because it is attainable with the least amount of delay and of immediate opposition. No doubt, in the prosecution of every great enterprise something approaching to a compromise has to be made, in order to secure the co-operation of those who cannot see so far or so wide as the originator of the movement. In such cases, the main duty of the originator is to beware that he does not sacrifice so much as to make the movement not worth further persisting in, and that he does not interpose permanent barriers in his path which shall for ever prevent him from progressing to the highest point of perfection.

The class of "codifiers" now under consideration are fond of speaking of "gradual" or of "progressive" codification. They desire to reconstruct large portions of the law, each severally by itself—in fact, converting all the law on each separate topic into a statute, the statutes being quite independent of one another, or only casually related. The subjects to be thus codified in turn would be chosen either in view of their apparent importance, or of the pressing need they stand in of having some process of re-organization performed upon them. The titles of the several subjects would be the ones currently in use, and would thus presuppose the retention of all the main divisions of the law which have been familiar from the most ancient times.

This notion of codification was that which seems to have prevailed at the commencement of the preparation of the Code Napoléon, though the systematic treatises of Pothier, and the actual prevalence of Roman law in a large part of France and its influence in other parts, secured the use of a logical language and of a method of classification to which each branch of the law, as it became successively codified, readily adapted itself. The same practice has been applied with success (as it would appear) to British India, in which the peculiar circumstances of the country would seem to have rendered it eminently suitable, or, rather, indispensable. In British India the character of the law has had a political importance which is wholly unlike anything that exists in England, or in most of the countries of Europe. The necessity of discovering some system of law which would neither shock the prejudices of natives, nor grievously disappoint the expectations of English settlers—which would preserve that which was sanctioned by custom, and yet afford a very wide field for the introduction of systematic legislation; which could be easily learnt and readily administered—this necessity concerned the very vitality of the English dominion in India, and provision for it must needs have taken precedence of all considerations for the future unity and completeness of the whole code.

Similar circumstances existed in Prussia under Frederick II., and previously to the influence of the French codes introduced into Prussia by Napoleon, when codification had already become one great question of the day. Though the code of Frederick II. was not confined to particular topics, yet it was very far from exhausting the whole body of law. By the "Patent of Publication," it was said that the code was to be merely a subsidiary system, to take the place of Roman, "common Saxon," and other foreign subsidiary laws and statutes. All provincial laws were to continue in force as hitherto, but they, too, were to be severally digested or codified within three years.

The objections to this partial codification are obvious on the face of it, and the only excuse for it is the undoubtedly superior facility of getting the work undertaken at all. Many persons who will stand aghast at the project of codifying the whole law, as too adventurous and rash a task for mortal man to grapple with, will engage cheerfully enough in the task of consolidating all the statutes and embodying all the principles of common law on a particular subject, even though that subject, like merchant shipping, bills of exchange, evidence, or jury trial, be one of enormous range. Nor will such persons be much more alarmed if the consolidating and embodying statute affect a precision in language and skill in logical arrangement of a kind entirely novel in legislative enactments.

In this way, no doubt, a considerable amount, or perhaps the whole, of the law might gradually be reduced into statute law, and form a body of codes or a code. Nevertheless, there would still hang round the work the vices of its mode of accomplishment. There could be no possible harmony of view between the different sets of codifiers working (it may be) at long distances of time without mutual concert, and with only a very imperfect reference to one another's work. This want of unity in conception and execution cannot but largely affect the character of the final work; and though that work, even with such shortcomings as are thus implied, need not be valueless, or may even be a great gain upon what went before, it is a serious mistake to expend the toil necessary in any case to the completion of a code upon a work which, for educational purposes, popular and professional, as well as for purposes of speedy and ready disputation in courts of justice, is something very far removed from the best.

It is time now to pass on to the second mode of interpreting the term *codification,* to the full appreciation of which the above remarks on partial codes will have fitly prepared the way. In this second sense of the term, a code is eminently a product of logical art. The persons who advocate codification in the sense now being considered, while they agree with the former in the importance they attach to certainty and publicity in the law, yet differ from these in attaching at least an equal importance to the claims of symmetry, of consistency of language, and of perfection in logical distribution. They hold that one great purpose of a code is to shorten and simplify labour. Another great purpose is to prevent litigation by removing, as far as possible, all grounds for dispute about the meaning of terms or the import of sentences. Now, the only means to secure both these objects at once is to rescue law from the verbiage, the cross-divisions, and the cloudy classifications in which the accidents of ages (and those mostly very dark ages) of forensic dispute have shrouded it, and to republish it in a form to which the most exact logician can take no exception. Not, however, that it is sought needlessly to alter terms, and to reconstruct familiar notions. On the contrary, just as little change would be made as was absolutely indispensable for the above ends, but also just as much.

There are, indeed, those who contend that law by its nature resists the process of being hemmed in by the logical confines which are suitable to mark the various departments of a physical science, and they go on to contend that to make much of rigid definitions and sound classification in matters of law is labour in vain. The objection to codification in the sense now being considered is so common a one, especially in England, that it is worth while examining with some attention the grounds upon which it rests. The meaning of the objection seems to be that the institutions upon which law is based are so peculiar, the transactions of mankind out of which refined legal rules grow so multiplied and so intricate, and the capacities of language so limited, considering the strain put upon it for the expression of law, that only a very moderate amount of scientific precision in this region can ever be hoped for or ought to be attempted.

It might be sufficient to reply to this sort of reasoning that every modern statute enacted by the British Parliament, with its distributed subject matter, its logical classifications, its attempted accurate terminology, and its interpretation clauses, not only aspires to keep pace with the subtleties of human action and the diversities of social and commercial operations, but proceeds upon a theoretic belief that the endeavour will be not altogether unsuccessful. Some statutes are very badly drawn and others are well drawn; but whether well or ill drawn, the standard by which the adequacy of a statute is universally and properly weighed is that of logical and scientific completeness. The praises, again, which are accorded to certain codified systems of law,—as the works undertaken under the auspices of Justinian,—are based on the rigid precision of the terminology, and the exhaustiveness of the classification, quite as much as on the value of the legal conceptions and the firm hold of them which the writers displayed. In the same way the absence of definitions is notoriously treated as a serious imperfection in the French codes, and the current criticism directed against the French and other celebrated modern codes is usually based on some purely logical shortcomings.

Thus it would appear that when once a code is made or while it is being made, the common voice of mankind demands accuracy in preference to looseness in the use of terms, and sound, in preference to unsound, methods of arrangement. Instead of making allowance for the difficulties of the codifier in view of the variety and complexity of human action, the attainment of the highest possible amount of exactness in the conduct of logical processes is imperiously demanded. Nevertheless, it is sometimes the very same persons who discourage the project of making a systematic code, on the alleged ground that the rigid logic attainable in the treatment of the physical sciences is not attainable in the treatment of law, who are most severe on the codifier who ill discharges his most appropriate and necessary functions.

It might almost seem as if this class of objectors believed that the persons who favoured the sort of codification now being considered were stricken with a mania for definition and classification, solely as such and wholly apart from any practical end to be served.

The sole purpose of definitions is to correct the consequences of the vague and uncertain, or often ambiguous, meanings which have generally become attached to terms largely used in the common speech of the people. The terms of law are very generally also popular terms, and have become infected with all the vacillation and flux incident to words bandied about in the common speech of unthinking people. Furthermore, these terms are apt to contract a variety of peculiar and artificial meanings from the practice of courts of justice themselves; and this fact is the more menacing, as it requires a special professional education to appreciate the various meanings, which are therefore likely to escape the attention of the legislator when he addresses himself to the amendment of existing law.

The demand for rigid classification is equally urgent, and is based on exactly the same considerations as the demand for it in the treatment of a physical science. It is not desirable, in the exposition of a body of laws, to have to handle the same matter over and over again. It vastly increases the bulk of the work, while it enhances the labour and impedes the facility of reference. Ordinary common sense suggests the adoption of an arrangement by which that which is common to a number of topics should be treated by itself and apart, and that which is peculiar to each of the topics should also be treated apart; in other words, there is a transparent convenience in making the general precede the special.

The objection under review, probably, is founded on a suspicion that this division into what is "general" and what is "special" cannot be always carried out in the exposition of a body of law. But it certainly is carried out daily in the creation of statutes which are broken up into chapters, divisions, clauses, sections, and subsections; the invariable principle of distribution being the precedence of what is general over what is special. Again, the objection in question seems to proceed upon a confusion of law and morality. There is no more notable distinction between these two fields than that one is capable of being exactly circumscribed in its whole area by the limitations of language, and the other is not. It is true that law, like morality, touches upon almost every department of human action, and every human interest. But morality addresses what is inward, and is occupied with individual cases and circumstances. Law is concerned with what is outward, and expresses itself in general rules. Now, whether it be true or not that language is adequate to cover the whole realm of human thought and feeling, it is certainly true that it is fully equal to describe and map out outward acts, and to designate such of the coarser mental antecedents of these acts, as can be matter of direct concern to the legislator and the judge. The very process of administering public justice implies a recognition of this fact. It is an oral process, depending wholly upon the oral communication of facts and the oral enunciation of the rule of law which seems to be applicable.

It would be a poor answer to a claim or a prosecution to allege that the acts of the defendant were of too subtle and complicated a nature to be susceptible of the application of law. It might indeed happen that—as in the case of prosecutions for opinions—the matter was really one which never could be made the subject matter of a judicial investigation; and as to which the only possible topic of inquiry would be the presence or absence of some act of outward conformity. Or it might happen that no law had yet actually been made, and therefore either that some existing law must be strained so as to meet the emergency, or that no remedy or penalty could be awarded or exacted. Thus, it is obvious that law implies, from its very nature, the capacity of describing in human speech all the human transactions which can be the subject of law; and good law implies (among other things) the describing them with exquisite precision. So far, indeed, is it from being true that the logical use of language is less appropriate to the exposition of a body of law than to that of a physical science, that it may be rather said that in the exposition of law, human language attains its worthiest and most appropriate use.

There is one sense, indeed, in which the objection under consideration might seem to be based upon an indisputable truth. It is the fact that the transactions of men which law seeks to regulate, and the modes of fraud and wrong-doing by which men endeavour to evade the vigilance of law, are so varied and so constantly new that it is impossible in anticipation to frame particular language which shall distinctly describe all the acts that it is the intention of the legislator to prevent. For this reason recourse must needs be had to two devices: one, that of incessant fresh legislation or periodical amendments of the code; the other, that of formulating principles, maxims, or general rules, the exact extent and limit of which must be gathered from a general study of the code, aided by such illustrations or explanations as may be appended to them. It is sometimes supposed that the possession of "principles" of law is the exclusive privilege of a system of unwritten law; and that the creation of a code implies either the reduction of all principles to minute and specific regulations, or else the statement of principles in such general and vague terms as practically to afford the judge no guide whatever. This last-mentioned consequence has undoubtedly followed in the case of the French codes, and an inordinate swarm of commentaries is the result. It has yet to be seen whether the practice of including illustrative cases,—such as are familiar in the Digest, and such as have been introduced with success in the codes of British India,—as well as an adroit use of definitions, and of interpretation clauses, will not prove, in the case of new codes, that all alarm on this head is wholly superfluous.

From the above examination of objections, it will be seen what is the essential conception of a code in the sense now being considered. It is not merely a written republication of the whole mass of existing law, but it also implies the greatest attainable perfection in precision of terminology and in skilful arrangement. The method of this arrangement will not, of course, be dictated by reference to merely abstract logical considerations or to scholastic refinements. In the treatment of every science, and, indeed, in all other business, modes of classification must depend largely upon the nature of the practical purpose in view. In the case of a code, convenience and rapidity of reference for judges and professional advocates is one part of the purpose in view. Professional and popular education is another part of that purpose. Another part is the supplying information on the general structure of the whole law to legislators and to foreigners. While yet another part of the purpose is the enabling each class of persons in the community to study thoroughly the portion of the law which peculiarly touches themselves, without obliging them to lose themselves in the intricacies of the whole code.

There is a third sense in which the word *code* is familiarly used, that of complete republication of the whole existing law of a State, after the fashion last described, coupled with, and embodying, all the fresh legislation which seems called for in order to render the code theoretically adequate to what the codifier takes to be the legal wants of the nation at the time. This is a conception of a code, which seems, almost insensibly, to creep into and to qualify the other conceptions. And it is natural this should be so, because the publication of any code whatever involves, at the least, that amount of legislation which is needed in order to give the code transcendent authority; and, in fact, the re-expression of existing law, when extended over a wide surface, cannot but involve (even in the hands of the most cautious and diffident codifier) a large amount of unconscious alteration in the substance of the law. Even such self-restraint as would confine itself to the re-expression of existing rules is, in the case of a code based on a systematic plan, practically impossible. There are gaps that must be filled, doubts that must be solved, contradictions that must be reconciled, on every side; and the codifier cannot proceed with his task without initiating such an amount of legislation as will at least make his work complete in form. But the transition from recommending essential legislation such as this to that of recommending legislation of a more ambitious sort is almost irresistible, and in that way it is hard to draw the line between the two corresponding meanings of the term *code*.

The above investigation of the various senses in which the term *code* is used suffices to indicate the nature of the several projects which are favoured in different quarters for the systematic republication of ancient systems of law. It is, however, to be remembered that the problem is a very different one in different countries, and may call for a proportionately different species of solution. Thus, all analogies from the use or success of certain kinds of codes in one country must be applied with the utmost discrimination and caution to the circumstances of another.

This heedless use of foreign analogies has wrought a twofold injury to the cause of codification in England. On the one hand, people have argued from the good success of a foreign code to the probability of an equally successful experiment in this country. The result has been that, when it is discovered that a foreign code has disclosed in the course of its operation serious defects, the conclusion has been hastily drawn that an English code is likely to fail in the same direction. On the other hand, it is frequently argued, from the unsuitability to the uses of the English nation of any code which should resemble a Continental one, that no suitable English code could ever be constructed. In order to impress this lesson more strongly it is worth while to estimate with some care the characteristic differences in the legal situation of England, and of such a country as France, which, for the present purpose, is the best typical instance to select.

In England, as in Rome, the development of law has been unbroken in continuity, and has extended over a number of centuries. Based originally upon great and durable institutions, it has spontaneously expanded as the material and moral necessities of the growing nation required, till it presents at the present day the appearance of a vast, uniform, organic structure. Nor, in this account of the actual state and history of English law, are the contrarieties exhibited by the two rival systems of law and equity forgotten.

As in Rome, so in England, equity has been nothing more than the accidental shape which the inevitable development of law has taken. The existence of a double series of courts and jurisdictions—one embodying the progressive, and the other the stationary, element of law, though neither of them wholly consistent in keeping its own province—has undoubtedly been a great practical inconvenience, and has brought upon the administration of justice notorious scandal on the ground of delay and uncertainty. But, in fact, the two systems have for ages flourished vigorously side by side; and each, while in appearance counteracting, has really propped up the other. But for "equity," "law" must have rotted away into a mass of lifeless technicalities, and become wholly discredited through its insufficiency to meet the exigencies of an energetically growing society. And but for "law," equity must have dissolved into a group of loose moral maxims, arbitrarily applied and casuistically invented.

Each of the two great systems in reality presupposes the co-existence of the other; and, so far from implying a breach, they testify in the most signal way to the essential unity which prevails in the general structure of English law. The new Judicature act, which abolishes the ancient division between courts of law and of equity, while retaining all the principles which have been recognized in either class of courts, will result in giving to this unity a living expression of the most commanding sort.

Nor must the irregularities, inconsistencies, and obscurities which have disfigured the form and substance of English law hide out of sight the richness of the material in which that law abounds. The severest critic that the English law has ever encountered has admitted as much as could possibly be needed to establish the value of the materials of that law. In his papers on codification addressed to the President of the United States (Works, vol. iv. p. 460) Bentham says, "All this " while, incapable as, in respect of its *form*, it is of serving, " in any tolerable degree, in its present state, in the " character of a *rule of action* and *guide to* human con- " *duct*, nothing could be much further from the truth, " than if, in speaking of the *matter* of which English law " is composed, a man were to represent it as being of no " use. Confused, indeterminate, inadequate, ill-adapted, " and inconsistent as, to a vast extent, the provision, or " no-provision would be found to be, that has been made " by it for the various cases that have happened to " present themselves for decision; yet, in the character ' of a *repository* for such cases, it affords, for the manu- ' factory of real law, a stock of materials which is beyond ' all price. Traverse the whole continent of Europe,—

"ransack all the libraries belonging to the jurispruden-
"tial systems of the several political States,—add the con-
"tents all together,—you would not be able to compose a
"collection of cases equal in variety, in amplitude, in
"clearness of statement—in a word, in all points taken
"together, in instructiveness—to that which may be seen
"to be afforded by the collection of English *Reports of
"adjudged cases*, on adding to them the *abridgments* and
"*treatises*, by which a sort of order, such as it is, has been
"given to their contents. Of these necessary materials,
"the stock already in hand is not only rich, but, one may
"venture to say, sufficient: nor, to the composition of a
"*complete* body of law, in which, saving the requisite
"allowance to be made for human weakness, every
"imaginable case shall be provided for, and provided for
"in the best manner, is anything at present wanting but
"a duly arranging hand."

It is further remarkable, in making an historical survey of English law, what a uniformity of mind and of legal temper seems to have prevailed among all the English judges at whatever periods they may have lived. That certain peculiar and eccentric modes of reasoning have been in vogue at some periods everybody knows. The antiquated doctrines about the common law reposing in the "bosom of judges" or "in the clouds" or being the "perfection of reason," as well as the curious arguments in favour of the law of descents founded on the tendency of all bodies to gravitate "downwards," have now for some time been exploded or relegated to the region of mere legal curiosities.

But in spite of these temporary vagaries, the race of English judges has had only one mind as to the true methods by which the existence or non-existence of an alleged rule of law is to be tested, and as to the sort of arguments which alone are applicable to the case. Except in the anomalous instance of the parallel principles upheld in courts of law and of equity, there have been no competing systems of law in this country to distract the loyalty of an English judge. He may have been occasionally tempted to allude to vague maxims of a "law of nature," or of "natural justice," but he has instantly corrected himself by explaining that the common law embodied the law of nature and all the principles of natural justice, and so the decision was alleged to be given in strict conformity with the principles of the common law.

From this review of the general history and present circumstances of English law, it will be readily understood what are the difficulties in the way of constructing a really systematic code. English law embodies in itself a great method, a great mode of thought, and a huge mass of scattered but invaluable material. The transition in England from an uncodified to a codified state of the law implies a mental and almost moral metamorphosis of the whole legal intellect of the country. English law, at present, is interpreted by rules peculiar to itself. A code must be interpreted by the common logical rules by which all other written language is interpreted. Thus one of the difficulties of codifying English law, and of using a code wisely when it is made, proceeds from the very compactness and unity of the system which is to be codified. And yet the incessant growth of new law must render an authorized republication of the whole at some date or other an inevitable necessity. The need of codifying is growing just in proportion to the ever increasing difficulties of the task.

Now, to contrast the condition of English law at this day, as above described, with that of French law at the date of the preparation of the Code Napoléon, it will be seen that the main demand in France was unity instead of duality or plurality in the law. It was not only that the Roman law prevailed in some provinces and the customary law prevailed in other provinces; but, even in the provinces ruled by customary law, that law only extended to a narrow range of subjects, such as fiefs, seignorial rights, the system of joint ownership (*communauté de biens*) between married persons, and the right of pre-emption on the ground of kinship. As to all the other matters of concern to an industrial and commercial society, such as guardianship, contracts, and testaments, some other legal authority had to be resorted to. This authority might be either a regal ordinance, or a custom in a neighbouring province, or (as generally happened) a rule of Roman law. But it was and is a matter of an indefinite amount of dispute as to whether the Roman law was adopted as a supplementary authority because, in some sense, it prevailed as law even in custom-governed provinces, or whether its rules were adopted only because of their invariably representing a "written reason." It will thus be seen that the chief need for France, in respect of legal reform, was a unity of legal authority extending throughout the whole country. This could have been achieved in no other way than by a code; and whatever imperfections have attached to the execution of the work, and however numerous the commentaries to which it has given birth, the general gain must, nevertheless, have been enormous.

It is needless to point out how insufficient is any analogy between the situation of France and that of England, either to aid or to injure the cause of codification in this country. A like insufficiency might be shown to exist in the popular analogy between the cases of England and British India, and also between those of England and the States of the American Union. This argument of the impotence of superficial analogies was handled in a masterly way by Savigny, when he resented the reckless importation of a general code for all Germany through a mere imitation of the work of Napoleon in France and in the countries which he subdued.

The truth is, that each nation must judge for itself whether the time has yet come at which it must needs codify its law. The elements that furnish the ground for the decision are various, and not always easy of calculation. Among them are such considerations as the actual indefiniteness or uncertainty in the state of the law as applicable to a large number of important questions; the duality or plurality of systems of law of co-equal authority; the actual voluminousness of the law rendering systematic arrangement for speedy reference a question of the greatest moment; the probability of an efficient code being made, considering the capacity of the persons who are likely to make it; and the habits of the community, as rendering a popular use of the code more or less probable.

The most serious objection that has ever been urged against codifying an ancient system of law under any circumstances whatever is that thereby the spontaneous growth of law is likely to be impeded, or diverted into unnatural directions. This objection touches upon far profounder considerations than any above treated, and has been powerfully urged in Germany—though it is also not altogether unknown in England. The objection is, of course, likely to be urged with the greatest effect in those countries in which codification is not imperiously called for, as the sole means of bringing into harmony two or more competing systems of law, or else as the instrument of enforcing on the people the policy of a new government. Where neither of these demands for codification is present, the value of a spontaneous or unconscious development of law is likely to be estimated at the highest. It is worth while examining more minutely what this alleged "spontaneous development" of law means.

Except in the case of foreign conquest or foreign influence of a very peculiar sort, every nation makes its own law. Part of the law, and that the larger and more important part, is made directly by the invention of the people themselves in the action of their daily life; and part of it is made indirectly, by the invention of a supreme political authority which the people have generated out of their midst. This latter part is, strictly speaking, as much made by the will and consent of the whole people as the former part, and that not fictitiously, but really; as that will and consent would be estimated not at any particular moment, but as extending over a length of time sufficient to enable the popular determination fully to express itself.

If a supreme political authority persists in counteracting the will of the bulk of the population, either the authority itself will be dethroned by constitutional or revolutionary processes, or the State will become so far disorganized as to be threatened with extinction, or the supreme political authority will be forcibly compelled to change its policy, and retrace its steps. Instances of each of these solutions are supplied in abundance both in ancient and modern times. The phenomenon is an extremely important one as exhibiting what is the true character of a supreme political authority at any given epoch, and what are the natural and effectual restrictions on that authority. It is thus not a mere utterance of demagogic rhetoric that all law is made by the will of the people. The proposition is rather a truism as thus stated, though what is usually meant is that the interposition of the people should be made more direct and immediate in the enactment of laws; and that the supreme political authority, instead of depending on the assent of the people as gathered in the long run, should be dependent on that assent as gathered at very brief intervals of time.

Thus, so far as occasional legislation goes, being emitted from time to time according to the exigencies which seem to call for it, it must necessarily be in tolerably exact agreement with the wishes, tastes, habits, and aspirations of the people at large. The adjustment, indeed, will not be very fine, as the influence of particular classes of people will now and again dominate over that exercisable by other classes; and the policy of individual statesmen or party will do much to make the current legislation bear in one direction rather than in another. But such interfering elements as these will, in the course of a few years, be counteracted by rival elements of the same sort, though acting in the opposite direction, so that the general result will be an exact representation in their laws of the tendencies and character of the general community.

It is true that, in this approximation of statutory law to the standard erected by the popular will, it is assumed that the popular will has the means of making itself known. If the rights of public meeting and of free discussion in the press are either ignored or trampled upon by the executive, there need be no correspondence at all between the will of the people and the acts of the legislature. In such a State, whatever be the outward form and title of the government, it is, in truth, nothing better than an arbitrary despotism. Sudden revolution or decay, prolonged, it may be, over centuries, are the only alternatives which can be looked for.

France, Belgium, Italy, and Spain, have been fortunate enough hitherto to adopt one solution. Turkey and the

Asiatic kingdoms have had the other thrust upon them. To Germany and England alone has it been hitherto given to escape the necessity of either alternative.

But the warning is sounded in the ears of every country, even the freest, to the effect that only by the fullest possible freedom for discussion and peaceable combination can a truly healthy accord be secured between the mind of a people and its laws; and, far short of tyrannical invasions of that freedom, even casual interferences with it, whether legislative or executive, are fraught with infinite and ominous mischief.

Thus it is a fact that the ordinary statute law of a State expresses the sentiments of the whole community. But it is also a fact that the unwritten law is likely to express the sentiments of certain groups of persons in the community with still more infallible precision. The unwritten law must be based partly on what people do and partly on what they want.

It is true that the personal instrumentality concerned in forging the law or in converting a practice into a law is a person who is generally outside the region in which the practice has grown up. But such a person, called as is he to judge in a disputed matter, is only one in a long race of judges. Even though each judge has his own peculiarities, his eccentricities of thought, his superstitions and his caprices, if the series of judges be long enough, it may be expected that what is wayward in one will correct what is wayward, but in a different direction, in another.

On the other hand, the wants, wishes, and habits of the community in which justice is administered are likely to continue much the same, with just such silent and graduated changes or deviations as the development of the nation brings with it. To meet this uniformity of progress, it is no doubt probable that a professional judicial temper will be framed, bringing with it artificial modes of thinking and classifying; but such a temper will be largely fashioned by the logical character of the business upon which decisions have to be given, and wil' therefore be steady and uniform, and will admit of being exactly described and evaluated.

In view, then, of all these circumstances, it might be expected that a system of unwritten law, in which customs, general maxims, floating principles, and ancient but familiarly cherished institutions, supplied the chief materials,—the rest being due to nothing else than the logical dress woven into shape by a long line of judges,— must represent with the greatest possible nicety, not only the actual will of the people, but the finest modifications of that will as progressively manifesting themselves. The certainty and familiarity of the law supply, in their turn, guides for action, so that the regularity of customary modes of intercourse becomes intensified through the action of the very cause which might have disturbed it.

Great, however, as are the conspicuous advantages of the easy play between courts of justice and the actual habits of mankind, yet the disadvantages are not to be overlooked. It was seen in an earlier chapter of this work that the true purpose of law is not only to give reality and vigour to the essential groups out of which the State is constituted, but also to ascertain and describe the true relations of the groups to one another and to the whole State. The peculiarity of an unwritten system of law,—based mostly, as it must be, on custom,—is that it gives validity to the transactions of small groups of persons, or of persons living in particular localities, without any concern for the degree or the mode in which those transactions affect the well-being of all other persons in the community.

Customary law is, indeed, a perfect mirror of the practices and wishes of numberless sections of persons in the community; but one custom has only a casual connection with another custom, and one branch of customary law with another branch of customary law.

The doctrines of English common law with respect to land and the simpler forms of contract and even procedure are instances of this; as also are the scattered topics which alone found a place in the great customary systems of France. It is not true to say of the usages enshrined in these different bodies of law that they express in the surest possible way the will of the people. They only express the will of certain persons, or of persons living in particular places or under particular conditions. To the persons whose will the law does express, it readily becomes familiar, and modifications in the usages are easily digested and reproduced in the legal system. But the law as a whole must continue to be made up of great inharmonious fragments, and the will of the whole people, as an organized community, is never consulted upon it directly or indirectly. So untrue is it that a system of unwritten law is eminently a representative of the will and spontaneous tendencies of the whole people.

It has thus been seen what are the peculiar characteristics of a system of statute law, and of a system of customary law. It has been asserted by some that the best system of all is one jointly of statute and of customary law. It is scarcely a matter of choice whether or not such a system as this last shall or shall not be introduced into a State, because there is no advanced State in which either statute law or customary law are unknown; or, in fact, in which the legal system does not consist very largely of both. The sort of law which is evolved, as of necessity, by judges in the course of applying already existing rules, is common to both systems, and, in fact, is an indispensable incident in the administration of justice. If the interpretation of written language and the import of general principles is not to be fixed by the concurrent voice of a series of judges in conformity with logical principles generally adopted, either endless uncertainty must prevail, or the logic of self-appointed commentators must take the place of the logic of the judicial tribunal. Hence it may be assumed that statute law, customary law, and law evolved in the act of administering law, are three universal elements in the laws of every State.

It remains to be seen how far the substitution of a code for some part of these elements may tend to enhance the advantages and diminish the disadvantages inherent in all of them.

In the first place, it is no doubt true that a code made in one generation is liable to project, directly or indirectly, the intellectual and moral notions which prevail at the day into times when such notions shall have become anachronisms. On the other hand, there is no such sure mode of securing the maintenance of a fair balance between the claims and interests of all classes of persons in the community, and of the State itself, as by the construction of a systematically arranged body of law. If any claim or interest is neglected, if any class is privileged unduly, if any unfairness or partiality works anywhere in the legal system, the publicity and orderly arrangement of a code must instantly bring it into the light of day.

So also with the anomalies incident to customary law. No custom will be consecrated by a code which cannot stand the criticism of the whole community. The recognition of partial and local customs will none the less sufficiently prevail by force of the general judicial principle of satisfying well-grounded expectations. With respect to that part of the law which insensibly grows with the administration of it, it must be expected to grow just as much under a code as in the administration of statute law.

The main remedy for this evil (if it be one), as well as for that due to the rigidity and inelasticity of a code, is to provide for its constant and periodic revision, on each occasion the most authoritative interpretations of language being inserted, and such new statutes as touch the organic structure of the code being also embodied. It must be assumed throughout that in a number of outlying and special departments statute law must be created independently of the code. The code will only be a systematic exhibition of the leading departments of the law. It will incorporate customary law and common law, and it will contain within itself the principles of its own revision and of its incessant adaptation to the national needs.

Nevertheless, the objection that a code has a special tendency to fix in a rigid groove the legal conceptions, the modes of classification, and the language, prevalent at the time at which it is made, is deserving of most attentive consideration. The objection, indeed, is much more potent if urged against making a code at one epoch in the development of a nation, than when urged against making a code at another epoch or at any epoch at all. It takes a long time in the growth of any nation, apart from direct external influences, for all the main departments of a fully expanded legal system to form themselves. The formation has to proceed slowly and almost tentatively, and often in a crooked and tortuous fashion. Sometimes, as in Rome and in England, a large portion of the legal conceptions come into being through one set of judicial processes, and another large portion through another set.

In all countries, as has been seen, customary practices, prevalent and changing moral theories, judicial idiosyncrasies, and political events, contribute to the composition of the general structure of the national law. The experience of one age corrects that of another; improved moral notions displace inferior ones; and growing social and commercial intercourse, between men and between nations, render innovation of the boldest sort from time to time quite indispensable.

While this process is actively proceeding, the crystallization of the whole legal system of the country into a code, even with ample provision for amendment, could not operate otherwise than as an arrest of the most beneficial mode of growth. The question, then, is presented whether this course of changing conceptions and progressive enterprise in the field of law is an unending one, or whether a period ever arrives at which it may be said that the formal shape of the whole body of law has become finally and definitely fixed. Another question lies close at hand, as to whether, assuming such a period has arrived, the nation can know for itself that it has arrived. In a word, can a nation tell for itself that the period has arrived at which it may safely proceed with the codification of its laws so as to attain the greatest amount of gain, and to encounter the least loss possible?

If the theory which has been advocated throughout this work be a sound one, to the effect that a nation is constituted out of a number of definite and ascertainable groups, and that the purpose of law is to give reality and cohesion to these several groups on the one hand, and, on the other, to ascertain their mutual relations to each other and to the State as a whole, then the answer to the first of these questions becomes tolerably ready. So soon as ever all the groups are completely evolved, their perpetuity and distinctness from one another secured, and their bearings in respect to the whole organization of the State precisely determined, the main steps in the growth of law are accomplished.

It is true that law may yet have to undergo the most important alterations in order to clear it from all the obstructions, the anomalies, the incongruities, the antiquarian curiosities, which, in the course of generations of struggle, have adhered to it. But this task of formally adapting law to the actual social conditions around is a tolerably rapid and easy one, so soon as ever an enthusiastic spirit of reform is fairly roused. How rapid and comparatively easy is that task, under such favouring circumstances, is sufficiently illustrated by the example of what was done at Rome in the time of Augustus, of the Antonines, and of Justinian; in France during the first revolution; and in England in the early part of this century, after the close of the French war. Thus it may be said broadly that there is a halting-place in the progress of every nation at which the chief and final lineaments of the legal system admit of being formally determined, though, of course, endless opportunity must survive for detailed modifications and even radical innovations.

The other question, as to the competency of a nation to judge for itself whether the halting-stage here described has yet arrived, can be answered with equal facility. The answer for any particular nation must depend on the degree of development to which the conscious reflection on the nature of law shall have attained in that nation. If the essential elements of the complete national life have been correctly calculated, and if the state of the national law, as addressed to the support and nutrition of those elements, has been critically surveyed, there seems to be no reason why a definitive conclusion should not be drawn as to whether the law has or has not as yet conformed itself to the conditions needed to justify codification.

But, even if the time properly and generally adapted to codification shall not yet have arrived, there may be special circumstances to justify the anticipation of that time. It may happen that all further development in the legal system is hampered and clogged by the rugged and obscure condition of the authorities to which reference is made in order to know the state of the law. It is quite possible that these authorities may be so, obscure, so multifarious, so contradictory, that either total anarchy is the result, or a technical and traditional system, wholly out of all living connection with the people and their requirements, is handed down from one generation of judges to another, and is servilely acquiesced in, and even lauded, by a narrow-minded legal profession.

Such was the condition of the common-law in England at the time that Bentham was so loud in his demands for codification. The rapid course of legislative reform since his day, to which allusion has already been made, has tended to rest the demand for codification on broader and deeper grounds than those on which he rested it.

Thus it appears that a premature codification may sometimes be properly brought about as a substitute for anarchy, and as a refuge from dangers greater than any which attach to itself. Most people, for instance, will admit that the codification of the French laws, at the time it was proceeded with, was an indispensable necessity; though they will, on reflection, probably confess that, had the composition of a code been waited for till the effects of the revolution had fully penetrated every portion of French society and given it its final shape, the code then made would have been better and more useful than the code now in existence.

CHAPTER XIV.

LAW AND GOVERNMENT.

THERE is yet another important aspect of law which, though necessarily glanced at in the earlier chapters of this book, yet still remains to be investigated with precision. This aspect is the one in which law is presented when it is regarded merely as a means of government, or as what may be called, in a large sense of the expression, a political instrument. In order to give practical value to the investigation, the question must not be proposed in too abstract a form; but, in speaking of government, the form of government to which all modern States are gravitating with a constantly accelerated velocity must be kept in view throughout. This form is undoubtedly the *democratical*,—if it be allowed to use the term, neither in an euphemistic nor dyslogistic sense, but simply as descriptive, that is, in the sense intended by the late M. de Tocqueville. It remains, then, to examine what is the position occupied by law in relation to government, as becoming constantly more and more democratically constituted.

It was noticed in an early part of this work that the activity of government is twofold in character. One portion of this activity is displayed in administration, that is, in selecting a vast hierarchy of persons to perform definite work; in marking out the work of all and each; in taking such measures as are necessary to secure that the work is really done; and in supplying from day to day such corrections or modifications as changing circumstances may seem to suggest. This task is of the highest degree of importance, and, in a very primitive condition of society, represents the largest portion of governmental action. In a very complete and advanced condition of society, again, the task of administration is one of inordinate magnitude and difficulty, but it is only a very subordinate agency in the whole process of government.

The rival agency is that of legislation, or the formulating of general rules, addressed to all persons, or to certain classes of persons in the community, and directing their actions in certain ways specified in the terms of the rule. In the place of the incessant supervision implied in administration, the persons to whom these rules are addressed are left to themselves, and only interfered with after the rules are broken. A large class of functionaries, judicial and executive, are called into being for the purpose of ascertaining whether these rules are conformed to or not; if not, who it is who fails to conform to them; of punishing such refractory persons; and of publicly expounding the true meaning of these rules, should doubts in reference to this meaning arise in any quarter.

It is obvious that these important rules,—the ultimate operation of which is thus removed from the immediate eye of the legislator, and in the general character of which public liberty is so deeply concerned,—must call for the most anxious reflection and the balancing of innumerable considerations.

It is at this point that the characteristic difference between a despotical or aristocratical, and a democratical form of Government tells upon the peculiar difficulties that are inherent in the enactment of laws. The more democratic is the condition, the more numerous are the persons who have to assent to the passing of the law, and the greater are the expectations entertained by the population generally of thoroughly comprehending the import of every law that is passed. The political consequences of this state of things are momentous, though some of them are more obviously beneficial than others. But the strictly legal consequences, which are immediately relevant here, are also very noticeable.

One of such consequences is that, inasmuch as the passing of every law involves the assent of a large number of persons, a quantity of time must be occupied, on all occasions on which the policy or language of the proposed law are open to question, with controversy, criticism, and lengthened expositions of the circumstances which seem to recommend or discountenance the adoption of the law. The results are the following:—First, in default of special devices to secure logical unity in the framework of laws (such as by referring every suggested amendment to a permanent legislative commission for incorporation in the body of the law originally proposed), the varieties of opinion which have characterized the debate are likely to reappear in the structure of the law itself, and so at a later stage to perplex the judicial consideration of what was its policy and meaning. The fact is, a law so constructed out of a number of compromises, and allowed to survive, if at all, only at the price of most of what its author held to be its essential features, cannot be said to have any definite policy; and to speak of the "legislator" or even the "legislature," as though the law flowed from a single responsible and morally constituted being, is, under a system of representative government, a scarcely appropriate form of diction.

Another result of the tedium and difficulty with

which disputable laws are enacted in a democratically constituted assembly is that it becomes necessary to delegate as much legislation as possible to subordinate authorities. There are many grounds for resorting to such subordinate legislation besides that of convenience or necessity; but the tendency must be to multiply subordinate legislation, even in cases where no other considerations recommend it than the impossibility of the central legislature otherwise getting through the business of the year.

The danger is that the choice between what properly belongs to the central body and what may suitably be left to subordinate bodies in dependence on the central body will be determined rather by accident or caprice than by principle. Thus there will be always a temptation presented to an assembly of popular representatives to avoid taking action in matters upon which it is known great difference of opinion exists, and in respect of which inflammatory feelings are aroused in all parts of the country. It is easier to avoid making enemies or losing friends by simply throwing the matter back on the people themselves. And yet this may imply a gross dereliction of governmental duty. The matter may be one as to which a numerical majority of the people outside the assembly has no claim to overbear the smallest minority; or as to which unity of action throughout the country is of more importance than unity of opinion; or as to which absence of legislation is even worse than wrong legislation. In such circumstances, as these the facility of simply ignoring the duties of a legislature, by handing over difficult topics to Local Boards, is to be noted as one of the perils inherent in democratic government.

The real value of subordinate legislation, as practised in England, by Local Boards, by School Boards, by Town

Councils, by Committees of the Privy Council, and even, under restrictions, by the heads of the Police force, is indisputable, and may be regarded as one of the most precious of modern political discoveries. Indeed, it is not easy to see how, apart from a large resort to this method of legislation, the joint purpose of disburthening the central legislature of needless business, and of inviting the co-operation of the people at as many points as possible in the task of governing themselves, could possibly be achieved.

A check on the unbridled extension of this form of legislation is suggested by the perils to public liberty involved in the comparative secrecy of local legislation, and in the difficulty of bringing general public opinion to bear upon abuses occurring either in the process of making or in that of executing the law. Other checks are suggested by the comparative incompetence of local authorities to take a large, far-sighted, and well-proportioned, view of the interests at stake, and the inconvenience of having different systems of management prevailing in different parts of the country perhaps closely adjoining each other.

One consequence of the popular conditions which Government, in modern times, has to satisfy, is highly ominous to the character of law. This consequence is the sort of irregular interference which the process of making law encounters at the hands of the mass of the people at large. In a democratically constituted State, the people are properly not content with choosing their representatives from time to time once for all, and then remitting to them the whole labour and responsibility of making the laws. The means of communication and information, which are essential elements in the social condition of modern States, result in bringing the daily debates of the Legislative Assembly under the eyes and watchful criticism of the whole people. These means of communication also bring to the knowledge of each other those who, in different parts of the country and otherwise isolated, are of the same mind with respect to the laws they wish to enact or change, and who thereby assume the character of a large and significant confederation. The result is of an ambiguous character, partly good and partly evil, the proportions of the good and the evil being determined by the amount of education and political self-control of the people.

In a large and highly organized State, liable to suffer inordinately from even a few hours of general lawlessness, and to feel even the occasional recklessness of a few of its members as a heavy calamity, it is of the utmost importance that the people as a whole should not only understand the law, but should zealously co-operate with its execution. The attainment of this result becomes increasingly difficult, because the larger and the wealthier is the State, the greater is the certainty (under present conditions of society) that it will contain among its members not a few who mostly look for their subsistence to abusing the general confidence produced by law. On all these grounds it is now a recognized part of the policy of all States, not ostensibly possessed of a despotical or aristocratical constitution, to do their utmost to meet the wishes of the whole people in the enactment of law.

Two difficulties are here presented. One is, that it is hard to invent a test by which the wish of the whole people shall be distinguished from that of a large and tumultuous fraction of the people. No sufficient test can really be imagined. The tests of numbers, of education, of rank, of wealth, of uproar, are all either inapplicable under the circumstances or else absurd. The comments of the daily press, in countries where it is perfectly free, are, no doubt, held by statesmen as an element in ascertaining the general inclination of public opinion; but, as often as not, it is the press which makes the opinion rather than the prevalence of the opinion which finds expression in the press.

In this uncertainty of a test for estimating public bias, an open field is presented for the manufacture of factitious and spurious counterfeits of a true and popular conviction. The majority of the population (as things are at present,—and for a long time to come no essential change can take place in this respect) have in ordinary times no political convictions at all. They are, therefore, easily open to moral pressure from the first persons of strong convictions who solicit them for their aid and sympathy.

There are large classes of laws—especially those which, by a favourite modern extension of the province of Government, touch upon the moral habits and the physical health of the people—which affect one class or order of persons in the community in a different way, or to a different extent, from that in which they affect all the rest. Thus, for instance, in many countries laws have been enacted, or have been called for, affecting solely the sellers of certain wares, or those belonging to certain trades or professions, or those earning their livelihood in certain definitely described ways.

The persons who are specially or immediately interested in the enactment, the modification, or the repeal, of such laws as these, are, at the first, only a small section of the population. But they thoroughly comprehend the subject, or, at least, one side of it—the one nearest to themselves. They are ready with all the arguments which tell in their own favour, whether real or fallacious. They may be, and are likely to be, sufficiently at leisure to be distracted by no considerations of ulterior policy or interests other than their own, or what they have taken up as their own. Steady concentration of mind on a single order of topics enhances the original narrowness of view, and favours the generation of a vehement condition of feeling. Here are gathered up all the elements of an unreasoning and selfish fanaticism.

This fanaticism is none the less dangerous because it is often cloaked in the becoming garb of scientific wisdom, and because it simulates (perhaps unconsciously and innocently) a sole regard for the general good. What is here relevant, however, is that, in estimating the weight of an alleged popular demand for legislation, the frequent existence of a fanatical cry for legislative changes is one of the most misleading of indications. It is only as the people become better educated and less servile to the leadings of the press, the platform, and the parade of scientific statistics, that they can be safely trusted to prescribe to legislators duties from day to day, and can be allowed to interfere at every moment in the process of enacting laws. But even then the position of a trained statesman—bound as he is to consider the far future as well as the past, the distant as well as the near, and to weigh in an accurately adjusted balance the merits of competing considerations borrowed from all parties—must always entitle him to resist a popular outcry, however vehement and however persistent. That people is the greatest which can rear out of its midst a race of statesmen who will be its faithful servants, and neither its masters nor its slaves.

It is for the statesman to interpret the genuine voice of the people, and to distinguish between a mere selfish and ignorant cry and the solemn promptings of an awakened national conscience. He must possess an infallible touchstone by which to discover, among competing parties, who are the true fanatics. He will attribute at least as much weight to a clearly expressed and fairly ascertained popular judgment, as to a well-reasoned scientific conclusion. He will be as ready to retrace his steps when, by an accidental step in legislation, he finds he has outraged a sound, healthy, and common sentiment, as determined to persist when he is persuaded the laws he supports are in harmony with such a sentiment. .

There is yet another aspect in which law must be regarded when treated as an instrument of Government. So soon as a law is made, and lifted out of the region of controversy, it begins to exercise a moral influence, which is no less intense and wide-spreading for being almost imperceptible. Though law can never attempt to forbid all that is morally wrong, yet that gets to be held to be morally wrong which the law forbids.

Similarly, whatever law recognizes and provides for is regarded (it may be insensibly and only by very gradual steps) as morally right. It is almost a necessary habit of thought to regard the State as a moral being, possessed of a will, a conscience, and moral responsibility. There is no need here to trace the order of thought by which this popular and universal conception grows up. It is sufficient to allege the existence of it as a fact, and to deduce the consequences of it. In obedience to this conception, law becomes accepted as the expositor of the national conscience, and the language of law as one of the readiest tests of the inherent rightfulness or wrongfulness of actions. In this way, by a constantly advancing educational process, to which the decisions of every court of justice are day by day making their contribution, the moral sentiments of the people are gradually brought into accord with the principles apparently consecrated by law.

A law-loving people may criticise, if they have the opportunity, a newly proposed law to any possible extent. But when once it is enacted, they will not only cheerfully obey it, but, by a peculiar action of the imagination, will unconsciously attribute to it a quasi-mysterious origin, and banish all memory of the competing views of expediency amidst which it arose. Thus a law of the most ambiguous value borrows the credit and reverence which is rightly due to the great mass of the laws side by side with which it is ranked; and where the possibility of practical resistance ends, criticism is likely enough to end likewise.

These considerations point to the fallaciousness of the notion of making experiments in legislation. There can, strictly speaking, be no real experiments in legislation; first, because a bad law, like some poisons when taken into the human system, at once changes the nature of the medium into which it is introduced; and therefore the apparent success of the law may only mean that what in a healthier condition of society would work badly and be resisted, does, in a depraved condition of society, meet with general approval; secondly, because some of the results only, and these the least momentous ones, admit of being catalogued in a statistical form, while all the other results, however much they permeate the whole of society, are far too subtle and obscure to be made the subject of a quantitative estimate. It is obvious that these remarks apply with much greater force to some kinds of laws than to other kinds; with very little force, perhaps, to some of the laws which merely regulate taxation; but with the greatest force of all to laws which, directly or indirectly, affect to curb or regulate immorality.

Lastly, law, when regarded as an instrument of government, must be treated as a necessary fact among all those facts of human existence and physical nature by which the character of the individual man and woman is perfected. The individual human being can only discover for himself his aim, his vocation, and the true use of his faculties by association with others. It is out of this association, first, in the primitive family, then in the primitive State, and then in that higher form of the State in which the competing claims and functions of State life, family life, and individual life, are reconciled and mutually adjusted, that human nature attains its true proportions. But this process of growth is not achieved without personal and national mishaps of all sorts, delusive adventures, disappointments, mistakes, and disastrous calamities. Nevertheless, the growth advances and man remains ever steady to his aim. That which steadies him and keeps him firm to his conscious or unconscious purpose, protecting all men against the imperfection of each, and protecting each against the pressure of all—kind and yet unflinching, personating the past, the present and the future—imperiously addressing all and yet whispering to each—is *law*.

INDEX.

A

ACCESSORIES, theoretical aspect of, 250.
Accident, as operating on Intention, 110.
Act, definition of legal term, 101.
—— various popular uses of the term, 100.
Acts, relation of, to Will and to Events, 101.
Administration, as part of the function of Government, 397.
Adoption, Roman practice of, as affecting the Family group, 130.
Advocacy, nature and morality of, 311-313.
Agency, nature and legal incidents of, 224, 225.
Anglo-Indian Codes, use of definitions and illustrative cases in, 65.
Appeal, grounds for constituting Courts of, 313, 314.
Arbitration, prevalent indisposition to, 348.
—————— real obstacles to, 349, 350.
—————— value of theories of, 347, 358.
Assurance, nature and policy of Contracts of, 225, 226.
Attempts to commit crimes, theory of punishing, 254.
AUSTIN, estimate of his qualifications, 4, 5.
—— founder of the Science of Law, 4.
—— his notes respecting *Dolus* and Malice, 245.

B

BAIL, theory of, and problems relating to, 264, 265.
Balance of Power, influence of doctrine of, 346.
Bankruptcy, notion of, and proceedings in, 209.
BENTHAM, his characteristic method, 3.
—————— his view of the relations of Law and Morality, 3.
—————— his influence on English Law, 7, 8.
—————— testimony of, to excellence of English Law, 381, 382.
BLUNTSCHLI, Professor, his Code of International Law, 343.
Burden of Proof, problems respecting, 300, 301.

C

CAPITAL PUNISHMENT, difficulties attending the use of, 271.
Cessio Bonorum, nature of the Roman remedy of, 209.
Character, grounds for allowing production of Evidence of, 287.
Child, situation of a, in respect of Intention, 105, 106.
Children, limitations on Rights of Ownership by, 161.
Chivalry, its functions in the development of International Law, 335.
Church, nature of the Established, in England, 136.

Church, various forms of an Established, 135, 136.
Circumstantial Evidence, meaning of, as opposed to Direct, 304.
Civil Injuries, distinction between Crimes and, 229, 235.
———————— theoretical view of, 290-292.
Civil Procedure, account of the law of, 290, seq.
Classification, purpose of, in Codification, 375.
Clauses, Interpretation, functions of, in reference to Interpretation, 65. .
Code, various uses of term, 366.
Code Civil, provision in the, for insufficiencies in the law, 74.
Code Napoléon, the, in reference to the word chose, 86, 87.
Codes, influence of modern, on Science of Law, 10, 11.
Codes of International Law, account of modern, 343, 357, 358.
Codes, use of Definitions and Illustrative cases in Anglo-Indian, 66.
Codification, a mode of Statutory Legislation, 75, 76.
——————— general account of Theories of, 360, seq.
——————— various uses of term, 366.
Cognitiones extraordinariæ, theory of the Roman, 297, 298.
Combination Statutes, policy of English, 212, 213.
Commands, relation of, to laws, 23.
Commentators, influence of, on judicial legislation, 67, 69, 70.
Commerce, theory and use of Tribunals of, 315, 316.
Common Law, English, doctrines of, as illustrating the growth and compass of Law, 390.
————————————— in relation to the history of the Science of Law, 6, 7.
—————————————— mode of development of, 63.
Communism, misapprehensions respecting, 159.
Compensation, as contrasted with Punishment, 37.

Conceptions, elementary account of, 77, seq.
Conspiracy, comment on English Law of, 255, 256.
Constructive Fraud, meaning of doctrine of, 199.
Conflict of Laws, influence of the, on Science of Law, 12, 25-28.
———————— problems presented by the, 318-321.
Conscience, growth of, as an element of Morality, 32.
Consideration for a Contract, meaning of expression, 204.
Constitutional Law, anomalous characteristics of, 16.
Contract, account of Law of, 190.
————— analysis of a legal, 195.
————— capacity for making a, 199.
————— distinction between a, and a Conveyance, 219, 220
————— Form and Evidence of a, 200-203.
————— growth of legal conception of, 94.
————— Marriage as a, 217.
————— meaning of "consideration" for a, 204.
————— Nature and Origin of, 191, 192.
————— relation of, to Obligation, 221.
————— Sale as a, 218.
Contracts, Immoral, 196.
————— "implied," nature of, 216.
Crime, real test of a, 96.
————— Sir H. S. MAINE's account of Primitive Law respecting, 230.
————— distinction between Moral and Legal notion of a, 236.
————— distinction of a, from a Civil Injury, 234, 235.
————— elements in determining Punishments for, 39.
————— essential notion of a, 232.
————— grounds for pardoning Political, 41.
Crimes in relation to Rights, 96.
————— policy of punishing Attempts to commit, 254.
————— policy of punishing Concurrent, 256.

Crimes, primitive relation of, to Civil Injuries, 229.
────── theory of modes of punishing, 278-288.
────── what acts are styled, 14.
Contraventions, place of, in French Code, 257.
Conveyance, relation of, to Contract, 219, 220.
────── or Transfer, theoretical nature of a, 182.
Copyright, how far strictly a Right of Ownership, 168.
Costs, theory of, 317.
Courts, distribution of, according to business, 315.
────── grounds for distributing into Superior and Inferior, 314.
Courts of Appeal, grounds for constituting, 313, 314.
Criminal Law, account of, 228, *seq*.
────── Responsibility, as affected by Age, 106.
Cross-examination, nature and value of practice of, 307.
Custom, conversion of, into Law, 50, 51.
────── Sir H. S. MAINE in reference to, 49, 50.
────── theory of, 49.
Customary Law, how it grows, 389.
────── theory of, 326.
────── Systems of France, as illustrating the growth and compass of Law, 390.
Customs, account of, in reference to Codification, 360.
────── adoption of, a mode of Judicial Legislation, 67, 68.
────── relation of, to a Code, 391.
────── Sir H. S. MAINE on primitive, 193.

D

DAMAGES, modes of assessing, in Contract, 214.
────── nature of Exemplary or Vindictive, 211.
Death, a fact provided for by Law, 183, 184.

Definitions, a mode of avoiding the necessity of Interpretation, 65.
────── purpose of, in Codification, 374.
────── use of, in the Digest, 66.
Delicts, distinction between, and Crimes, 229-235.
────── theoretical view of, 290.292.
Democratical form of Government, as affecting Law, 396, 397.
Depositions of witnesses taken out of Court, practice of receiving, 306.
Digest, meaning of a, as opposed to a Code, 367, 368.
Diligence, estimate of, in Contracts, 207.
────── nature of, as related to Intention, 116.
Direct Evidence, meaning of, as opposed to Circumstantial, 304.
Discretionary Punishments, theory of, 39, 286.
Divorce, problems for the Legislator in respect of, 125.
Dolus, analysis of notion denoted by term, 243-245.
────── Mr. Austin's notes in reference to, 245.
Drunkenness, as affecting imputability, 109.
DUDLEY FIELD, Mr., his Code of International Law, 343.
Duty, Analysis and History of the Legal term, 88-97.
────── definition of legal term, 97.

E

EASEMENTS, classification of, 172.
────── nature of "Negative," 172.
────── nature of "Positive" or "Affirmative," 172, 187.
────── nature of, as subjects of Ownership, 169, 171, 186.
Emancipation, Roman practice of, as affecting the Family group, 130.
Endowments, English modes of providing against abuses in, 139.

Endowments, nature, varieties, and policy of, 137-140, 165.
English Common Law, doctrines of, as illustrating growth and compass of Law, 390.
English Law, general characteristics and history of, 382, 383.
Equity, a constantly recurrent phenomenon, 56-58.
——— as a method of adjusting Laws, 35, 36, 56.
——— functions of, in developing early Law, 56.
——— fusion of Law and, 56.
——— historical relations of, to Law, in England, 380.
——— history of English, 34, 35.
——— older sense of the term, 34.
——— true nature of English, 56.
Events, nature of, as contrasted with Acts, 101.
Evidence in the shape of Confessions by the Accused, treatment of, 275-278.
——— meaning of Direct and Circumstantial, 304.
——— Hearsay, 305.
——— of Character, grounds for allowing production of, 287.
——— of Experts, problems relating to the, 309.
——— of prisoner excluded in England, 274.
——— principle and grounds of excluding, 302.
——— theory of rules of, 299.
Exculpation, theory and grounds of, 246-250.
Executors and Administrators, theoretical functions of, in England, 184.
Executive, the, as vested with the Prerogative of Pardon, 41.
Exemplary Damages, nature of, 211.
Experts, problems relating to Evidence of, 309-311.
Extenuating circumstances, theory and value of French verdict of, 270, 271.
Extensive Interpretation, meaning of, 66, 67.
Extradition Treaties, theory and policy of, 263.

F

FAMILY, Law in relation to the, 117, 124, seq.
——— Group, preservation of the, an object of Law, 123.
Felony, history of distinction between, and Misdemeanour, 252, 253.
Feudalism, its influence in the development of International Law, 336.
Fictions, function of Legal, in developing early Law, 55.
Foreign Law, incorporation of a mode of Judicial Legislation, 67, 69.
"Fractional" Right, meaning and illustrations of a, 171, 187.
France, Customary Systems of, as illustrating growth and compass of Law, 390.
Fraud, nature and operation of, 114.
——— as affecting the validity of a Contract, 198, 199.
——— Constructive, meaning of doctrine of, 199.
Frauds, English Statute of, Policy of, 202.
FREDERICK II., his Code only a subsidiary system, 370, 371.
——————————— forbids "Interpretation" of Laws, 61.
French Codes, numerous Commentaries on, 377.
——— Law, characteristics and history of, 383, 384.
FROUDE, Mr., his testimony to the severity of the English character, 274.

G

GERMANY, effect on treatment of Law of philosophic tendencies in, 3.
Government, as an ingredient in the conception of the State, 122.
——— functions of, in the creation of Law, 6.
——— in relation to Law, 122.

Government, relations of Law and, 396, *seq.*
Grammatical Interpretation, meaning of, 66, 67.
Growth of Law, account of the, 47, *seq.*
GROTIUS, influence of his work in the development of International Law, 338, 339.
Guardianship, in reference to the support of the Family group, 129.

H

HABEAS CORPUS ACT, nature and policy of the English, 264-266.
Hæreditas, function discharged by the, at Rome, 184.
Hearsay Evidence, meaning of, and problems as to treatment of, 305.
Husband and Wife, principles for ascertaining the rights and duties of, 126.

I

IGNORANCE, classification of forms of, 111.
——— how far treated as excusable, 112.
——— legal provisions for cases of, 113.
——— of Law, effect of, 111.
——— presumptions in respect of, 110.
Illustrations, a mode of avoiding the necessity of Interpretation, 65.
Impeachment, Pardon not pleadable to an, 40, 41.
Implied Contracts, nature of, 216.
Incorporeal Thing, meaning of expression, 86, 167-169.
India, British, Codification in, how far a precedent for England, 384.
——— laws of, influence of, on Science of Law, 10, 11.
———Village Communities in, 131.
Indian, Anglo, Codes, use of Definitions, and Illustrative cases in, 66, 303, 377.

Infancy, Qualifications of Intention due to, 105.
——— presumptions in favour of, 106.
Insane, problem as to Punishments for the, 288, 289.
Insanity, Judicial and Medical aspects of, 108.
——— Presumptions in respect of, 107.
Intention, analysis of, 104, 115.
——— modes of ascertaining, 105.
——— nature of, as qualifying Acts, 103, 115.
Intercessio, nature of the Contract of, 208.
International Law, account of, 322, *seq.*
——— distinguishable from Morality, 323, 324.
——— influence of, on Science of Law, 11, 12.
——— Mr. Austin's theory respecting, 323, 324.
——— Private, influence of, on the Science of Law, 25-28.
"Interpretation," devices for avoiding the necessity for, 65.
——— meaning of "extensive," "restrictive," "grammatical," and "logical," 66, 67.
"Interpretation Clauses," a mode of avoiding necessity of Interpretation, 65.
Interpretation of Contracts, modes of, 205-207.
Interpretation of Law, a permanent logical process, 24.
——— forbidden by FREDERICK II.'s Code, 61.
——— function of Judge in reference to, 62.
——— grounds for, 59-61.
——— modes of providing for, 61-65.
Interrogatories, practice of using sworn answers to, as Evidence, 306.
Intestate Succession, theoretical nature and history of, 183, 184.

J

JUDGE, function of the, in the Interpretation of Written Law, 62.
—— function of the, as contrasted with that of the Legislator, 53, 54.
—— function of the, in assigning Punishment, 39.
Judicial Authority, Classification of Law made by, 76.
Jurisprudence, meaning of French term, 63, 64.
Jury, nature and policy of the institution of Trial by, 267-270.
Jus in personam, meaning of the expression, 88, 94.
Jus in rem, meaning of the expression, 88, 94.
JUSTINIAN, value of works undertaken by, 373.
Juvenile Criminals, problem of punishments for, 288.

L

LAND as a subject of Ownership, 166, 167.
—— early property in, 163.
Language, use of, as a vehicle of Law, 376.
Law, criticism of AUSTIN's and BENTHAM's views of, 324.
—— Constitutional, anomalous characteristic of, 16.
—— Criminal, account of, 228, *seq.*
—————— classified as made by Legislative Authority, 76.
—— Customary, a permanent element in Law, 391.
—— Customary, how it grows, 389.
—— theory of Customary, 326.
—— Definition of a, 48, 324.
—— doctrines of English Common, as illustrating growth and compass of Law, 390.
—— as an instrumentality of Government, 122.
—— regarded as a medium of Political action, 404-406.
—— and Government, relations of, 396, *seq.*

Law, account of the growth of, 47.
—— English, influence of BENTHAM upon, 7, 8.
—— English Common, its relation to the history of the Science of Law, 6, 7.
—— fusion of, with Equity, 56.
—— historical relations of, to Equity, in England, 380.
—— English, general characteristics and history of, 382, 383.
—— Foreign, incorporation of, a mode of Judicial Legislation, 67-69.
—— French, Characteristics and History of, 383, 384.
—— of Civil Procedure, account of, 290, *seq.*
—— classified as made by Judicial Authority, 76.
—— International, account of, 322, *seq.*
—————— influence of, on Science of Law, 11, 12, 25.
—————— theory of the evolution of, 326.
—————— distinguishable from Morality, 323, 324.
—————— relation of, to a Code, 391.
—————— Mr. Austin's theory respecting, 323, 324.
—————— Private, influence of, on Science of Law, 25-28.
—— Interpretation of, a permanent logical process, 24, 59.
—— confusion of, with Morality, 2, 29, 375.
—— its true relation to Morality, 32-34.
—— Modes in which it comes into being, 5.
—— of Nations, account of, 322, *seq.*
—— of Nature, appeal to a, a mode of Judicial Legislation, 67, 72-74.
—— of Nature, function discharged by notion of, in respect of International Law, 333.
—— permanence of elements of, 23.
—— in reference to Religious Bodies, 133-137.

Law, Roman, influence of study of, on Science of Law, 9, 10.
—————— as an ingredient of French Law, 384.
—————— its contributions to International Law, 332.
—— Science of, materials of, 18.
—— in relation to the State, 117, seq.
—— Statute, a permanent element in Law, 391.
—————— how far it expresses the sentiments of the community, 388.
—— theories as to the development of, 21-23.
—— Unwritten, how it grows, 388, 389.
—————— logical conflicts incident to Interpretation of, 24.
—————— Principles are not confined to, 377.
—— Written, ambiguity in meaning incident to, 24.
Laws, Conflict of, influence of, on Science of Law, 12.
—— Moral influence exerted by, 404.
Legal Fictions, functions of, in developing early Law, 55.
—— Profession, theory of the existence of a, 294, 311-313.
Legislation, as part of the function of Government, 397.
—————— fallaciousness of the notion of making Experiments in, 405.
—————— grounds and modes of Judicial, 64-67.
—————— Local, dangers incident to secrecy of, 400.
—————— Statutory, various modes of, 75, 76.
—————— Subordinate, perils incident to use of, 262.
—————— perils and value of, 399, 400.
Legislative Authority, classification of Law made by, 76.
Legislation, British Indian, influence of, on Science of Law, 10, 11.
Legislator, functions of the, as contrasted with those of the Judge, 53, 54.

Legislator, meaning of expression, The, 398.
Lex domicilii, meaning of expression, 320.
—— fori, 320.
—— loci actus, 320.
—— loci contractus, 320.
—— loci rei sitæ, 320.
Libel Act, Mr. Fox's, theory and operation of, 269, 270.
Liberty, analysis of conception of, 90.
—————— estimate of modern securities for public, 257-266.
—————— nature of Political, 98.
—————— relations of, to Right, 91.
Lien, nature of a, 208.
'Literis,' nature of Roman Contract, 202.
Local Legislation, dangers incident to secrecy of, 400.
Logical Interpretation, criticism of expression, 67.
Lunacy, Judicial and Medical aspects of, 108.
Lunatics accused of Crime, treatment of, 288, 289.
—————— Limitations on Rights of Ownership by, 161.

M.

MAINE, Sir H. S., his Work on "Ancient Law," 47.
—————— on primitive rules antecedent to true Law, 325.
—————— extracts from his "Ancient Law," in reference to Ancient Codes, 365.
—————— in reference to early Codes, 154.
—————— on primitive Contracts, 193, 201.
—————— on the primitive relation of Contract to Sale, 218.
—————— his account of the Roman obligatio, 168.
—————— his account of primitive Law respecting Crimes, 230.

MAINE, Sir H. S., his observations on Custom, 49, 50.
—————————— his work on Village Communities, 47.
—————————— on the history of early Wills, 183.
Malice, analysis of notion denoted by term, 243-245.
—————— Mr. AUSTIN's notes in reference to, 245.
Mandatum, Nature of Roman Contract of, 224.
Marriage, Nature, Conditions, and Forms of, 124.
—————————— growth of legal conception of, 92.
—————————— as a Contract, 216, 217.
Men and Women, relative claims of, 126, 127.
—————————— historical evolution of relations of, 127, 128.
—————————— Legal relations of, 129.
MILL, Mr. J. S., extract from his Essay on BENTHAM, in reference to English Law, 362.
Misdemeanour, history of distinction between, and Felony, 252, 253.
Misprision of Treason, account of English offence of, 255.
Monarchy, influence of, in the development of International Law, 336.
Moral Theories, account of competing, 30-32.
Morality, Confusion of, with Law, 2, 29, 375.
—————————— its true relation to Law, 32, 33.
—————————— relation of International Law to, 323, 324.
Motive, legal use of term, 102.
Murder, suggestions for classifying offence of, 270.
—————— problems respecting Punishment of, 283.

N.

NATURE, Law of, appeal to a, a mode of Judicial Legislation, 67, 72-74.

Negligence, nature of, as related to Intention, 115, 116.
—————— estimate of, in Contracts, 207.
Negotiable Instruments, meaning and use of, 201, 222, 223.
Neutral Commerce, influence of English doctrines respecting, 341.

O.

OATHS, Judicial, criticism of use of, 308.
Obligation and *obligatio*, relation of, to a Contract, 221.
Obligations, transfer and descent of, 222.
Obligatio, Sir H. S. MAINE's account of the Roman, 168.
Owner, meaning of term, as contrasted with Possessor, 182.
Ownership, growth of legal conception of, 93.
—————————— Origin and early History of, 150, 151.
—————————— account of Laws of, 148, seq.
—————————— elements of a Law of, 160.
—————————— progress of conception of, 153, 154.
—————————— analysis of a Right of, 170, 171.
—————————— Moral aspects of, 155-159.
—————————— Possession in relation to, 152, 178-181.
—————————— theory of German Jurists respecting, 157.
—————————— Political limitations of, 188.
—————————— Modes of Protecting, 188.

P.

PARDON not pleadable to an Impeachment, 40, 41.
—————— Prerogative of, theory of, 40, 41, 271.
Patria Potestas, institution of the,

as supporting the Family group, 130.

Penalty, nature of a, as contrasted with Compensation, 37.

Person, analysis and history of term, 78-81.

Persons, artificial or fictitious, account of, 83, 84.

Personal Property, history of distinctions between, and Real, 164.

Physical facts, as supplying permanent elements to Law, 25.

Pleading, nature and history of, in England and Rome, 296, 299.

Prerogative of Pardon, theory of, 40, 41, 271.

——————— lodged with Executive, 41, 271.

Police, danger of fostering a system of Detective, 277.

——— perils incident to employment of, 260.

——— offences, multiplication in modern times of, 257.

Political Authority, nature of a supreme, 48, 49.

——— Crimes, grounds for pardoning, 41.

Pope, influence of the, in the development of International Law, 337.

PORTALIS, M., upon French term *Jurisprudence*, 63, 64.

Possession, nature of, in respect of Ownership, 175-181.

——— analysis of conception of, 176.

——— *bona fides* in relation to, 177, 178.

——— meaning of "Natural," 176.

——— Right of, as contrasted with "Right to possess," 178.

Possessio ad Interdicta, meaning of Expression, 177.

——— *ad Usucapionem*, meaning of expression, 178.

Presumptions in respect of Ignorance, 110.

——————— in favour of Infancy, 106.

——————— Insanity, 107.

Presumptions, theory of, as affecting Burden of Proof, 300, 301.

Prisoner, evidence of the, excluded in England, 274.

Prisoners, history of treatment of, in England, 273.

Private International Law, influence of, on Science of Law, 25-28.

——————— Problems presented by, 318-321.

Procedure, forming Rules of, a mode of Judicial Legislation, 67, 70, 71.

——— an element in development of Law, 51, 52.

——— account of the Law of Civil, 290, seq.

Proof, Burden of, problems respecting, 300, 301.

Property, account of Laws of Ownership or, 148, seq.

——— history of distinction between Real and Personal, 164.

——— early, in Land, 163.

Punishment, nature of, as contrasted with Compensation, 37.

——— Judicial discretion in assigning, 38, 39.

——— theory and policy of Criminal, 278, 288.

Q

QUASI-CONTRACTS, Nature of, 215.

R

REAL PROPERTY, history of distinction between, and Personal, 164.

Reformation as one purpose of Punishment, 280, 289.

Relevant facts, possibility of enumerating, 303.

Religious Bodies, Law in relation to, 133-137.

Representative Institutions, estimate of value of, in respect of securing Liberty, 258, 259.

Res mancipi and *Res nec mancipi*

account of distinction between, in Roman Law, 164.
Restrictive Interpretation, meaning of, 67.
Right, analysis and history of legal term, 88-97.
—— "Fractional" meaning of a, 171.
Right of Ownership, analysis of a, 170, 171.
Rights, possibility of the State having, 99.
Roman Law, its influence on Science of Law, 9, 10.
—————— its contributions to International Law, 332.
—————— Institutions of, for the support of the Family group, 129, 130.
—————— analogy of its development with that of English Law and Equity, 380.
—————— as an ingredient of French Law, 384.

S

SALE, as a Contract, 218.
Sanction, BENTHAM's conception of a, 3.
—————— relation of a legal, to Morality, 32.
SAVIGNY, his objections to Codification in Germany, 385.
Science, order of treatment of any, 1.
Science of Law, Mr. AUSTIN founder of, 4.
—————————— materials of, 18.
Servitudes, nature and classification of, 171-173, 186.
—————— classification of, in Roman Law, 173, 187.
—————— nature of "Positive" or "Affirmative," 172.
—————— nature of "Negative," 172.
—————— meaning of "Personal," 173.
—————— meaning of "Rustic" and "Urban," 186, 187.
Social theories, as explanatory of the Science of Law, 20-22.

Specific Performance, nature and limits of the remedy of, 210.
State, analysis of the meaning of the term, 48, 119.
—— gradual formation of a, 89.
—— historical development of the, 121.
—— functions of the, 123.
—— function of the, in respect of Crime, 231-233.
—— the, in reference to Government and Law, 122.
—— the, Law in relation to, 117.
—— the, Modes of influence of the Governing Authority of, 15, 16.
—— the, regarded as a Moral Being, 404.
—— the, possibility of its having Rights, 99.
—— true conception of the, 120.
—— various uses of term, 118.
States, analogy of, to human beings, 329.
—————— mutual relations of, as influencing the Science of Law, 25.
—————— theoretical equality of, 346.
Statesman, functions of the, in respect to legislation, 403.
Statute, a, principles of Interpretation of, 64, 65.
—————— Law, how far it expresses the sentiments of the community, 388.
Statutes, mode of drawing English, 373.
Statutory Legislation, various modes of, 75.
Stoppage in transitu, nature of the remedy of, 208.
Subordinate Legislation, perils incident to use of, 262, 399.
Succession, theoretical nature and history of Intestate, 183, 184.
Supreme Political Authority, functions of the, in respect of the creation of Law, 325.
Supreme Political Authority, possibility of the existence of, in a Society of States, 327.
Suretyship, nature of the contract of, 208.

INDEX. 417

T

TERMS, account of elementary, 77, seq.
Text-book writers, influence of, on Judicial Legislation, 67, 69, 70.
Thing, analysis and history of the legal term, 85-88.
―――― a Person sometimes treated as a, 87.
―――― reference to legal term, in the *Code Napoléon*, 86, 87.
―――― meaning of Incorporeal, in English Law, 86.
Things, divisions of, co-subjects of Ownership, 165.
Titulus Justus, meaning of expression, 176.
Treason, ground of the criminality involved in, 235.
―――― historical account of, in England, 252, 253.
―――― English statute of 23 Edward III. respecting, 251, 252.
―――― Misprision of, account of English offence of, 255.
Treaties, influence of, on International Law, 344.
Trial, circumstances of an early, an element in the development of Law, 52.
The XII. Tables, Commentaries upon, how concocted, 63.
Trustees, various modes of appointing, 143.
Trusteeship, necessity for institution of, 141, 142.
Trusts and Trustees, nature of laws relative to, 141, *seq.*

U

UTILITARIAN TEST, Mr. AUSTIN'S views of the use of the, 4.

V

VATTEL, his distinction between the "necessary" and "voluntary" Law of Nations, 340.

Village Communities, SIR H. S. MAINE'S work on, 47.
―――― Community in reference to the progressive organization of the State, 131.
―――― Group, importance of the, 132.
Vindictive Damages, nature of, 211.
―――― theory of Punishments, objections to the, 282.

W

WARD, Mr., his testimony to the influence of Chivalry, 335.
Warrant, meaning and theory of a, 264.
Wars, influence of International Law on, 345.
―――― modes of preventing, 351, 352.
Wife, Rights and Duties in respect of Husband and Children, principles for ascertaining, 126.
Will, legal use of term, 101, 102.
―――― theoretical nature of a, 183.
Wills, Sir H. S. MAINE on the History of early, 183.
Witnesses, grounds of excluding, 302.
―――― practice of receiving Depositions of, taken out of Court, 386.
―――― problems relating to Evidence of Scientific, 309-311.
Women, historical evolutions of relations of Men and, 127, 128.
―――― legal relations of Men and, 129.
―――― relative claims of Men and, 126, 127.

Y

YOUTH, as affecting the capacity for making a Contract, 198, 199.

www.ingramcontent.com/pod-product-compliance
Lightning Source LLC
Chambersburg PA
CBHW020536300426
44111CB00008B/684